MY FREEDOM AND ME

The inspirational true story of one woman's
amazing adventure...
told by the woman who experienced it.

MY FREEDOM AND ME

The inspirational true story of one woman's
amazing adventure...
told by the woman who experienced it.

Abigayle

AMBASSADOR INTERNATIONAL
GREENVILLE, SOUTH CAROLINA & BELFAST, NORTHERN IRELAND

www.ambassador-international.com

My Freedom And Me

*The inspirational true story of one woman's amazing adventure...
told by the woman who experienced it.*

Printed in the United States of America

ISBN: 978-1-935507-10-9

Cover Design & Page Layout by A&E Media

AMBASSADOR INTERNATIONAL
Emerald House
427 Wade Hampton Blvd.
Greenville, SC 29609, USA
www.ambassador-international.com

AMBASSADOR PUBLICATIONS
Providence House
Ardenlee Street
Belfast, BT6 8QJ, Northern Ireland, UK
www.ambassador-productions.com

The colophon is a trademark of Ambassador

Dedication

This book is dedicated to Richard and Rene, without whom I couldn't have done it. Thank you for helping me share my story with the world.

Chapter 1

August 31, 1998

Maybe this is just a dream… and I'm **not** really sitting in the driver's seat of a 21 year old, 27 foot long motor home, with $100 in my pocket and everything I own in the world tucked neatly into cupboards and drawers, (which isn't much - but more than enough). Could I really be driving off into the unknown - completely alone… and yet rejoicing in the fact that I have been given the gift of another day, no matter what it holds?

Maybe I'm still at home in my bed, fast asleep – and soon I'll open my eyes and feast them upon a rushing river, teeming with wildlife and set against a backdrop of lush green pastures and wild snow-capped mountains, (the Siskiyou National Forest). That amazing view has been the first thing I've seen every single morning for the past seven years; with the ocean for my front yard and the river for my back. All I had to do was open my eyes… and there it was, seen in full array through the floor-to-ceiling windows that served as the only wall between me the water rushing by not 20 feet from my bed. I can still smell the saltwater and hear the sounds of crashing waves and calling seagulls. And now, as hard as it is for me to believe, it's all over - thanks to the great West Coast flood in the winter of 1996/97. That devastating hundred-year flood took more than just my home, business and earthly possessions; it took away life as I knew it in my beloved little ocean-front town of Gold Beach, Oregon. But the best part is… it actually **gave** more than it took away.

Just a year ago, I could **never** have imagined that I would find myself in this situation; alone and driving a big old RV, with absolutely no idea where I'm going or what the future holds. The fact is, I'm not even sure what the next HOUR holds; let alone the next year, or decade. But I DO know one thing; no matter what happens from this moment forward, the last seven years living in paradise was a gift that will always be with me… indelibly printed in my heart forever.

And yes, I was just kidding about being asleep - because obviously I'm wide awake and savoring each and every moment. I may not know what the future holds, but whatever it may be, I'm armed with unshakable faith in God and armed with the love and guidance of my Savior, Jesus Christ… and THAT is enough. So look out world - here I come!

Right now I'm driving north from Gold Beach, Oregon on Highway 101, the infamous, (and often narrow and curving), stretch of road that will take me 300 miles to my first destination; Portland, Oregon. I just wish I could spend more time admiring the beautiful Pacific Ocean landscape and watching the mighty waves as they crash into the high, craggy rocks that look almost like sentinels marching to the shore. I wish I could admire them one last time… but unfortunately, I can't. Why? Because right now it's taking every bit of my concentration to keep this big old motor home, (towing a heavy car behind me on an old-fashioned tow-dolly I borrowed from a neighbor), on the narrow, winding road. So for now, I'll have to settle for the oh-so familiar and soul-soothing sounds of the never-ending waves as they break and then recede; break and then recede… back into the mighty Pacific Ocean. That way I can keep one eye on the road and the other one on the temperature gauge… which is unfortunately in the **"red"** zone. Drat! I've only been driving for 20 minutes, so how could the engine already be overheated? That certainly can't be a good sign!

And just to make things even more interesting, this is my maiden voyage (as far as driving a motor home goes), and I know next to nothing about engines. I've lived most of my life in Oregon, (possibly the only State that still doesn't allow "self-service" gas stations), so I've never even pumped a gallon of gasoline into a car. Come to think of it, I've never touched a dip-stick, added oil or water, or even changed a tire. That was one of the benefits of having two "car-loving" sons, but it sure does leave me feeling painfully ignorant and mechanically helpless as I set off on this journey to "I know not where". Oh well, I'll just have to learn as I go… put my trust in God, and take it one hour at a time. (Wow - what an adventure this is going to be!)

So here I sit… in a very uncomfortable semi-truck type driver's seat, (1977 version), concentrating on the never-ending broken yellow line, (and my temperature gauge), and looking back over all the other "lives" I've managed to cram into my 47 years on this planet. I was so sure when I moved to Gold Beach seven years ago, that **this** time I'd finally found the place I would call home for the rest of my life. At last, my childhood dream had come true… and I was living on the ocean/river, and building an equestrian beach resort. It was to be a place where "horse people" (like me), as well as riding clubs both large and small, could bring their own horses and ride on five miles of unbroken sandy beach and explore hundreds of miles of wilderness trails winding through the breathtakingly beautiful Siskiyou National Forest. Although the project wasn't quite finished, (it would eventually consist of a campground/RV park, motel and restaurant - complete with meeting rooms and horse-training facilities), we were *open for business* and I thought I had truly found my destiny.

But boy-oh-boy was I ever I wrong! And yet, strangely enough, I don't feel the least bit sad. I have complete and unshakable trust in my Lord, so instead of crying and worrying about where I'll go next or how I'll buy the gas to get there… all I can think about is how blessed I was to have HAD those seven years in paradise, and how eager I am to get started on whatever it is the Lord wants me to do next.

So, if you, my dear readers, are going to ride along with me on this most wonderful and exciting adventure, I should probably start out by introducing myself and telling you how I got into this most unusual situation.

You can call me Abigayle, which has been my pen-name since I was in grade school. That's how old I was when I first realized that writing poetry and songs, as well as public speaking, debating and most importantly… making people feel good was to be my true calling. I'm a devout Christian woman who loves animals and flowers and pretty rocks. I'm a horsewoman, ex-world champion foosball player, downhill skier, one-time disc jockey, legal secretary, saleswoman, sports lover, resort developer, amateur musician and self-appointed "cheerleader for the people", (to name just a few). And did I mention that I'm a single mother, grandmother of three, sister, and daughter?

I don't usually like talking about myself, (nor having my picture taken), but I'm fairly tall for a woman, (almost 5'8"), and a bit more slender than I'd like to be. People tell me that I have unusually intense bright blue eyes that seem to gaze directly into a person, focusing only on the soul, (and ignoring the unimportant things like facial hair, skin conditions or even eye glasses… sometimes to my own embarrassment). My hair is long and blonde, and not because it "looks good" but because I simply refuse to spend any more time than absolutely necessary on my physical appearance. A quick braid, or a few twists held up with a clip, and I'm ready to go. Although I do enjoy wearing nice matching outfits and beautiful dresses, I'm every bit as comfortable in sweats and blue jeans. I've only been to a beauty parlor once in my life, and that was the day I was named queen of the Senior Prom, many years ago. I've never been one for wearing much make-up, nor have I ever owned a pair of high-heels. Whatever the good Lord saw fit to give me is enough… so "Hair by Heavenly Father" is my stock answer whenever people ask me, "Who does your hair? Although my fingernails are always clean and nicely trimmed, I've never once had a manicure or pedicure, nor would I consider the idea of having cosmetic surgery to improve upon my looks or hide the tell-tale signs of aging.

But the thing that most people notice about me is my never-ending (and sometimes irritating, I'm sure), supply of energy and unbridled enthusiasm.

I can't seem to talk without using my hands, my arms and sometimes even my whole body. I've been called both dramatic and animated by just about everyone who knows me, and the faint, (but just beginning to show), smile lines on my face have no choice but to become deep and permanent... because **I'm always happy**. I live my life with passion and joy, (full-tilt, no matter the circumstances), because to me... each and every moment is a gift, and the fact that Jesus died for my sins (thank you, Jesus), is MORE than enough reason to rejoice. His sacrifice was the greatest gift ever given, and because of Him, I will always be rich! No, my treasures aren't the monetary kind, (at least not since the flood), but I've been blessed with unshakable faith - and a deep and abiding love... not only for God and Jesus - but for **all** my brothers and sisters on this planet, as well as every plant, animal, pretty rock, rainbow and puffy cloud in the sky. God created it all — and I revel in His magnificent handiwork!

I was born in Tillamook, Oregon...a small town on the Central Oregon Coast and famous for its gourmet cheese. And whether or not the fact that I came into this world; born in a little beach-front town had anything to do with it or not, the ocean has always been a big part of my life. I'm pretty sure I must have, as they say, *saltwater in my veins*, because whenever I lived inland, I literally felt "withdrawals" if I went too long without seeing the crashing waves and smelling the salt air. I left Tillamook when I was only 4 weeks old, boarding a huge ship with my 16 year old mother and heading for Panama to join my father who was in the Army. But no matter how hard I tried, (especially being a single-mother), it took me until I was 40 years old to figure out a way to make a good living **and** live on the ocean again... which is when I moved to Gold Beach in 1991. Gold Beach is a town of 1,500+ people and that is where I began the "project". At last, I had figured out a way, and I was ecstatic; barely able to comprehend the fact that I would be able to look at the ocean every single day! But as I made my unbridled enthusiasm blatantly obvious to everyone I met, the townspeople simply chuckled and shook their heads; warning me that eventually the excitement of living where you can see the beach from everywhere in town, would fade. But they were wrong! My amazement and appreciation not only didn't fade - it grew stronger every day, and then every year… and I never once stopped being absolutely stunned by the beauty. Not a single day went by that I didn't feel like pinching myself to see if I was dreaming; unable to believe that I could actually be living in the midst of such jaw-dropping beauty. (And what better place could there be for a poet?) It was perfect, and I loved it.

But then, who wouldn't love spending countless hours walking on the beach, searching for agates and shells and gathering driftwood… which I then happily made into plant-holders and a jig-saw puzzle-like driftwood fence that surrounded my home. I had always dreamed of riding my horses in the surf and playing frisbee with my two Labrador Retrievers in the sand, and there I was… doing it every day for seven glorious years. What a blessing! But now it is finished - and as I drive away, (probably for the last time), it's almost bittersweet; both happy and sad all at once.

As you can probably imagine, it would have taken something really huge, (much bigger than a mere flood), to make me leave my beloved town… and believe me, that's exactly what it was; HUGE. In fact, it was so life-altering that sometimes I still can't believe it happened, but it did. And why me? I'm certainly no one special. And yet, for some unimaginable reason, our most gracious Savior saw fit to actually *speak* to me… and **that** would change anybody's life. But I still don't understand "why me?" I'm just one more sinner, repenting every day and praying for guidance and strength. The *visitation* and the miracle of the Bible is quite a story; one I will not only share with **you** - but with everyone who will listen as I travel. (I'm just not sure "how" yet…)

Why would the Lord speak to someone as unimportant as me? I'm ashamed to admit that it's been almost 25 years since I attended church on a regular basis and I'd never read the entire Bible, cover to cover… so how could He possibly have not only *spoken* to me, but allowed me to witness an absolute miracle, (along with at least a hanf-dozen other people); a miracle so amazing that it's the reason I'm driving this big old RV right now, all by myself, with no money and no plans.... and **still** so filled with joy I could burst. I'm also ashamed of myself because it **took** a visitation and a miracle, (not to mention a major flood), to rid me of all those earthly possessions I had mistakenly thought were so important. In other words, it took a good, swift kick from my Lord and Master to put me on the right path... so shame on me, and thank you Heavenly Father!

But I finally got the message... and from that moment forward, my life would never again be about "me". Instead it would be about how I can use my gifts to comfort and encourage others, and give all the glory to God. So here I go, exhausted but grinning from ear to ear... leaving all the hopes and dreams I thought were mine behind - with absolutely **no fear**, no sadness and no doubt. My Lord has called me and He'll be leading all the way. **He's** my pilot, my guide, my strength, and my soft place to fall when I need one. Now I have just ONE fear; and that is that I might disappoint Him.

And that's why it doesn't matter if my engine overheats or if I break down in the middle of nowhere. I'm a woman on a mission... and some-how, I'll figure it out as I go along. But I do know, beyond a shadow of a doubt, that my Lord loves me and always has my best interest at heart.

Which is why I found myself smiling and eager this morning, (instead of crying), as I watched while helpful neighbors hooked up the big old borrowed tow-dolly to this 21 year old RV. And that's why I was still filled with joy as they drove my 1986 Thunderbird, (I had so lovingly named "Rosy"), onto the tow dolly so I could haul her 300 miles to Portland, find a buyer, and then use the money to pay for this motor home.

And that's why the all-consuming joy and excitement continued to fill me, even as I started the motor up for the very first time and waved goodbye to my friends and neighbors, as well as my beloved little town of Gold Beach... the home of my lifelong dream. And no, I didn't even shed a tear when I took one last look at the 24 ocean and river front acres my partners and I took from wild and inaccessible to a destination resort. And my joy continues even now - as my engine gets hotter and I say goodbye to each and every breathtakingly beautiful and achingly familiar landmark I pass for what I know could be the very last time.

Amidst all the loss, I found some joy I didn't expect; sort of a "side benefit", because for the first time in my adult life, I am completely FREE. I have no plans, no money, no savings account, no credit cards, no telephone, no home, and no job. Both of my sons are grown now, (my youngest is 25 years old), and the equestrian resort project… which took every waking hour of my day, is gone. I have no Board of Directors to please, no phones to answer and no customers to take care of. There are no horse stalls to clean, no meals to prepare and no plans to formulate and carry out. It's so strange that I still can't quite comprehend it – but I really think that for the very first time… everything I do today is up to me, with no pressure and no expectations.

And it may sound crazy, but once the flood took all my possessions, from family pictures to clothing, from a lifetime of carefully collected antiques to all my mementoes from the past, I realized that it was actually a GOOD thing, (a helping hand from God), because if it hadn't been for that flood, I might have spent the rest of my life living on the beach. I'd still be gathering driftwood and agates, watching amazing sunsets and riding my horses in the surf. Yes, it would have been a wonderful life, but it would have been all about ME… and it would have been selfish. I've been blessed with so many gifts, (as we **all** have), but with gifts come responsibility, and the joy of sharing them. So now, at the spiritually tender age of 47, I finally get it. God has been preparing me for something all my life, and even though I still have no idea what it might be, I'm humbled and honored if He thinks I can be of service. (I wonder if the American Indians would have called this journey a "vision quest"?) Well, whatever it is… it's a brand new chapter in my book of life and I plan to relish every single moment.

And right now everything would be perfect if it wasn't for my temperature gauge still climbing higher into the "red-zone". The man I'm buying this motor home from warned me that it had been parked for several years so he couldn't guarantee the engine, but even THAT didn't daunt me in the least. Why? Because when you're on the right path, a way **will** be prepared, which is why I wasn't worried. In fact, it was only 24 hours before I had to be off the property, (which had been auctioned off on the courthouse steps), when at the last minute, a casual acquaintance offered to sell me this RV… really cheap. I had been prepared to go in my car if I had to, but nope; already I was being provided for. Now I'll always have a roof over my head, a bed to sleep in, a stove, a refrigerator and even a toilet! Talk about "camping first class". And now, no matter what happens, I'll always have a place to call HOME. (I just carry mine with me.)

But even though I know absolutely nothing about engines, I DO know that an overheated engine isn't a good thing… so I guess I'll have to pull over every once in a while and let it cool down. Then when it does, I'll start it up again, drive as far as I can until it overheats… and then pull over and let it cool down again. Hopefully, by continuing to do that, I'll eventually make the 300 miles to Portland where I'll have my two mechanically gifted sons fix whatever's wrong with the engine.

But isn't it wonderful? Even if I **do** break down, I have everything I need. Only a hundred years and fifty years ago, I'd have been traveling over unpaved and rutted roads in a covered wagon, probably drawn by oxen. But here I am, sitting on a comfortable (?) seat and doing nothing more than pushing my foot down on a little pedal on the floor. I'm like a turtle, carrying his home on his back). In fact, I'm so darn lucky (actually "blessed" is the correct word), that I think I'll name my new/old motor home "Lucky". Yup, that's what I'll do. "Hello Lucky. I'm Abigayle, and we're a team now, so let's see if we can't make it to Portland before you get so hot you burst into flames."

Hopefully I'll be able to sell Rosy (my 1986 T-Bird), for at least $2,000… which is what I need to pay for Lucky, and then anything I get over that amount will be the money I'll begin my journey with. Alan, my best friend (and one of my business partners in the Gold Beach project), has offered me a place to park at his house while I advertise and sell Rosy, and then – this cozy little home on wheels will be all mine. Yes, I'll admit it's a far cry from 24 ocean and river front acres and a 4000 square foot home and shop like I had in Gold Beach, but it's enough... in fact, it's more than enough. Because **I have Jesus**... and he told me, "Do not worry – everything will be fine."

The hardest part is leaving my children and grandchildren, but at least while I'm in Portland, I'll get to spend some farewell time with them, as well as my parents and my brother. I've set up several meetings with attorneys regarding the corporation and our potential lawsuit against Curry County, (yet another story about the flood), but for now, let's just say that thanks to the help of my two aunts and my uncle, (who are also my business partners), and by selling the land, my horses, and everything else left of value after the flood, the corporation was barely able to avoid bankruptcy. But there are still many legal issues to be addressed... and once those loose ends are tied up, (and my father and my sons have fixed Lucky), It'll really be time to hit the road - destination; unknown. I can't wait!

And that's when it happened. I was just sitting there, driving and thinking about everything, when suddenly the engine died. There was no noise – no warning of any kind... just quiet instead of the ear splitting sound of that big old Dodge 440. I pushed my foot down on the gas pedal all the way to the floor, but nothing happened. And to make matters even worse, I suddenly had no power steering or power brakes. I was on an uphill grade, so I couldn't even coast far enough to get completely onto the narrow shoulder before coming to a complete stop. Great! I'd only been on the road for half an hour and there I was - broken down in the middle of nowhere.

chapter 2

Still August 31, 1998

The past few weeks had been pure mayhem and I spent every waking moment handling a myriad of extremely stressful and time-consuming corporate and personal business matters. (And did I mention ending a marriage and having major surgery during that time?). I didn't get even two hours of sleep the night before I left, so I was already emotionally and physically drained when the motor died. I was so darn tired I just sat there in the driver's seat, laying my head on the steering wheel and wondering what I should do.

OK – first things first. I tried restarting the engine but nothing happened. No click, click, click… no moan or groan of an almost dead battery; no sound at all. That meant I couldn't get any further onto the narrow shoulder, so I needed to get help as soon as possible - before a car came around the corner and hit me. Next, I needed to survey my surroundings and see what my options were, but unfortunately, there wasn't a single house or business in sight - which meant I could either hitchhike, (no thank you), or see if the one dirt road I spotted 100 feet or so from where I was stopped, might be someone's driveway. If so, I could use their telephone to call AAA. The choice was easy; so I climbed out of Lucky and began walking up the deeply rutted dirt road. "Please, Lord, let there be a house with a phone up here?"

It was an unusually hot August day for the normally temperate Oregon Coast, so by the time I rounded the first corner on that dusty marrow road I was already damp and eager to find a house. As it turned out, I didn't have much further to go – because there, tucked neatly into the thickly wooded hillside, sat the house I'd been hoping to find. Thank you Jesus! Help was at hand and I felt a sudden burst of energy; enough to jog the last 100 yards to the house. Apparently the owner must have seen me coming because I never even got a chance to knock on the door and it just magically opened when I raised my fist.

"Hello sir," I said to the clean-cut young man who appeared in the doorway. "I'm afraid I'm in a bit of a pickle and I was wondering if I could use your telephone. My RV broke down on the highway up there and I need to call AAA."

"Sure," he said without a moment's hesitation and a welcoming smile. "Come on in and make yourself at home." And what a lovely, rustic home it was, complete with three young children intently playing a game at the kitchen table while his sweet faced young wife stopped doing dishes in the kitchen just long enough to smile and greet me. What a wonderful place to raise a family, I thought.

And thank goodness for AAA, because they promptly arranged to send a tow-truck from the town of Bandon (about 20 miles to the north), so it looked like disaster had been averted. After a short visit with my new friends; I happily thanked them for their hospitality and headed back down the long dirt road to the highway. Even though I hurried, (and by MY standards, that's saying a lot), by the time I reached Lucky, the tow truck driver, (a tall, over-all clad young man) was already standing there waiting for me.

"Looks like you picked a pretty dangerous place to break down," he said with a smile that said he hadn't been waiting long enough to become irritated yet. "But at least I see you've already unhooked your tow car – so that'll save us some time," he continued.

"What do you mean?" I asked. "I didn't unhook anything."

"Well, then… if *you* didn't do it, it's a mighty good thing you broke down when you did because that trailer's just sitting there – and who knows what could have happened if you'd kept driving."

Well, I knew exactly "**who** knew" what could have happened… so I offered a short prayer of thanks as the tow truck driver led me to the tow-dolly and showed me what he meant by "unhooked". I'm probably not using the right terminology, but bear with me as I try to describe what we found.

The housing on the tow-dolly that fits over the *ball* is held in place with a steel pin. Somehow the pin had vibrated loose and was hanging by a cord – no longer holding the ball in place. Then I guess the bumpy road must have caused the housing to bounce up and down… and apparently that last pothole must have done the trick, because there it was, just sitting on TOP of the ball at an awkward angle, and ready to fall off at any moment. I couldn't believe my eyes… and I just stood there thanking God that the trailer hadn't come lose and killed some innocent family following behind me.

And if that wasn't enough of a problem, there were also safety straps that my neighbors had wrapped around the front tires of my car, securing its position on the trailer, and they, too, had somehow come undone and were now lying in the road alongside the tow dolly. I could just picture them flying alongside the trailer as I drove – like banners on a parade float. My stomach started spinning when I realized what that meant. My car had been just sitting there on the trailer, (completely unsecured), as I negotiated the tight corners and steep hills that Highway 101 is so famous for.

So it was actually a blessing that Lucky's motor quit running when it did, and although I'm sure my helpful neighbors meant well when they hooked up the tow-dolly for me, I think I'd better learn how to do a few more things for myself from now on. It never once crossed my mind to double check their work; instead I just assumed that everything was fine and drove away without giving it a second thought. **Lesson number one**… for today anyway.

But then my ignorance about motor homes reared its ugly head when the tow truck driver suggested that he take a look at my engine; just in case he could fix the problem without having to tow me to the repair shop in Bandon. "So," he said, "take me to your doghouse and I'll see if it's something I can fix,"

What doghouse, I thought to myself... wondering whether I'd heard him right? Why would someone who drives a tow truck, (and supposedly knows about engines), ask such a dumb question?

"Sorry, but I don't have a dog with me - so why would I have a dog-house," I asked... and that's when he began to laugh.

"No," he finally managed to say in between chuckles, "The *doghouse* I'm talking about is the place where you access your engine."

So, here we go again, I thought, and for just a moment I wondered if he might be as ignorant as I am about motor homes. Doesn't *everyone* know where the engine is? This time, instead of a verbal answer, I simply walked around to the front of Lucky and pointed to the grill. "It's in there," I said matter-of-factly... and once again, he began to laugh. (I'm sure glad someone was seeing the humor in this situation.)

"No, ma'am," he said, still grinning. "That's where they keep the bat-teries and the radiator. The *doghouse* is how you access your engine from **inside** the RV," he explained patiently.

Well, I'll be! Here I thought that big hump between the driver and pas-senger seat was to set things on. Oh well, at least now I know where my "doghouse" is and how to get to my engine; **lesson number two,** and I've only been on the road for an hour.

Together we walked to the passenger side of the motor home and I opened the door so we could step inside the RV. He then used a screw-driver to remove the carpeted hump from between the two front seats, taking the time to smile at me as he pointed and said, "See? Your en-gine's right in here." He then spent the next few minutes eliminating some things he thought could be the problem before finally announcing, "Sorry, but I don't see anything obvious, so I guess I'll have to tow you to the RV repair shop in Bandon."

"That's OK," I answered, doing my best to mask my disappointment as we headed for the door. "Thank you for trying, anyway."

And that's when the strangest thing happened. As we were leaving the RV, he exited first and was standing next to the door as I climbed down the steps, as if he were going to offer me his hand for stability, like any gentleman would assist a lady. But instead, he calmly reached out and grabbed my rear end and squeezed! I was shocked (to put it mildly)! I couldn't believe he'd done that! Up to that point, he'd been nothing but polite and respectful, even calling me ma'am, so what could he have been thinking? And besides that… he couldn't be more than twenty-five years old, and I may have long blonde hair and a trim figure, but I'm still a 47-year old grandmother - and a LADY.

So naturally, I let him have it with both barrels. Shame on him for behavior that was both rude and insulting! After I finished my calm but severe admonishment, he sheepishly apologized… and then offered to make up for his bad behavior by taking me out to dinner in Bandon while they repaired Lucky. Unbelievable! What gall.

Like I'd even consider going anywhere with a man who would grab my rear end. But in the back of my mind, I couldn't help but wonder if there was anything I had said or done that might have unintentionally encouraged him? Yes, I was wearing shorts, (after all, it was a hot August day and I have no air conditioning), but they were almost knee length and quite loose fitting. And besides that, I've always been the "girl-next-door" type, wearing little or no makeup and never revealing or tight fitting clothes. What could have made him think that I would be receptive to his rude (and obviously lustful) behavior? Oh well, I'd have to ponder that later but in the meanwhile, I hurriedly climbed into Rosy, (my T-bird), to follow him to the repair shop. At least I had my own car to drive so I wasn't forced to ride with him in the tow truck.

When we got to the repair shop, I signed the necessary paperwork, and he quickly and quietly disappeared, (thank goodness). Three mechanics began working on Lucky, while I waited inside, writing in my journal and hoping that the repairs wouldn't cost more than the $100 I had in my pocket.

"Excuse me ma'am," one of the mechanics announced as he replaced the doghouse and tightened up the screws. "We've checked everything we can think of and we can't find a darn thing wrong with the engine. I'm afraid we'll have to charge you something for our time, but we don't have any idea why your motor quit running like it did. It's working just fine now."

So…maybe it WAS an act of God – and Lucky stopped just in time to prevent a major catastrophe. Or maybe there IS something wrong with the engine and they just can't find it. But, whatever the reason, I'm sure I'll find out sooner or later; probably while crossing the steep coastal mountains between here and Portland. Oh well, at least I could get back on the road again – a whole lot shorter on funds, (one hour of mechanic's time) and highly motivated to get out of Bandon before my friendly tow truck driver decided to return for another try.

But I'm not worried, because…
Isaiah 12:2
Behold, God is my salvation: I will trust, and not be afraid;
for the Lord JEHOVAH Is my strength and my song;
He also is become my salvation.

chapter 3

September 1, 1998

<small>THE NEXT MORNING</small>

I'm afraid I didn't make it very far on my first day on the road because by the time I left the RV repair shop, it was mid-afternoon and I was already exhausted. Another couple of hours of driving, and I decided to call it a day.

It was my first night sleeping in Lucky…and it was absolutely wonderful. I'm so happy and comfortable in my little home on wheels. And speaking of *wonderful*, that's exactly how I feel right now. Due to countless business meetings and dozens of doctor appointments in Portland over the last seven years, (yet another story for another time), I've driven this stretch of highway more times than I care to remember… and almost every time, I took a few minutes to pull over at this pretty little viewpoint at the base of the coastal mountains to admire God's handiwork. But all those other times, I was in a hurry —with just enough time to stretch my legs and admire the view. But last night was different; this time no one was waiting for me; this time I could stop for as long as I wanted… so this time I decided to spend the night parked right here.

And it was amazing! All I had to do was turn off the engine, close my curtains, and there I was… at *home*. Who cares if Lucky doesn't have a generator, or if I don't have an air conditioner or television? I have freedom… and I have peace. So here I sit at my little kitchen table, drinking a cup of tea, (since

I do have a propane stove and a refrigerator), looking out the window at the beautiful coastal mountains, with its peaks and valleys in every shade of green imaginable… and thanking God for keeping me safe and comfortable.

I think now would be a good time to tell you about the miracle and the visitation that changed my life forever. It's an amazing story and I can't wait to share it with the world!

It was the winter of 1996/97 and the entire West Coast was flooded, (including my own home), as the river I once fished for salmon and steelhead from my deck gradually circled the house, turning it into an island. The quiet little river was now a raging torrent, carrying with it the debris of too much clear-cut logging upstream and every sort of human-garbage you could think of. I even saw someone else's deck go rushing by as it narrowly missed my own. Even though the living room was already under a foot of water and the bathtubs and sinks had been transformed into spouting fountains, I still wasn't ready to leave and was using my video camera to record every dramatic moment. When suddenly, four firemen burst into my living room in full gear and demanded, (in no uncertain terms), that I leave the premises immediately… an order I reluctantly obeyed. The 24 ocean-front acres directly across the street from my house was the Horse Motel and RV Park, and although it was even closer to the ocean than my home, it was slightly elevated, (in the 500-year rather than the 100-year flood plain), which is why I decided to spend the night on the property, in the main bathhouse, completely surrounded by water but still feeling safe from the raging river.

It was almost midnight when the Curry County Road Department began bringing their heavy equipment onto the our property and informed me that the only way they could drain the flooded valley for two miles upstream was to cut a path through our entry road - which would then allow the water to drain directly into the ocean. And that was the end of our seven year project. Without the entry road, the property would be inaccessible and my childhood dream would be over before it was even finished. Of course I insisted that the Road Department put their assurance in writing that they would repair any breach they made, but they matter-of-factly denied my request, saying that it was an emergency situation (imminent domain) and that there was no time for paperwork or promises.

And that's why I spent the entire day after the flood videotaping the actions of the Road Department as they destroyed the entrance to our property, (just in case they refused to repair it and we ended up in court). But that also meant I didn't have time to assess the damage to my own home until the second day after the flood and I have to admit that I dreaded seeing the carnage the floodwaters had left behind. My two sons, Scott and Jeremy, had driven the 300 miles from Portland to Gold Beach in the midst of the raging flood, often forced to go around *road closed* barriers in their 4-wheel drive Bronco and literally risking their lives to get to their mother's side. I think that was the worst part of all; thinking that my two sons might actually lose their lives trying to help me save "stuff". But God was with them, and there they were, standing beside me as I took my first look at the devastation inside my home.

I've been through a hurricane and even watched Mt. St Helens erupt from my living room window, turning day into night and covering everything with inches of ash, but I've never been through a major flood before, and the damage was even worse than I had imagined. My house, which had been moved off it's foundation, was sill in one piece (and NOT floating in the Pacific Ocean like the Fire Department thought it could have been). But everything I owned was not only wet - but brown; coated with "flood sludge" (which is a filthy combination of silt, road oil and septic overflow). And even those possessions I had placed high enough up to escape the several feet of flood water were already fuzzy green with mold and the smell was nauseating. It was a complete and total disaster... and I'm ashamed to admit it, but I couldn't stop the tears of self-pity that were rolling down my cheeks.

Several of my neighbors had offered to help me and my sons, so together we were all loading wheelbarrow after wheelbarrow with the soggy, stinking contents of my once cozy home, and setting aside the few things that could be washed or repaired. As soon as each wheelbarrow was filled, it was then hauled out to the yard and dumped in a big pile where it would await transportation to the Curry County Landfill.

Next to the pictures of my children growing up, the thing that hurt the most to lose was my large collection of books, proudly displayed in the living and dining room on a 15 foot long, floor-to-ceiling bookcase. I've been a poet/writer all my life, so my books were my treasured friends and it broke my heart to see them destroyed. Because the bookcase wasn't secured to the wall, the bottom shelf held the biggest and heaviest books, while the second one held the smaller ones. The third shelf was occupied by paperbacks and pictures while the fourth shelf was reserved for foosball trophies. I told my kindly crew of helpers that I wanted to be the one to empty the bookcase... giving me one last chance to say goodbye.

So there I was, crying quietly, as I dumped armload after armload of slimy brown books into the wheelbarrow, and yes, I'll admit it; I was feeling pretty darn sorry for myself. Not only was my childhood dream of building a "horse motel" on the beach gone after only being open for a few months (even though it wasn't completely finished), but my plans for the future were gone as well. No flood insurance meant no rebuilding... and since we hadn't been open the one-year minimum needed to establish a business record, we didn't even qualify for SBA or FEMA disaster relief. Of course I was grateful that no one had lost their life, but opening this business had been my life-long dream... and now **it** gone, along with almost everything else I owned. And that's when I saw it!

I had just finishing loading my first heavily laden wheelbarrow full of books when I noticed something **white** on the bottom shelf of the bookcase about 10 feet ahead of where I was working. But how could that be? Every thing the water touched was slimy and brown, yet there it was; one shiny white book. Still unable to believe my eyes, I walked over and carefully pulled that big white book from its place on the bottom shelf and I was stunned! It was not only untouched by the stinking brown flood-sludge but it was COMPLETELY DRY! There could be no doubt that it was a miracle... because that amazing white book was the King James Version of the Holy Bible!

It was a very large, white, leather-bound family version, with room for genealogy and family history, and it had been one of my most valuable possessions for more than 20 years. During the flood, when the firemen evacuated me, the water was already up to the second shelf, so all the floor level books were completely submerged and the water was still rising. Yet He, the great I Am, the Master of All, had protected that book - and the meaning was crystal clear, to me anyway. There is **nothing** on this earth that can take away what's REALLY important; and there it was - HIS book, HIS word and HIS teachings... untouched, undamaged, and still sparkling white and dry.

For just a moment, I stood there in stunned silence... hugging that miraculous Bible close to my heart, knowing that it had been touched by the hand of God, and that's when I felt something indescribable happen. In that one single moment, my tears of pain and frustration were gone and I no longer felt sad or tired. It was as though when I held that Bible in my arms, hugging it close to my heart... all the earthly emotions I had been working so hard to get rid of (like anger, lust, greed and envy – to name but a few), simply floated away, almost as if I could feel them leaving. Where just moments before I had been crying and sad, as I held that big white book in my arms, suddenly all I felt was "peace" and "joy".

I actually began to laugh out loud as I yelled for my kindly helpers. "Come here, everyone," I shouted. "Hurry! You're not going to believe what I just found." All 10 (or so) of them ran into the room... wondering what I could possibly be shouting about - and they, too, were stopped dead in their tracks. The spot where I had removed the book from the bottom shelf was now just an open space and as one or two of them reached their hands down to touch the books on either side of where that Bible once sat, their hands were covered with brown slime... just like all the other books. You should have seen their faces as they realized what had just happened, especially since most of them had never owned nor read the Holy Bible. But at that moment, there wasn't a doubter in the room and the message was clear to everyone. The flood could destroy property, but it could *never* destroy anything God didn't want destroyed. Every one of us had been given a first-hand demonstration of not only His power, but of how important the Holy Bible is... and not a person in the room scoffed or tried to deny it.

As what we had just witnessed began to really sink in, I was truly ashamed of myself for having dared to mourn such trivial things, like earthly possessions or even my business. I thought to myself, "How could I have been so shallow? I should have felt blessed to have had them for as long as I did." But I'd been so wrapped up in "earthly" desires that I had somehow let myself lose sight of the "big picture", and that miraculous demonstration; that one single moment… changed me, (and my life), forever. I don't have to **own** anything to be rich… Jesus, our Savior, has already taken care of that - by giving us the true riches; the keys to the Kingdom.

Most of the people who had volunteered their time to help me were patrons of the tavern next door, (commercial zoning) and as they ohhh'd and awww'd over the Bible, it became quite clear that they had been equally touched and were choked with emotion. Several of them even commented that "maybe it was time they read that book". And yes, there were still tears on my cheeks, but now they were tears of wonder and joy because it was obvious that today… not just me, but everyone in that house, had been touched by the hand of God.

So, after about an hour of excited discussion among my now spirit-filled and amazed helpers, I set that big beautiful white Bible on a clean dry surface (which was no simple task) where I could look at it as I once again began putting the remaining water-logged books into the wheelbarrow. But this time I wasn't crying. Nope, this time I was smiling and happy… praising God and thanking Him for setting His now even **more** humbled daughter straight.

But then something else happened; something so unbelievable that this time I didn't yell for the others to come running. This time I was shocked into complete silence and disbelief. But there… on another section of that same bottom shelf of the bookcase, I found another completely dry and undamaged book; one that I hadn't noticed before because it was reddish brown in color and didn't stand out like the big white Bible did. But there it was… a second book - dry and untouched by the flood. But how could that be? How could I even utter the name of that second book in the same breath as the Holy Bible? I couldn't! Why? Because it was MY book of handwritten poetry.

I've been a poet since as long as I can remember. According to my family, I was barely two years old when I refused to repeat the familiar nursery rhymes and insisted on creating my own. When I graduated from high school in 1969, a friend bought me a big beautiful gilt-edged book filled with nothing but blank pages on which to record my poetry. Over the years, I had filled that book with verses I thought the world would never see - and I didn't care whether they did or not. So why would God have protected that unimportant book? Then it dawned on me. Could I have been misusing the gift of words the good Lord had given me? I had used it to earn money and impress people. I had used it to relieve my pain and confusion and to ask heart wrenching questions. So why would the Lord bother to protect such a worthless book written by such an unimportant person? This time the message **wasn't** clear, but I knew He was trying to tell me something… and I needed to know what it was.

So two days later, when we finally finished emptying the house, I decided to ask my Father in heaven directly. For the first time in my life, I told my family and friends that I planned to take a few days off to catch up on my rest, but instead spent three full days and nights in my slightly tilted, green fuzzy bedroom; fasting, praying and reading that miracle Bible. No television, no telephone, no food and no earthly distractions whatsoever; just me and the Bible, praying for an answer from my Lord. I didn't set a "three-day limit" on my fast and prayer quest for answers, and I would have continued for as long as it took, because nothing was more important than understanding what my Lord was trying to tell me.

It was on the morning of the 4th day when I finally received my answer. It happened as I was kneeling in prayer on my deck, (which was now hanging over the river at a slant because two of the support beams had been washed away), when I heard the *words* that will be imprinted on my heart and soul forever.

"It's time to use your gift for MY work now. I will do my part – but YOU must do yours. Do not worry, everything will be fine." But it was the strangest thing. I didn't hear those words with my ears. No... they just seemed to surround me, as though they were coming from everywhere all at once. And what was even **more** amazing was the fact that I **recognized** that powerful and all-consuming voice! It was more than familiar than that of my own sons or my parents, and I began to sob with joy. I **loved** that voice so much I thought my heart would break, and I can't begin to describe the intense feeling of warmth and peace that flowed through me as I listened. But then, as the voice stopped speaking, I struggled to find my own voice. I desperately wanted to ask for more instructions. I needed to know HOW! How could someone as insignificant as me use my gift for His work? I'm just a poet and a lover of life and people, and now one with no money or assets. What difference could I possibly make? And **how** did He want me to do it?

But no matter how hard I tried, I couldn't move and not a single sound would come out of my mouth. It was as though my body was no longer mine and it wasn't until I don't know how much later (since time lost all meaning), that I slowly opened my eyes and realized that I was laying face-down on the cold rain-soaked deck. It was so eerily silent... there wasn't even the sound of a sea gull crying or a branch rustling in the wind, and yet I still felt His presence. Me, a writer who can talk your ear off, and I can't find the words to describe the love and the comfort... like being held in the arms of my Savior himself? I can't because there are no words. But I know one thing for sure - I didn't want to move... afraid that the most amazing and wonderful feeling I'd ever experienced on this Earth would be gone when I did.

But finally I raised myself back to a kneeling position and realized that for the second time that week I had experienced a life-altering event, (as I'm sure it would have been for anyone), and I literally shouted for joy, with my arms raised to the sky as though reaching for my Lord, "I understand, now," I yelled. "I know what you want me to do. I just don't know HOW. But from now on Lord, I'll never again use the gifts you have blessed me with for any-thing but YOUR work. I belong to you and I will read that Bible over and over again, and I'll use the gift of words you gave me to comfort and encour-age others to do the same. I don't know if that's enough, but I trust you to lead me. And thank you, Jesus," I sobbed. "Thank you so much".

Wow! My Lord had actually spoken to me! In my wildest dreams I had never expected such a direct answer to my appeal for understand-ing. I was just hoping for guidance from the Holy Spirit, or perhaps the strength to discover the answer on my own.

But there it was... beyond refute. He had actually spoken to me. He had told me to use my gift for HIS work and that **"everything would be fine"**. But the part about "He would do His part – but I must do mine" really had me worried. What if I didn't know what MY part was? What if I let Him down? With everything I owned gone, what could I, a 47 year old grandmother/poet/songwriter, do to make a difference? To that ques-tion, I had no answer, but I wasn't worried. If He had brought me this far, surely He would lead me the rest of the way. All that mattered at that mo-ment was the impact that deep, powerful and familiar voice had on me. I will hear it in my mind forever... and now I had experienced a completely NEW kind of love; one that put the others to shame. My life now belongs entirely to God ... and from that day forward, I would use my ability with words, whether it was through songs, poems, stories, public speaking, books or shouting from the street corner - only for His glory!

I was still kneeling on that slimy, slanted deck, smiling and sobbing, arms raised to the sky when the **THIRD** miracle occurred, and this one was **far** more binding than any signature on a legal document. There, right above my head, was the absolutely incontrovertible evidence that I had just made a covenant with my Lord. So close that I could almost reach up and touch it, was the brightest and widest rainbow I had ever seen! It looked like it was painted in the perfect blue sky and it stretched from one end of my deck to the other, a distance of not more than 25 feet. Having spent most of my life living in rain-rich Oregon, I've seen hundreds of rainbows and I understand the scientific explanation about the refraction of light on the particles of moisture in the air… which is why they can **only** be seen in the distance, and why you can never find the "end of the rainbow".

But there it was… directly over my head - and so bright the colors couldn't possibly be duplicated on Earth, at least not by a human being. I had gotten the message – and we had made a covenant. l would never again be afraid of anything that happened. In fact, truth be told, I'd have to work hard to make sure I didn't needlessly risk my life from now on - because the thought of being with that loving voice again made death feel like something to look forward to - rather than to fight against. "Yes my Lord. I am yours. From this moment on, I live for you!"

I wish I could have captured that feeling forever, or saved it on film, but I couldn't. All I could do was humbly bow my head and weep. But they were tears of gratitude and tears of love. But there was a new sadness now… because I realized just how much I **MISSED** my Lord - and a feeling of deep "homesickness" came over me. Earth just didn't feel like "home" anymore.

But I sure wish He'd given me some instructions. Since the flood had left me with no business, no home and no money - how could I possibly make a difference in this most confusing and misguided modern-day world? But right then, even that didn't worry me, because my heart was filled with such complete confidence and overwhelming peace of mind, that I knew my Lord would somehow show me the way… in HIS time. After all, He did say *"do not worry; everything will be fine."*, so that meant He would guide me, and He would protect me, and anything that happened would be according to His will, even if it was difficult or painful. Whew! What a relief! What a miracle! And me… a sometimes silly, often comedic, and always happy "Pollyanna" type middle-aged woman… had been called into service by my Lord. It was truly beyond my wildest dreams. So now you can see why nothing daunts me, (not that I was ever very good at being daunted anyway…), and why I seem so cavalier about lack of money or having no plans. I'm just the co-pilot and God is the pilot. What more could I ask for?

And no matter who believes me (or who doesn't), I'll continue to tell the story of those three miracles to everyone who has ears to hear, and by doing so, they will NOT have been just for me - but will be magnified a thousand-fold in the telling. I had no doubt that those miracles WEREN'T intended simply for me, but for me to USE as a way to glorify God and encourage others. Somehow, I will find a way to share them with the world; now I just have to figure out how.

And then… while I was still kneeling on my crazily tilted deck, (completely awestruck and deep in thought about what I should do next), another feeling so strong and so overpowering came over me that I KNEW it had to be the Holy Spirit. It was suddenly clear that no matter how much I loved my little beachfront town of almost 2000 people, I would have to leave it behind. I still had no clue as to HOW I could best be of service, but I DID know that I'd never find the answer enjoying life here in Gold Beach. I needed to sojourn among my brothers and sisters all over the country. I needed to understand what they were going through - and discover to how I could possibly make a difference in their lives. So here I am; on my way to "I know not where" to do "I know not what", and now you know the reason.

In every ending lies a new beginning…. and I can't wait to get started! So, on that note, it's time to open my curtains, start up Lucky's engine, and… "On the road again"; (I always did love that song.) What an adventure!!!! Thank you, Jesus!

John 10:4 and 27
4) And when he putteth forth his own sheep,
he goeth before them, and the sheep follow him;
for they know his voice.
27) My sheep hear my voice, and I know them
and they follow me.

chapter 4

Still September 1, 1998

"And the beat goes on…" but today was even **better** than yesterday - because I actually made it **50 whole miles** before Lucky broke down again.

It happened about an hour after I left the beautiful mountain viewpoint where I spent my first night on the road… while I was driving the winding, steep coastal mountain pass that connects the Oregon coast with the interior valley (and Interstate #5 – which would then lead me north to Portland), I was just driving along, happy and humming, enjoying the spectacular scenery, when suddenly I almost jumped out of my seat.

"BOOM…BOOM…BOOM!" It was so LOUD it sounded like the engine was trying to break out of the "doghouse". All I can say is thank God it happened next to a wide spot on the shoulder of the road, (which is a pretty rare thing on this particular stretch of highway), because I was able to pull over immediately, (however "immediately" you can in a 27 foot motor home) and turn the engine off. I couldn't believe it was happening again - and in that first moment of dismay, I let my head fall forward until my forehead was resting on the highest point of the big black steering wheel. It's funny the things you notice when the adrenalin is pumping through your veins… but the steering wheel felt cool and comforting where it touched my forehead, and I just wanted to stay there with my eyes closed - rather than face whatever had happened to my motor. I knew from the ear-splitting sound that it **had** to be something really serious, but since the mechanics in Bandon couldn't find anything wrong yesterday, what could it possibly be?

I sat there just long enough to take a couple of long deep breaths, trying to calm down and figure out what I should do next, (why do these things always have to happen in the middle of nowhere?), when I heard it. That's when I heard the sound of a very loud one-ton truck engine as it pulled up directly in front of me; headlight to headlight. I'd only been sitting there for maybe two minutes when I raised my head and saw what could have been a mirage in the desert. But this was no mirage. It was a very familiar big white flatbed truck, driven by my ex-business partner - and still best friend, Alan.

What in the world was HE doing here, I wondered in amazement as he climbed out of his truck and walked, (or should I say "sauntered"), toward me? I'll always remember the look on his face as he shook his head back and forth slowly, like a disapproving big brother… eyes dark and flashing. But his oh-so familiar dimples told a different story as his "aren't you glad to see me" smile gradually lit up his handsome face. Just a few more steps and he'd be here, so I hurried to pry open the little 6 inch screened panel that served as my driver's side window. (Who ever heard of a window you couldn't roll down?)

"I must be seeing things," I said to him as I shook my head in disbelief. "Alan, what are you doing here?"

"Rescuing you, it seems, my fair lady," he answered as he bowed slightly from the waist and tipped his baseball cap… much like a knight in shinning armor greeting a maiden in distress. "So what seems to be the problem," he asked?

"I don't have any idea," I answered, not bothering to fight my tendency to talk so fast that people have trouble keeping up with me. "I was just driving along - and all of a sudden I heard this really, really, really loud noise that went 'boom, boom, boom and it came from right over there…

under the passenger seat," I gushed as I pointed. "And now I think my engine is ruined! But Alan, how did you know where I was? And how did you know I was in trouble?"

"Well, it's like this," he explained, sporting his best, if somewhat sheepish, 'hope you don't take this the wrong way' grin. "Your two sons and I were just sitting around talking and wondering when you'd make it to Portland when we decided that we didn't like the idea of you being out here all by yourself. Yes… we know you can do anything you put your mind to," he said, perhaps a bit defensively, (and unnecessarily so, I might add - since "pride" was one of those earthly challenges I felt float away when I first held that miracle Bible in my arms after the flood), "but these roads are tough for anyone, especially when you're towing a heavy car. And since you told us that the motor home you bought hadn't been driven for a few years, we kind of figured you might have some problems. We drew straws to see which one of us would drive down here and make sure you weren't stuck on the side of the road somewhere. I got the short straw - so here I am, my lady," he said, with yet another knightly bow and an even brighter smile.

"And I'd say from the look on your face right now, Miss Abigayle, it's a mighty good thing I showed up when I did," he said, this time allowing a bit of "I told you so" in his voice. And why not, I thought? He deserved to feel proud of himself - and I didn't feel one bit insulted by the fact that they were worried about me. How could I? Surely, once again, God had provided… and we all know that He often uses other people to carry out His wishes. Today, it was Alan, and I'd never been so happy to see anyone in my life, (except maybe the night my sons drove through the life-threatening storm to get to me in Gold Beach after the flood).

Miracles come in all shapes and sizes, and this one just happened to be 5'10" tall, weigh 180 pounds, and drive a flat-bed construction truck FILLED with tools.

"But I still can't believe your timing," I said in amazement; and more than happy to give him another well-earned pat on the back. "It only happened a few seconds ago. In fact, I didn't even have time to figure out what to do next... and there you were," I gushed in heartfelt gratitude. "Thank you, Alan. Thank you for being my guardian angel today!"

"Yup, that's me... Your own personal guardian angel... at your service ma'am," he said. "And from what you just told me, I think I know what your problem might be."

"Really? Oh, that would be wonderful," I said with a deep sigh of relief. But dared I hope that Alan not only knew what was wrong with the engine, (without even hearing the noise), but that he might actually be able to fix it right there on the side of the road?

"Let me get my tools out of the truck while you move everything off your doghouse," he said as he began walking away toward his tool filled flat-bed. And yes, I admit it... I was kind of proud that I actually knew **where** my "doghouse" was, and I hurriedly removed my water container, some maps and two packs of Lifesavers from the carpeted engine cover before heading for the side door to let Alan in.

In a matter of minutes, he was intently studying the engine while I sat quietly in the passenger seat - praying that his diagnosis was right and watching every single move he made in case I might learn something that would help me the NEXT time Lucky broke down.

"Uh-huh... just as I thought," he announced. "Here, let me show you what happened. See that big long bolt right down there," he explained as he pointed his finger down into the engine. "That's what holds the alternator in place and somehow it either vibrated loose, or the mechanics who worked on it yesterday forgot to tighten it back up. The noise you heard was the sound of the fan blade striking that bolt every time it turned. The fan blades are pretty badly bent - but it still seems to be working, so I think we'll make it to Portland," he announced as he re-tightened the bolt and re-secured the alternator. "When we get there, we'll check it out before you leave town."

Wow...what a blessing. I'm not much of a gambling woman, but if I was... I'd have to put the odds at a million-to-one that Alan would show up in the middle of nowhere, **just** when I needed him most. (Thank you,

Lord.) If he hadn't come looking for me, I'd have been stuck walking for who knows how many miles, hoping to find a town not only big enough to have an RV repair shop, but a mechanic skilled enough to not only **find** the problem, but one who wouldn't leave any OTHER bolts or screws loose. And then I'd have to hope I had enough money to pay him, (which I highly doubt). So thank you, Alan; thank you for caring enough to drive 150 miles just to make sure I wasn't in trouble, and thank you Lord for sending him. And to top it all off - I just learned **lesson number three**; I know where the *alternator* is.

And he was right; we made it to Portland. I wish I could say the rest of the trip was uneventful - but far from it! I'd have **never** made it if Alan hadn't insisted on following me in his truck. But with his help…all obstacles were eventually overcome and the first leg of my journey was over. Lucky quit running two more times during the last 150 miles; the first being a clogged gas filter and the second a broken gas gauge, (which is why I ran out of gas). I should have known I couldn't be getting THAT good of gas mileage - but then I've never driven a motor home before so I didn't think to question the gauge.

This particular model has two 30 gallon gas tanks, and even though both were full when I started, I couldn't figure out how to switch from one tank to the other. Luckily, (after a bit of searching), Alan thought to look on the floor **under** a carpeted mat and next to the driver's seat, for an almost completely hidden lever. How dumb is that? And it's not even marked so you can tell which way to turn it for each of the two tanks. (Who designs these things anyway?)

But we eventually made it to Portland… and here I am; much the wiser and a little worried about being so mechanically challenged. My two sons, Scott and Jeremy, were waiting at Alan's house when we arrived - and after many hugs, kisses and "thank you's", I filled them in on the rest of my adventure. I'm afraid that may have been a mistake because when I told them about the tow truck driver squeezing my bottom, no amount of pleading could stop my son Jeremy from angrily calling the tow truck company and… shall I say "raising Cain" over their driver's unprofessional behavior towards his mother. I doubt if that young man will make such a foolish mistake again; at least not while he's on the job. (Actually, I hope he still HAS a job, after Jeremy got through with his boss.)

But there's always something to be learned; even from the unfortunate incident with the young tow truck driver. From now on, no matter how hot it is, I'll **never** wear *shorts* when I'm traveling. It'll be baggy sweat pants or long skirts for this lady. It's a shame I can't just be comfortable, but I guess that's life in this day and age …so I'll just have to make some adjustments.

And now the first leg of my incredible journey is over – and I'm safely parked at Alan's house in Lake Oswego, (a rather high dollar suburb of Portland). He's such a gracious host that he even surprised me by setting up a little RV pad right next to his garage. It has electricity, water, (and with the help of my two sons and 200 feet of thick black cable cord and telephone wire), television and a telephone. How blessed can I be? It's a hot Indian summer evening, and yet here I am, cool and comfortable in my cozy little "fort" of a home named Lucky… happy, safe and surrounded by people I love. It doesn't get much better than this!

chapter 5

September 15, 1998

Another beautiful day parked at Alan's house... and you know what?
I think I could get used to living like this. Even when I was a little girl,
I loved making forts; whether they were stomped out in the tall grass of
an unused pasture or under a table covered with blankets, they always belonged to me... a place where I felt separated from the rest of the world;
a place for dreaming and wondering. And that's what life in Lucky is like;
my very own little fort. Although my childhood wasn't what *most* people
would call normal, I was blessed with a wonderful extended family, and
when my father and mother divorced for the second time, (when I was 7
years old), and my mother disappeared from my life, that's when my loving extended family stepped up to the plate and made sure that I always
had a place to call home.

I was raised by my aunts and uncles, grandparents and whenever possible, my father and eventually... his new wife, Roma. And this is no a
sob-story - because like everything else that's happened in my life... it
turned out to be a blessing in disguise. Unlike so many unfortunate foster
children, **my** stand-in parents were family, and they loved and welcomed
me with open arms. I would spend 6 months with my grandparents, then

a year with my aunt and uncle, and then back to my father for a few months, (as he did his best to be a single parent). But his job was demanding and required him to travel, so eventually he would have no choice but to drop me off at another one of my aunt's houses. I really didn't mind moving so much, or not having a home where I really felt like I belonged, but the one thing that **did** break my heart was being separated from my little brother, Ronnie. I was almost three years older than he was and when my mother left, I appointed myself as her replacement, at least in MY childish eyes. But alas, two extra children were a heavy burden for one family to bear... so we were usually separated, and that's the one pain I will never forget; the nights I cried myself to sleep because I missed my dad and my little brother, Ronnie.

But now that I'm an adult and can look back on those years through grown-up eyes, I realize that my rather unconventional upbringing was simply preparation for my life in service to God. Why? Well, for several reasons; one; because I learned how to find joy in the midst of loss - and security based **not** on my surroundings but within myself. And two; because children learn by mimicking their parents (from vocabulary to life-skills), which meant I was blessed to have **eight** fine examples to learn from.

And there were other benefits too, like how changing schools at least once a year (sometimes more), taught me to depend upon **myself** for acceptance and approval, rather than my peers. And I was so blessed! My family was well educated, kind and generous. They not only worshipped God and accepted Jesus as their savior, but they helped instill those important values in me. I was eight years old when I was baptized and from that moment on, the Holy Spirit shined brightly within me. But I still missed my mother... and it felt like there was a hole in my heart; a missing piece of the puzzle that no one but she could fill - except God, that is. And now, reflecting on those early years, I realize that it was partially because of those difficult circumstances that HE, my Heavenly Father became the ONE constant in my life; the ONE in whom I found, (and still find), my strength and my exuberant love of life, no matter what obstacles and disappointments might come my way.

By the time I was 10, every time I moved it was like beginning a new adventure; almost like being born again. Every time I registered at a new school, I could be anyone I wanted to be, with a clean slate just waiting to be written on. In one school, I would be the "smart" girl and in the next, I would be the "athlete". Not everyone gets so many chances to start fresh in the eyes of those around them and I'm pretty sure that it was because of the sometimes painful changes in my life, that I developed my ability to find joy in **every** situation – good or bad… and that's also how I learned that every *ending* is really just a new *beginning*. That has been my lifelong motto; and one that is apparently still serving me well today.

The summer before my freshman year of high school, my father remarried for the final time. Her name was Roma and she was a patient, kind and loving woman. But as wonderful as she was, I'm afraid I'd already been motherless too long to give her a fair chance to fill that roll in my life. But eventually, through much kindness and patience, she became more like a highly respected friend or big sister, and I love her with all my heart to this day. I'm ashamed to admit what a hard time I gave her those first few years, but I thank the Lord that she was wise enough to understand my refusal to accept her as my mother and she continued to treat me with nothing but understanding and patience. At last, my father had found the "love of his life" and even though I certainly didn't make it easy, she did everything she could to nurture and encourage me through those tumultuous teenage years. And there was another big bonus to my father's marriage to Roma; we could live together as a family again, which meant that for the first time in my 14 years of life, I got to spend all four years of High School in one place, Oregon City, Oregon (a suburb of Portland) and I must say…it was everything I had ever dreamed High School would be.

Of course there were many bumps along the road, as with everyone, but because I had become so self-reliant and confident, some of my bumps were funny… rather than difficult. For example, I was just entering the 9th grade when my father, Roma, my brother Ron, and I, (along with my two horses, and a dog named Coco), moved to Oregon City. As I mentioned before, I didn't mind changing schools every year, but there was one thing I DID miss out on by moving so much and, (silly as it sounds), it was the chance to become a cheerleader. I've always loved sports, but in the early1960's, girls weren't allowed to compete in sports. The closest we could come was cheerleading… and that's one thing I really wanted to do; to cheer my team on. And now that we had settled down in one place, I was absolutely **sure** that I could finally make that dream come true. Looking back on those years, I can't imagine why I thought "cheerleading" was so important, yet now I see that it, too, was actually training. My gift of writing, (and inspirational speaking), means my job is to "encourage" others"… so I guess you could say that the Lord called me as a "cheerleader for the people", and those years in high school were just part of my preparation for that role.

Now… here comes the funny part. It was the first day of my freshman year in Oregon City. Because we had moved to town only two weeks before school started, we were still unfamiliar with the area. My step-mother, Roma, drove me to school on my first day and as we sat in the car in front of the building, (hoping that we were in the right place), I wasn't the least bit nervous. In fact, I couldn't wait to meet my new friends; friends I wouldn't have to leave behind this time. We were a little early, so Roma and I just sat there in the car talking, and all I could think about was how I was finally going to get to be a cheerleader.

"Gee, this school looks small," I commented, as we sat in the parking lot. "I'll bet I won't have any trouble at all making cheerleader here," I announced with my usual confidence.

She smiled, and in her own kind and supportive way said, "Yes, my dear, I'm sure you'll have no trouble at all."

But then the other kids started showing up… and guess what? They were all less than 5 feet tall. "Boy," I said, with more than a hint of sarcasm, "I'll definitely make cheerleader here, because I think this is the GRADE school."

Together we laughed at our mistake and then asked an arriving teacher how to get to the Junior High School, which we soon discovered was MUCH larger and held MANY more students. (And they were a lot taller too!)

That was in the first week of September, and I quickly discovered that the cheerleading try-outs were only two weeks away. That didn't give me much time to get acquainted with the other kids, but even that didn't daunt me. As I said before, one of my more dominant character traits is the fact that I'm not "daunted" easily, which some might consider a good thing - while others might call it a recipe for disappointment. But I've always believed that "where there's a will – there's a way", and this time would be no different. So what if I was the "new girl in school"? So what if most of the kids had known each other all their lives, and so what if I was a stranger? I'd simply "blow them away" with the biggest and best cheerleading campaign they'd ever seen - and before it was over… they'd be so impressed that EVERYONE would vote for me, and my dream would finally come true.

We'd moved to Oregon City from Medford, Oregon, where sports reign supreme and football in full pads and uniforms begins in the fourth grade. Cheerleading try-outs in Medford were handled like a major election; with signs posted, buttons handed out and all the frills that went with a serious campaign. It never once dawned on me that it might be different here in Oregon City, so on that very first day, I was already planning the mind-blowing campaign that would lead me to victory.

And Roma, bless her heart, spent hours helping me paint huge posters which I planned to put up on the walls of Thora B. Gardner Jr. High School. We made buttons to hand out and even made a *sandwich signboard* which I would wear proudly as I walked from class to class.

So early one morning, about a week before the elections, we had the school janitor let us into the building early, (before the other students arrived), so I could get the best spots in which to place my posters. It took almost an hour… and after our work was finished, Roma gave me a big good luck hug and went home, while I happily donned the big sandwich signboard, (which advertised my cheerleading skills and encouraged people to "vote for me"), and rather clumsily headed for my first class. (Those sandwich sign boards are hard to walk in!) I do have to admit that even now, as I tell you this story, I find myself laughing out loud. I was so darn determined - and so sure that nothing was going to stop me!

But as often happens... things didn't go exactly as planned; in fact, far from it. As I walked down the hall toward my first class, I could hear the snide comments and rather loud snickers from groups of students clustered together as I passed by wearing my sandwich board sign. It wasn't long before they began tearing down my posters and tossing both them and my buttons into the trash cans. But if I thought that was bad... it got worse. The snickers turned into full-blown laughter and apparently, I, the new girl, became the "joke of the day". I had no idea why, but not one other person put up a single poster... and now the ones Roma and I had so painstakingly spent hours creating were filling the garbage cans. Oh well... I just picked those posters right up out of the trash cans, smoothed them out as much as possible, (after taping together the ones they had ripped apart), and put them back up on the wall, again and again, usually with an audience of disbelieving students staring at me in disbelief. It didn't take long before I figured out that cheer-leader tryouts at Thora B. Gardner Junior High School were nothing but a glorified popularity contest. No one campaigned and no one put up posters. No one handed out buttons... except me, that is, and I'm sure no one even *thought* of wearing a sandwich sign board. But one thing was for sure... now EVERYONE knew who the new girl was.

You'd think that their cruel disdain would have embarrassed me to tears... but nope, it didn't daunt me for a moment. Rather than tuck my tail and admit defeat, I just walked up to one of the largest groups of snickering students and said, "Gee, I guess I must have moved to Hicks-ville, huh? Where I'm from... the BIG schools, they know the **right** way to elect a cheerleader. Maybe you guys ought to try it - instead of wasting your time laughing at me. It's really fun; unless, of course, you **like** being a country bumpkin."

Well, needless to say, I **didn't** get elected... and even after numerous speeches that week about how the BIG schools did it, not one single person followed my example and began campaigning. But that didn't matter... because and there would always be next year. I was absolutely **sure** that by that time, I'd know everybody in the school and I WOULD be elected cheerleader - which is exactly what happened.

At the end of that 9th grade year, the class moved up to the three-year Oregon City High School building, (a very big deal to 14 year olds, and a very big school with over a thousand students), and the very same kids who had torn down my signs and spent the week mocking me - became the same ones who elected me to the Junior Varsity cheerleading squad for my Sophomore year in High School. I love to dance, and without bragging, I had more "pep" than the rest of the squad all put together, which is why I was re-elected every year for the next three years, (co-captain my Senior year) and even got a college scholarship to Oregon State University for "cheerleading", as well as "drama and speech".

But the moral to the story is that I never once let the embarrassment of those first few weeks affect my confidence in what I could accomplish. And believe me, as the years went by, my "gall" – or "courage"... depending on who was doing the talking, became somewhat of a legend in Oregon City, and the snickering insults gradually turned into sometimes grudging respect. See? Just one more example of the "training" that I have no doubt will come in handy when I stand up in front of my first audience, playing my guitar and sharing my poetry, songs and God filled stories. I'm prepared for the fact that some people will laugh and think I'm a nut, because I know others will be touched... and if even ONE person goes away feeling better than they did when they came in, it will be more than worth it!

And after all, I did get the last laugh; especially when I donned the "prom queen" crown my senior year. And the BEST part of all was that I did it **without** becoming part of the snobby "popular" crowd. I did it by encouraging the **rest** of the students that THEY were the ones who held the power. I became their self-appointed representative... constantly reminding those who were miserable because they were pimpled, fat, poor or just plain lonely that they didn't **need** to be standing on the outside looking in, (aching to be popular), because that wasn't what was important. So what if some kids were better looking or had more money. So what if they had nicer clothes or drove expensive cars? They were few in number... and the **rest** of the students were many, so THEY held the real power. I also reassured them continually that someday when the star athletes were "has-beens", living on nothing but memories of their glory days ... and when the beautiful, shapely popular girls became fat and stuck in bad marriages to those has-been jocks, that THEY, the smart ones, the hard workers, the ones who were forced to develop their talents and abilities because everything didn't come easy to them, would be the REAL winners.

Needless to say, I was pretty much hated by the "in" crowd, and they considered me an "outsider"; but one they couldn't do anything about. But why should I care? I was a friend to everyone else... and with them behind me, it was the "in" crowd who no longer controlled the elections or decided who got to be cheerleader or prom queen, or anything else. It's no wonder the usual "clique" that all too often controls everything in most high schools, (making everyone else's life miserable), hated me... but I took that as a compliment. After all, I got MUCH more joy from encouraging the "others" to recognize their value - and much more satisfaction as I convinced them to quit comparing themselves to people who were no better than they were. As I found out when I went to the **only** high school reunion I've ever attended (25th year), my encouragement made more of a difference than I could have imagined. Twenty-five years later, as I entered the formal dance, I can't count the number of people who came up and told me that they never forgot the encouragement and the respect I had given them. Believe me, no one was more surprised than I was, (nor humbled)... but here I am - once again trying to figure out how I can do the same thing; this time on a much larger scale.

But even then, as I played the lead in school plays, and led the debate and speech team; even as I was a driving force behind the cheering squad, was elected prom queen and girl of the month for being peppiest and most school spirited, (surprise-surprise), I still attended church every single morning before school, every Wednesday night and every Sunday morning and evening. I wrote and shared my poetry about eternity and God... and how HE held the only **true** power every chance I got. and I told everyone who would listen that life on Earth was just a flutter of an eyelash in comparison to eternity. I wanted everyone to know that God loved them, and so did I.

Now, if only I'd listened to the doctors who told me that I was permanently damaging my vocal cords by screaming until I was "voice-less" EVERY single week at the pep-rally's and football and basketball games for three years. But nope – not me! I was 16 and immortal. What did the doctor's know? I already had a deep, rather husky voice to begin with... so by the time I got a college scholarship for cheerleading, drama and the speech/debate team, my vocal cords were well on their way to being permanently damaged. Funny how at 18 you know **everything** – and the older you get, the more you realize you **DON'T** know. And the doctors were right, because although I can still carry a tune, I'll definitely never be the one to record my own songs. Oh well. I'd rather let someone else take the applause anyway... just as long as the song gets sung!

So, as I sit here in my little fort of an RV named Lucky - enjoying some well-earned idle time parked at Alan's house, (and reminiscing about my early years), as I once again I find myself on the verge of driving off into the unknown. And, as always before, I will not be daunted! I'm on a mission, (even if I'm not sure what it is yet), but no matter what God has planned for me, I'll give it everything I have, knowing that each and every "teardrop is a blessing" (one of my own songs). I'll learn from my mistakes and continue to count on the Lord for guidance and forgiveness. Even though I've really enjoyed this time in my home town and will treasure the opportunity to say goodbye, not only to my friends and family, but to life as I have known it for 47 years, I can't wait to get started on my "new" one!

And so far, things are going really well. My two sons, (Scott and Jeremy), caulked all the windows and doors in Lucky, tuned up the engine and checked out everything they could think of. My father made me a set of short battery cables so I can hook the interior battery up to the start-up battery. That way, when I have trouble getting this big old engine to turn over, I'll know what to do. They also gave me some lessons in RV living, so now I know the difference between "black water" and "grey water", how to empty my holding tanks and even how to jump start my engine. How's that for progress? Jeremy showed me how to open the awning, although I'm not sure I'll remember, and my dad pointed out my two five gallon propane holding tanks. (Wow – I didn't know I was carrying explosives?) Unfortunately, my refrigerator doesn't work on electricity like it's supposed to, but at least it works on propane - so that's a good thing. Both my sons and my father are worried about my electrical system because the converter isn't recharging my battery when the motor's running - or even when I'm plugged into power, but since I don't have the money to buy a new one, I'll just live with whatever I have and be grateful that I have it. Dad gave me a battery charger, so I'll just recharge my start-up battery whenever I'm plugged into electricity. Since camping and backpacking in the wilderness has always been one of my favorite pastimes… electricity's a bonus; not a need.

I've also had several disappointing meetings with lawyers since I got to Portland a couple of weeks ago, and it appears that the suit we had been planning to file against Curry County for refusing to replace our access road to the RV Park, isn't going to happen after all. You'd think that someone who's been a legal secretary/assistant for almost ten years would have known that a government "by" and "of" the people can't be sued for punitive damages, but I didn't. They tell me it's because it would be like suing yourself; one of the *people*. But even if I had known at the time of the flood, I couldn't have let everyone for two miles upstream suffer just so I could be successful. There were not only homes in jeopardy, but many family businesses that had been in operation for generations who would have been ruined if the water hadn't been allowed to drain. To me, (and probably to most people, since I'm certainly no one special), my JOY can **never** come as a result of someone else's PAIN. It just wouldn't be right.

I did find out that you can sue for "actual damages", but the court costs would exceed the amount we could claim – because the *actual* cost is that of the gravel and dirt they removed and isn't nearly enough. We hadn't been in business the required **two** years to prove our "business losses" in court, so punitive damages would have been the only way to recoup enough to rebuild. But enough on that subject – because right now I'd rather concentrate on the things I CAN do and not worry about the things I can't.

And I know just how to lighten the mood. I'll tell you another funny story; one that happened just this morning. I suppose I should put the blame on my two sons, Scott and Jeremy, because they're such practical jokers that I'm always on guard… watching and waiting for their next attempt to fool me. That's why I was sure it had to be them when I heard someone sneaking around the side of my RV. I was sitting on the couch reading a book when I saw a hunched over shadow pass beneath my window. The shades were partially pulled down in order to cut down on the glare of the sun on this warm and sunny September day, but there was just enough room for me to peek outside and see what the noise was. That's when I saw the back of a white-blond head with a short military style haircut, (just like my youngest son, Jeremy), quietly and slowly making his way beneath my window. Well… I thought. I'll just surprise HIM instead. So I gave the shade a quick pull, which made it snap noisily as it rolled all the way to the "up" position and then I yelled at the top of my lungs, (fully intending to startle him), "I seeee youuu… You can't fool me!"

But I'm afraid my joke backfired when **I** was the one who got fooled… to put it mildly. The toe-headed person huddled beneath my window, (who I thought was Jeremy), heard the shade snap and my loud voice calling him and quickly jerked his head up… and to my complete amazement – it **WASN'T** my son. Nope, and shock of all shocks… he was carrying a rather large rifle. He looked me directly in the eyes, (quite sternly, I might add), gave me the "shush" sign with one finger over his lips, and then quietly continued on his way around my RV. I was flabbergasted when I saw the lettering on the back of his shirt! **It was the Portland SWAT team** and apparently they were moving in on someone in the house next door. I'm not sure who was more surprised - me or the toe-headed SWAT officer, but I rather sheepishly pulled my shade all the way down and stayed quietly inside my motor home until they were finished.

I was so embarrassed. I can sure be an idiot sometimes! Oh well, at least I didn't ruin their plans to launch a surprise attack because no one was at home... but it was definitely a morning I'll never forget. And this time, **the joke was on me!**

Well, I guess I'd better fix some lunch now because my sons will be here any minute; but this time, I'll make sure it's really them.

Lucky camping at Mittry Lake, AZ.

Chapter 6

September 28, 1998

2 WEEKS LATER

It seems like I just got here, but it's almost been a month already… and I can't shake the feeling that it's time to quit sitting here enjoying myself and get moving. I'm not sure **why** I feel that way… because Alan has made it more than clear that I'm welcome to park at his house for as long as I want, but I feel like I'm being tempted by a "trap of ease". It would be so **easy** to sit here reading my Bible, writing, playing music and visiting with my children and grandchildren. Who wouldn't enjoy that? But I'm not accomplishing anything and once again, it's "all about me".

I still haven't figured out the **best** way use the gifts God gave me to encourage others to find the soul soothing peace and contentment that I have found. I only know that once you have **unshakable faith** and **complete trust** in our Messiah… our Savior… our Lord, Jesus Christ, you are truly **free** for the first time; free from carnal bondage; free from doubt and fear, free to love unconditionally and find joy in even the worst of times. I want everyone to feel that, and it's time to get started doing what I can. But how?

I knew that I had to leave my beloved little beach town behind… and I also knew that I wouldn't find the answer parked here at Alan's house, but it sure has been wonderful... and I'll treasure this month of time spent with family and friends forever. But now, after much prayer and studying my miracle Bible, I think I've figured out "step one"... or should I say "destination one". It's just a beginning – but I have no doubt that "step one" will lead to "step two", and so on. So here we go, destination one: Gold Beach, Oregon.

Once I really thought about it, the choice was easy for two reasons: One; I sold Rosy yesterday and now I need to pay the man I got Lucky from, and he lives in Gold Beach. Of course I could simply mail him a check... if I still had a checking account, but with zero funds I have no need for a bank. So when I put **that** together with reason number two, which is a bit more complicated... it makes even more sense.

So now the big question is **"how can I best present my art and my stories in some way that will not only encourage and inspire those listening... but will glorify God?"** I guess this is **experiment time,** because I need to see how the people will react to my poetry, songs and stories - and then adjust accordingly.

And that's why I've decided that my first trial-run should be in front of the most **difficult** audience possible. Not only will I see how they react, (and use that as a guide for future shows), but after sharing my art, (and my testimony), with the **toughest** critics first... it'll seem all downhill from there; kind of like how when I started Lucky up for the first time and drove from Gold Beach to Portland, I was towing a big car over the steep and winding roads. But this time, (with just Lucky - and no heavy trailer tagging along behind me), it will seem like a walk in the park in comparison.

And there's a third, (much less important), reason; one that I must admit is completely selfish... but I'd sure love one last chance to say goodbye to my beautiful little village on the sea. So that's it then; the decision is made. "Poetry on the road" (journey by Abigayle), will begin where it started - in Gold Beach, Oregon.

Putting on my first show in my own home town will be tough - because for the first time in the seven years I lived there, I'll be introducing myself as "Abigayle", inspirational poet, songwriter and "cheerleader for the people". They've only known me as a businesswoman, horsewoman, project developer, and (thankfully, because it will certainly help), as a devout Christian who always dealt with people fairly, gave all credit to God, and made the time to encourage or counsel anyone who needed it. I can't image what they'll think when **Abigayle the poet** drives back into town. I'm pretty sure their first reaction will be surprise - since not one of them even knows that I write poetry, and second; they'll be wondering if the pain of watching my "dream" auctioned off on the courthouse steps was more than I could take and I've lost my mind.

And I can understand why they might wonder... because if I were in their shoes, I would. After all, an inspirational poet is the complete opposite of a business woman and land developer... which is what makes this challenge so difficult and why that's where I'm going to start; Gold Beach.

When I first moved there in 1991, I was a complete stranger... and once again, because no one knew who I was, I was free to start fresh and present myself as anyone I chose to be. That's why no one in Gold Beach knew me as Abigayle the poet and songwriter or even as a world foosball champion. They didn't know I'd been a paralegal, disc jockey, animal trainer or even a single mother, (since my youngest son was already 18 when I moved to town). To them I was just another out-of-town businesswoman... looking to make a buck; and they were right. In Gold Beach, I found myself in the battle of my life trying to build my childhood dream of a Horse Motel, and I had no choice but to be 100% business. Even so, it still took almost 5 years to get the permits and if the "good ole' boys" who had been running Curry County like it was their own private domain for so many years, had their way, we'd have never opened the doors for business.

From finding the perfect piece of land... to incorporating and selling shares to raise the money to purchase the property, (let alone build on it), it was a major struggle from day one. There were countless permits to be obtained, (from local, Federal and State), and a long drawn-out fight with just about everybody in City Hall, from Sanitation, Zoning, Planning, Building Department to the Road Department - and those good ole' boys did their best to thwart me at every turn.

Because these *unnamed power brokers*, (the "powers that be" in that area), had ruined the dreams of so many other people over the years, when the local newspaper began printing story after story about our battles, we somehow became the champion of those who had gone before us... and had eventually given up and left town in defeat. Many of them wrote us letters, begging us to fight on - not just for ourselves, but for them... which is exactly what we did. And now, seven tumultuous years later; (seven years of joy and pain, success and failure), I can just imagine the stir it will cause when I return and RE-introduce myself as *Abigayle, Inspirational Poet and songwriter.* Whew! I get butterflies in my stomach just thinking about it.

Believe me, seven years ago when I started the project, I had absolutely no idea what a hornet's nest I was getting into. As with many sparsely populated rural counties, the locals didn't take kindly to outsiders moving in, especially ones who wanted to make big changes... and it didn't take long for them to make it more than obvious that we weren't welcome. The 24-acre ocean and river front parcel we purchased for the project had been a lumber mill that burned down in the 1950's. No one had ever bothered to rebuild it, and so... as it always happens, nature had gradually reclaimed the old mill; covering the crumbling smoke stacks, log ponds and burned out buildings with river willows, blackberries and scrub Alder. And because the land was situated on a saltwater estuary, (where the river meets the sea), it was teeming with wildlife and the local citizens had been very happily using it as their private park, (and access to the beach), for almost 30 years... until WE came along.

And just to make things even MORE interesting, I found out AFTER buying the property that three other people; all members of that Good Ole' Boys clique, (gee, reminds me of high school), had **also** tried to purchase and develop that same piece of property - and all three of them had failed, which explains why we got the land so cheap, (compared to what it should have been worth). Apparently, even THEY - with all their highly placed connections and *palm greasing*, couldn't get the necessary permits to develop the land. The old log ponds were classified as "wet-lands", the river is a protected salmon and steelhead bearing stream, and we were on a saltwater estuary, all three of which have been declared "environmentally endangered zones". So it wasn't just the City of Gold Beach or Curry County that had to be dealt with; it was the Division of State Lands, the Army Corp of Engineers, EPA, FEMA, OSHA, and a dozen more, including every registered environmental group in the country. Apparently, even the richest and most powerful businessmen in Gold Beach had no influence over those agencies, so even they eventually gave up… and then my partner Alan, my two sons and I drove into town, with very little money - but a very big dream.

We must have looked like, a circus caravan when we first arrived in Gold Beach. It's a small town, with one main street (Highway 101), and one stop light, which means that everyone sees everything, including us. Our *parade* consisted of two big trucks, a large rental van, two cars and a horse trailer… all in one long line as we headed for the project property on the southern edge of town. As we drove through "downtown" Gold Beach, people actually stopped whatever they were doing and stood and stared as we passed. Since the realtor was local, the story had spread and everyone already knew not only **who** we were, but **what** we were here to do. (There's nothing more efficient than a small town gossip mill!)

And to top it all off, we were *outsiders* … strangers who were going to bring about change; and "change" isn't well received in a town of less than 2000 people who barely tolerate the summer tourists – and do so only because of the revenue they bring in. But who could blame the lo-cals for being skeptical? Not me, which is why the very next day I began going from door to door, person by person, explaining what our plans for the project were, showing them the drawings and sincerely asking them for their input. As time consuming (and nerve-wracking) as that chore was, I thoroughly enjoyed sharing my dream of an equestrian center on the beach with all those strangers; strangers who I hoped would some-day become my friends. I'll never forget how nervous I was as I parked my little station wagon in each driveway, got out and then watched as the people inside peeked between the drapes before answering the door, (most likely wondering what I was doing at their house). But at least the doors were opened, (most of them, anyway), and I'd smile and introduce myself by saying, "Hi, I'm your new neighbor who bought the old mill property and since our plans affect you… I was hoping we could talk about the project and maybe address any concerns you might have."

Once I saw how they reacted, I actually enjoyed it … just as I came to love the people I met; my brothers and sisters in Christ who deserved to be treat-ed with respect and consideration. I also loved the way they welcomed me inside… perhaps a bit skeptically at first - but by the time I left, it was with hugs and well-wishes, (and one less person to feel threatened by our plans).

At *almost* every door I made new friends, except for those few who were obviously dead-setagainst us just because we were changing some-thing they didn't want to see changed. But even in those cases, they at least realized that I **cared** about their opinions… and it was obvious that they appreciated it. Most of the people I visited loved the idea of watch-ing horses riding on the beach, and I reassured them that we would keep the beautiful trees and natural landscape intact. I wanted them to under-stand how much I, too, loved the beauty of nature and that we would be doing our very best to enhance - rather than destroy God's handiwork. I also assured everyone I spoke to that they could continue to use the property as their shortcut to the beach - and that my door would always be open if they had questions or concerns.

I'm a died-in-the-wool political conservative… but when it comes to appreciating the beauty of God's handiwork; I can "hug" a tree with the best of them. My plan was to make money by building a resort that actually enhanced nature, rather than destroying it. I believe that busi-ness and environmental protection can work hand in hand… and it was my goal to prove it.

But in looking back on those first few years, I can't believe how naive I was about the dirty underbelly of the business world. Pollyanna, (a nickname so often used to describe me and my unshakable positive attitude), had absolutely **no idea** how many almost insurmountable challenges we would have to face. It had all seemed so simple; just buy the property, build my dream, and bring jobs and new tourists to a town that was already suffering from the near collapse of the fishing and logging industries, (which had kept it afloat for more than a hundred and fifty years). What could be wrong with that?

But I'm afraid that wasn't the case, which became painfully clear the first time my business partner and contractor, (Alan), and I walked eagerly up the courthouse steps and submitted our plans to the Curry County Building Department. Where I had expected enthusiasm, (because of the much-needed revenue and new jobs we would be bringing to town), we got nothing but absolute and unequivocal rejection. The Head of the Building Department, (whose name I won't mention), sat in his little office, taking nothing more than a cursory glance at our plans before pushing them away and saying smugly, almost as if he was enjoying it, "Sorry; NO WAY you can build an equestrian resort on that piece of land." He then stood up, (his way of announcing that the meeting was over), and opened the door for us to leave.

As you can imagine, that didn't go over very well with me, so as Alan stood up… with abject disappointment darkening his face, and said, "Well, I guess there's nothing we can do but try and find a buyer for the property, then." I couldn't believe my ears! There was no way I would EVER give up that easily – so I just continued to sit right there in my chair as both men stood at the door waiting for me to get up.

"Why CAN'T we build our resort there?" I asked. "And what can we do to change whatever the problem is? If we go down, sir, we plan to go down fighting, so what advice can you give us?"

From the look on his face, it was obvious that he didn't want to discuss it… but since it was also obvious that I wasn't going anywhere, he finally sat back down and offered a more detailed explanation. According to him, even though the property was zoned C-4, (commercial use), you can't have livestock in a commercial zone. A *resort* for horse clubs would be a combination of both business and livestock zoning, and **that's** why it was impossible.

I argued that just a quarter of a mile up the road from our property, INSIDE the city limits, (which our property was not), sat the Curry County Fairgrounds, right on the ocean... complete with barns, riding arena, campsites and hoses stalls - which they rented to the public so they could ride their horses on the beach. In fact, that's where **my** horses had been boarded from the day we drove into town, so if the Curry County Fairgrounds could do it — why couldn't we? But still, he refused to listen to my arguments or offer an answer to my question.

"Ma'am, if **you** won't leave my office - then **I** will; and you can sit here for as long as you like. I'm finished," he said as he rudely turned his back and walked out the door. It sure looked to me like he was in someone's pocket - which was something I'd been completely unprepared for. Instead of encouraging us, as I'd expected, he was actually trying to make sure that we **didn't** build the resort... and that just wasn't right. Is that the way things are done in the business world? Well, we'd just have to see about that!

On that fateful day of our first visit to the Building Department, I hadn't **yet** discovered that Gold Beach was run by a small group of powerful and rich "good ole' boys" who decided what DID or DID NOT happen in their town. And now that I look back on it, I get the feeling that the Head of the Building Department was actually looking forward to reporting the results of our meeting to someone... someone he thought would be mighty happy to hear that our plans been thwarted.

But true to my usual form - and to the complete amazement of my partner, Alan, as we walked to the reception area, I looked "Mr. Head of the Building Department" directly in the eyes and politely, (yet firmly), said "I'm sorry, sir, but there simply HAS to be a way - and I WILL find it... no matter how long it takes, or what I have to do. This town needs jobs, and a new market segment of tourists is a win-win situation for everyone, and whether you believe that or not, I think that most of the residents will - so I guess I'll just have to prove that!"

As Alan and I reached the car, I admonished him for giving up so easily. In response, he argued that he'd been a contractor for more than 20 years and he had learned to recognize an impossible situation when he saw one. "Well, they haven't met me yet," I argued, "and we WILL find a way." I WOULD build my dream - and when it was done, our new equestrian resort would become one of the most popular horse vacation spots in the country.

My dream of building a "horse motel" in Gold Beach began when I was in grade school. We lived in Medford, Oregon and my father was going fishing at the coast, (Gold Beach), and asked me if I'd like to come along. I said, "Sure, if I can I bring Prince."

Prince was my horse… and the love of my life when I was 9 years old -and I, like almost every other horse owner, both young and old, dreamed of galloping him through the surf and riding on the soft sandy beaches. But alas, my father said, "Sorry sis, but we'll be staying in a motel and they don't allow horses."

"But why not," I argued? "Don't they have motels for horses?"

"No dear," he said with a patient grin. "I'm afraid motels are just for people."

"But that's not fair," I argued with my 9 year old logic. "Someday I'm going to build a motel for horses **and** people," I announced with determination, "right there in Gold Beach." And even though I'll never know for sure, my father surely must have thought it was just one more in a long line of childhood dreams that would eventually be forgotten and replaced with something new.

But he was wrong. I **never** forgot that dream, not even for a moment, and eight years later, when I graduated from high school, numerous friends wrote things in my yearbook like… "If we ever lose touch, we'll just look for the horse motel in Gold Beach." And then, when one year after High School graduation, I married my high school sweetheart, even **he** had to agree that our future would include a horse-motel in Gold Beach someday before I said "yes". The marriage may not have lasted, but the dream did… and finally, there I was - in Gold Beach… and still determined to make my dream come true.

Perhaps it was a good thing that I'd never attempted such a big project before, especially with so many environmental concerns, because if I'd known how long, expensive and difficult it would be, I might not have started it in the first place. I can't count the highly public battles we waged during those first 5 years. In fact, I could easily write a whole book about what it took to fight City Hall and Curry County for the permits, annex the property to the city so we could get sewer and to create and then "vote in" a completely NEW building zone; one that would allow **both** industry and livestock. It took going over the heads of local government, (both city and county), and using everything from State Senators to the state-wide press, and I found myself embroiled in the biggest battle of my life.

The problem was that the other team didn't play fair. So many times I was tempted to simply cut my losses and give up, (especially as sick as I was at the time, (another story for another time), but I couldn't. It would be like letting the "bad guys" win. And so we fought on. And I also can't count the number of times that if the proper palm had been "greased", our requests might have been granted, but I refused... strictly on principle. (Call me Pollyanna – but the good guys win... as long as they persevere - and we would persevere!)

And yes, 5 years later we eventually prevailed... but because the permit process took so much longer than we had anticipated, all contingency funding had been depleted and I was forced to sell just about everything I owned to keep the project afloat. Thankfully, my father and his wife Roma, as well as my aunts and uncles also believed in my dream ... so with their financial help, in the summer of 1996, (even though the project wasn't fully complete), we finally opened the doors for business. I still have a picture of me standing in front of our **"sorry full"** sign, and believe me... I was on top of the world. Now that we were open, maybe it wouldn't be long before we could finish the project. And maybe we could even afford what was **very** expensive flood insurance.

But even as determined as I was, I don't think we could have done it without some rather unexpected help; help that paved the way for my acceptance as one of the Gold Beach community - rather than being looked at as an "outsider"; help that could only have come from a power much greater than my own; something I dare to call Divine Intervention. Having had at least enough experience in business to know that it's always easier to fight from the "inside", than the "outside", I joined the local Soroptomist Club, served on the Board of Directors for the Chamber of Commerce and volunteered for every town event possible; from heading the "promotions committee" for the Curry County Fair - to being in charge of decorations for the biggest yearly fundraiser in Gold Beach; "Las Vegas Night. I tried to make myself invaluable... and it worked - but only to a point. The story I'm about to tell you did **more** than all of those things put together... and I know it HAD to have been the helping hand of my Lord at work. Here's what happened.

I've always loved prowling through museums, so it was somewhere in the middle of our "war" with the good ole' boys that I decided to spend a rainy afternoon exploring the local Historical Society Museum. There I was... reading the captions beneath all the turn-of-the-century photographs, (mostly schoolhouse pictures), when I saw my maiden name. I was especially surprised because my last name has a very unusual spelling and everyone who shares it is a close relative. When I saw that name beneath several school pictures of the class of 1892, I eagerly approached the elderly lady working behind the counter for more information.

"Excuse me," I inquired politely. "I wonder if you could tell me something about those school pictures."

"Sure, I'd be glad to help. I'm almost 90 years old and I was born right here in town; course' they called it Ellensburg back then, so I guess I oughta' know as much about those old pictures as anybody," she stated proudly as she slowly hobbled her way over to the wall of photographs. "What would you like to know, young lady?"

"That's my family name," I explained as I pointed to the wording beneath one of the pictures, "and I was wondering if you knew anything about them?" I asked.

"I sure do," she replied emphatically. "Are you saying this is **your** last name?"

"Yes, it is, and there aren't many of us around – so I'm sure these folks must be my relatives."

"Well then, dear," she said with a welcoming smile. "I reckon you'd better give me a big hug then – because I almost married your great-granddaddy! If you've got some time, I've got a whole passel of stories to tell you."

And I did have the time… which is why it was more than three hours later that I walked away from that little museum with the biggest genealogical mystery in my family solved. The missing branch of our family tree had been located at last… and amazingly enough – it was right here in Gold Beach. I couldn't wait to tell my aunts, because all three of them are devoted to genealogy and I knew that they would be thrilled to find out what happened to my great-great grandfather, Frank. All the family had been able to discover was that he was a Texas Ranger turned Confederate solder, who… when he returned to Texas after the Civil War, loaded his wife and six children into a covered wagon and headed for Oregon. After that, no sign of him could be found. And now, we knew where he had ended up; right here in Gold Beach. Isn't that amazing? Before I left the museum that day, I joined of the Curry County Historical Society… and the following week, the front page of our weekly town newspaper sported the big, bold headline "Pioneer family returns to Gold Beach". No longer was I merely a stranger moving to town; now I was a long lost founding-family member finding her way home..

Mrs. Miller (the curator) was most eager to talk… and told me the amazing story of how my great-great grandfather's wagon train had become trapped in the winter snow as it was crossing the wild, (and nearly impassable – still today), Siskiyou Mountain Range, and how one brave rider struck out for the coast; hoping to find help before the entire wagon train froze to death or starved. And then she told me about how that lone rider, my great-great grandfather, found the help he needed in a little community called Ellensburg; which was eventually renamed Gold Beach. And she also told me (with a wink) that at the time, there was an extreme shortage of young marriage-aged men, (and LOTS of young women), so when the townspeople found out that there were at least 15 strong, able bodied and unmarried men on that wagon train, they risked all odds and set out in the middle of a terrible snowstorm to rescue them. And **that** was how I discovered that my great-great grandfather was one of the early pioneer families in this area. She even showed me a local map and pointed out where his original land grant had been, as well as the land grant belonging to his son, (the man she almost married), my great-grandfather William.

Wow!! And if that wasn't amazing enough, what was even MORE amazing was how fast the news spread in such a small town. Even before the local newspaper headline made the story common knowledge, I was welcomed by almost everyone I met. No longer did they look at me like a stranger who was taking advantage of their beautiful town. Now they considered me family. I could just imagine the disappointment on the faces of those "good ole' boys" when they got the news; knowing that I wouldn't be quite so easy to stop now that I was a member of one of the *founding* families. I can't tell you how excited I was, and before I left that museum on that fateful day, I made photocopies of everything they had regarding my ancestors, from birth, marriage and death records to newspaper articles. I then hurried home to call my aunt, who quickly corroborated the names and dates and declared the family genealogical mystery solved. But to me, there was still a much bigger question. When I was only 9 years old, how did I know that I *belonged* in Gold Beach and why was I so SET on never giving up on that dream? I guess some things defy logic - but to this day, I believe it was destiny.

Mrs. Miller told me many wonderful stories, and even gave me the name and address of a 92 year old man who had lived next door to my family homestead when he was a young boy. The very next day I went to see him, (Mr. Gardner), and he welcomed me with open arms. "Why I was just a young whippersnapper when your folks left town," he said, "but they gave my daddy something to hold onto in case anyone ever came to get it. No one ever came… so I guess I'll give it to you right now, young lady," he announced with a smile. "Just give me a minute and I'll go find it."

When he reappeared in his living room, he was carrying a large manila envelope, which he carefully opened. Will wonders never cease! There was the original signed land grant, as well as numerous local newspaper articles about the family; stories that brought me to both laughter and tears. I couldn't believe my eyes. These were the missing pieces of my family history…and to me, they were priceless treasures.

And that same afternoon, Mr. Gardner drove me out to the original land grant where my great-great grandfather had settled. I was literally mesmerized as I imagined what their lives must have been like and how they must have felt when they were forced to leave their beloved home behind. I'll bet they never imagined that their great-great-granddaughter would be standing here right now, more than a hundred years later… following in their footsteps. Mr. Gardner told me the whole story about how they were driven out of town (and why) and I was not only saddened by their loss - but even **more** determined to succeed at building my own dream. Apparently my great-great-grandfather had also had a dream - and it wasn't that much different from my own.

His land grant was a magnificent piece of ocean front property that was so beautiful it has since become a State Park, with old growth trees so tall you can barely see the sky and a creek, (named after him), that cascades down the hillside… turning into a waterfall as it tumbles over the cliff and into the mighty Pacific Ocean. He loved that land so much that he dreamed of building a hunting lodge; a place where Easterners and foreigners could stay while he guided them in search of deer, elk, cougar and bear. The early railroad was supposedly on its way at the time, so he decided to risk everything he owned and built the lodge, counting on the train to bring the hunters and tourists through the dangerous Siskiyou Mountain passes. But unfortunately, as history so often tells us, the railroads were highly unpredictable, (and their routes all too often controlled by both politics and an earlier version of the same "good ole' boys power struggle" we were running up against today).

Eventually my great-great grandfather lost his battle... because when the railroad finally reached the Siskiyou National Wilderness, they decided it was impossible to bridge the huge canyons and steep terrain, and they turned further south... into Northern California. And because that train never came, he lost everything - including his land. When I went to visit the property, I found the stone chimney and a few of the larger beams that were still rotting on the fern covered ground and I just stood there... looking over the cliff at the crashing waves and smelling the sweet pines, and imagining what **he** must have felt like when he said goodbye to his dream. Now here I stood, almost in his exact footsteps, and our battle was just beginning. But now I had yet **another** reason to fight. Now I would be fighting for BOTH of us.

After months of back-breaking hand-clearing, we carefully prepared the property for construction with the least amount of damage to the natural beauty of the land. I was out working on the project site one day when an unexpected visitor appeared. It was my new friend, 92 year old Mr. Gardner, and his pickup truck was loaded to the brim with flowers and trees. "These are for you, my dear," he announced with a warm smile and a big hug. "I dug them up off your family's old homestead and I thought they'd look right nice here on your new place."

How do you thank someone for a gift like that? I couldn't find words... so as the tears began to fall, I just hugged him and said, "May God bless you, Mr. Gardner!" It was the perfect way to bring the old and the new together, and I spent the next several days selecting the perfect locations and planting my treasures; treasures from the past.

I really did love my little town on the Pacific Ocean. I opened my front door to the sight and sound of crashing waves and magnificent sunsets... and when I looked out my back door, there were the Siskiyou Mountains, tall and majestic, with rich green fields where cattle and deer grazed and through which the gentle river flowed. I could sit on my deck and catch salmon and steelhead and I spent countless hours watching the river otter play and the salmon making their way upstream to spawn. The area was teeming with wildlife and before long I had to turn the little yellow raft I kept tied to my deck upside down because so many ducks and geese were using it as a landing pad. The Curry County Road Department finally put up a "duck crossing" sign in front of my house because I had befriended so many of them that I earned the name "duck lady" and they were constantly crossing between the project property and my house… parading in a single line, sometimes mixed in with the wild geese.- and always making me wonder why they chose to walk when they could so easily fly across the road. I think maybe they just liked holding up traffic.

As far as I was concerned, I was living in Heaven on earth and not a single day went by that I didn't say "WOW"! "Thank you Heavenly Father for leading me here… and thank you for helping us through every single battle we waged". But we weren't done yet, as construction was to be completed in three phases… but at least Phase I was complete – and we were "open for business". It felt like victory, and it was… **but then came the flood - and it was all over.**

And now it is done. I have bid farewell to both my town and my dream and it's time to start out on a whole new adventure. That's why I think it's more than fitting that my first stop should be Gold Beach. When I get there, I'll pay for Lucky, arrange to borrow the Soroptimist meeting room for my performance, (which I'm sure they'll let me use since I've been a member for 7 years), make up some flyers, place an ad in the local paper and maybe even do a spot on the local radio. Then I'll put on a show of my songs, poetry and the miracle of the Bible. To tell you the truth, I don't really think I'm that good, (at least nothing special), so I know there's a good chance they'll laugh at me… but that's ok. I'll share my art – and even more importantly, I'll share my heart… and bear witness to the miracles that have changed my life. So what if they laugh at me? At least they'll hear the message… which is one of joy, hope, faith, love and complete trust in God.

But I sure wish I could get rid of these darn butterflies in my stomach. Gold Beach will be such a tough audience! It reminds me of how Jesus said that preaching was most difficult in his own home town. That's because the people had a preconceived notion about him as a carpenter and as the son of Joseph. Not that I'm worth being put in the same breath as Jesus… but I think the way I feel the same way about putting on my first show in Gold Beach. Most of the people in town think of me as the daring business woman who fought against all odds to make her dream come true, while others think of me as an accomplished horsewoman and animal lover. I'm often called the "duck lady" or the "flower lady", (for obvious reasons when you look at my property), while others know me as a very vocal member of the Chamber of Commerce Board of Directors or as a Soroptimist Sister. A few might even call me "one tough cookie who doesn't know when to quit". (I'll bet the good ole' boys are in THAT group.) But at least there was one thing EVERYONE knew; (both friend and enemy) and that was my deep and abiding love of God and Jesus.

Boy, won't they be surprised when they see the "real" me; Abigayle, inspirational poet, songwriter, story-teller and "cheerleader for the people:? Whew… there go those butterflies again!

So early tomorrow morning, I'll start up Lucky's engine and drive away - away from my sons, my grandchildren, my father and step-mother Roma, Alan and even my brother Ron. (He doesn't let me call him "Ronnie" anymore.) And this time, let's hope that I make it all the way to Gold Beach without breaking down!

chapter 7

September 29, 1998

THE JOURNEY BEGINS!

There's just never a dull moment, is there! I was so excited when I woke up this morning that I practically jumped out of bed... eager to greet the day on which I would officially begin my most exciting adventure ever! The new day was just dawning, and the late September sky was shades of gold and red as I removed everything from the countertops, unhooked my electric chord, cable wire, telephone line and water hose... and at last I was ready to roll!

But as I took my place in the drivers seat and turned the ignition key; nothing happened, not even a click. I thought that maybe since I'd been parked for a month, and my sons said my converter wasn't working properly, that my battery was dead, so I got out the little "mini" jumper cables my dad made for me and hooked the interior battery to the exterior battery and tried it again... and again... but still nothing happened.

Oh well, I guess that's what sons are for, because I called mine and they hurried right over. Alan had to leave for work, but before he left he said that if it turned out to be my battery, I could have the new one he had just put in his truck. That was so generous, especially since he wouldn't let me pay him for it, so I'm hoping that maybe he'll be able to recharge mine and use it in his truck.

And guess what? I figured it all out last night. After I set aside the $2,000 I need to pay for Lucky, I'll still have enough money left to fill both gas tanks, (30 gallons each), and my two propane tanks, (5 gallons each), and still have $150. That's more than I had when I LEFT Gold Beach so I was feeling darn pretty good. And to top it off, Alan surprised me yesterday with several bags of groceries - so obviously I'm being well taken care of.

And the problem DID turn out to be the battery, so it only took a few minutes for Scott and Jeremy to put in Alan's new one - and then...I was ready to roll. I'd been so anxious to leave Portland and begin my REAL journey, that all I'd felt was excitement - until it was actually time to say goodbye and I realized how much it would hurt.

As I drove away, I could see them both in my rearview mirror, just standing there waving ... and it was as though I was leaving my entire life behind; all the places I've known and the people I love. The tears started rolling down my cheeks and all I could think of was how blessed I was to have had the wonderful years we spent together. I have no idea when I'll see them again, but I will always be able to picture them as little boys... racing to see who could gather the most wood for our campfire. I can re-member Jeremy's first Little League t-ball baseball game when he hit the ball, ran to first base and just kept right on running... all the way across the field and into the school - with the parent-filled stands laughing so hard I wished I could capture that moment forever. I can still see my two sons sailing down the ski slopes, leaving me far behind... with me holler-ing all the way for them to "slow down and be more careful".

For so many years it was just "the three of us against the world"... and I am so very thankful that the Lord saw fit to put those two wonderful young men in my care. I love them with all my heart, as well as my par-ents, my brother, my aunts and uncles and my grandchildren... and even though I've only been gone for a few hours, I already miss them more than I thought possible.

But shame on me; I shouldn't be sad... because those memories are mine forever, and now that my boys have become grown men, my job of getting them ready for the world is finished and the Lord has assigned me a new job. I am leaving Scott and Jeremy in my Lord's most loving hands, (as they are His sons too), and now it's time to quit dwelling on the past... wipe away these darn tears and start concentrating on the future and what I can do to make a difference.

And this time I've already made it halfway to Gold Beach without a single break down. How about that! But since Lucky's still overheating, I decided not to push my luck, (no pun intended), and stop for the night at the half-way point, (my favorite little viewpoint), to give the engine a chance to cool down - and me a chance to rest before I actually drive into Gold Beach. After all, there's absolutely no reason to hurry.

Even when I drove Lucky to Portland a month ago, my sons and Alan were waiting and wondering when I'd arrive, but this time is different. This time I'm driving into complete "nothingness"; **just my freedom and me**. I don't think I've EVER been in a situation like this before, so it feels kind of strange; and I can't help feeing guilty; like I should be hurrying to **do** something. That's why I decided to stop right here at my little mountain viewpoint where I spent my **first** night on the road, and think. It actually felt comforting when I pulled into the exact same parking spot and turned off my engine. It felt like I had come home... so I guess "home" really **is** where the heart is... and for tonight anyway, **this** parking spot is my home.

The scenery at my little viewpoint is breathtaking and it's so peaceful and quiet. I'm sitting by my window, gazing out over the glimmering blue water surrounded by tree covered mountains and wondering about what my future holds. Up until now, my entire life has been nothing but one non-stop blur of activity ... and now that the whirlwind has passed, I have a feeling it might take some time to adjust.

And good news; so far, Lucky's running like a top, (thanks to my sons, my dad and Alan), and I plan to arrive in Gold Beach around noon tomorrow. Yes, I've left a big chunk of my heart back in Portland... but tomorrow's a whole new day, a gift from God, and I look forward to seeing what it holds.

Now I just have to figure out how to make the $150 I'll have left after paying for Lucky last long enough for me to prepare for, publicize and put on my first performance. First, I'll need to find a place to park Lucky, (cheap). By the time I place an ad in the paper and print flyers for my show, I'll be lucky if I have enough money left to fill my gas and propane tanks when I leave Gold Beach. And even though I've never been a big eater, (I tend to think of food as "fuel for my tank"), my cupboards will definitely need to be restocked if I plan to stay alive long enough to do whatever the Lord has in mind.

Money problems or not, I still refuse to charge admission for my show, nor am I passing a plate for contributions. Logic tells me I SHOULD be concerned, but how **can** I be when all I have to do is close my eyes and I can hear that wonderful, familiar voice I love so much saying *"Do not worry - everything will be fine"*. *"I will do my part but you must do yours."* Now if only I could be SURE what MY part is …but I'm not, so all I can do is my best, and leave the rest to God.

So then why is my stomach doing flip-flops? It's probably because I'm driving back into my beloved little town of Gold Beach and seeing the property I put so much of my heart and soul into… now occupied by someone else; someone who lied and cheated their way to get it, (another story for later). And as far as I know, my ex-husband, Jon, could still be living in Gold Beach and although I harbor no anger or resentment, (in fact, I love him like a brother and pray for his happiness), it still upsets me to think about bumping into him. And what I'm even *more* nervous about is putting on my first show in 10 years… and for such a difficult audience. To say that I'm *rusty* is a major understatement, and I can't help but wonder what they will think? Will they like my poetry and songs, or will they laugh and think I've lost my mind? I don't know… but I sure do wish those butterflies would settle down.

I think I'll take a nice relaxing walk along the riverbank. Surely the magnificence of nature will calm me down… and then I'll read my Bible and pray. That always works!

Look out Gold Beach – here I come!

chapter 8

September 30, 1998

Something absolutely wonderful has happened, and I can't wait to tell you about it.

The rest of my drive to Gold Beach was smooth and uneventful and my heart soared as I rounded the last corner... and there, tucked in the most beautiful little cove I've ever seen, was the town I love. As I crossed the mighty Rogue River on the beautiful arched bridge, I felt as though the land itself was welcoming me home, and all my butterflies disappeared.

I parked Lucky at what I thought was the cheapest RV park in town - and boy-oh-boy was I ever in for a surprise. It was $25 for one night, and at that rate, my $150 would be gone before I knew it. I almost climbed back into Lucky and drove away, but then I thought...no, I'll just spend **one** night here and find some place cheaper tomorrow. The problem is that Lucky is my only transportation - so I have to be parked in town so I can walk where ever I need to go.

Oh well, I could probably use the exercise anyway... so I parked Lucky for the night and then used my newfound RV knowledge, (thanks dad), to hook up to water, electricity and sewer. Then I walked to the nearest phone booth where I called Dean, the man I bought Lucky from, to let him know that I was back in town and had the money to pay him. He's known as quite the shrewd businessman, (if you know what I mean), so I had been both surprised and grateful when he had so generously signed the RV title over to me before I left for Portland, trusting me to bring him the money - with no contract and no promissory note of any kind. When I spoke to him on the phone today, I could tell he was relieved to see that his trust hadn't been misplaced when he said, "I'll be right over". As I waited, I used the idle time to start sketching a flyer for my first "Poetry on the Road" performance.

It was 3:00 in the afternoon when he finally knocked on my door and after a few minutes of taking care of financial business, he asked, "So, what are your plans now?"

"Well, I'm not exactly sure," I answered, "but finding a cheaper place to park is definitely number one on my list." Then I told him that I was going to kick off my 'Poetry on the Road" journey with a performance right here in Gold Beach, and I could see the surprise on his face - the same surprise I'm sure I'll get from EVERYONE in town when they find out.

"So, you're a poet, huh?" he said with BOTH eyebrows raised. "I've never really liked poetry much - but it sounds interesting," he said politely.

"I've **always** been a poet; Dean. I just put it aside while I got the project started, so now it's time to get back to what I **really** do." Dean is not what you'd call a religious man, but for some reason the spirit moved me so I told him the story of the Bible and the visitation and explained that that was why I would be spending the rest of my life using my gifts to serve God.

"Would you like to hear a sample?" I asked.

"Sure," he answered, politely but obviously without enthusiasm. "Like I said, I'm not big on poetry - but I'll listen."

And so I began... selecting one of my favorites, "The Book of Life".

When I finished the poem, his entire demeanor had changed, and he now spoke with genuine enthusiasm, "Wow, that's really good. You ARE a poet; I mean... you're the real deal. You even made **me** feel better and I've got to tell you, things have been pretty tough in my life lately.

Thanks Abigayle," he said with a handshake and appreciative smile. "I really needed that!"

"You're welcome Dean. It was my honor. I've been working on a flyer for my performance," I said as I showed him my rather crude drawing, "but I'm afraid I'm not much of an artist."

He looked at my drawing of Lucky towing a book of poetry and driving on a winding road under a big bright rainbow. "Well, I'm afraid I'm not much of an artist either or I'd give you a hand, but maybe I can do something else to help." That's when he took out the money I had just given him and smiled as he handed me back a one-hundred dollar bill. "I'd like you to keep this, Abigayle. It's not much, but maybe it will help a little."

Do you believe it? My $150 just turned into $250... which means I can afford a monthly spot at the local trailer park, (cheap because it's what we called the "Gold Beach Slums"), and still have $75 left over for food, gas and flyers. I think they charge $175 a month at the old trailer park so I'll drive over there first thing in the morning and find out. That'll give me a whole month in which to design a logo, distribute the flyers and practice my performance. Thank you Jesus – and thank you Dean for allowing the Lord to work through you!

How's that for amazing? I just knew my Heavenly Father would take care of me!

Well, I'd better get back to work on the flyer, and now... thanks to Dean, I have a plan!

chapter 9

October 1, 1998

THE NEXT DAY

What a day… what a day… what a day!

I left the more expensive RV Park at noon and headed for the one and only crummy, (and cheap), trailer park in Gold Beach. It might be considered the "Gold Beach slum", but at least it's right in the center of town and overlooks the ocean - with a short but steep path to the beach. In fact, it overlooks the fairgrounds horse barn, which was built right on the sandy beach and where I kept my horses stabled for almost three years.

When I think of all the hours I spent at that barn… and I never once bothered to look up the hillside and see the old, rundown and weather-beaten trailers parked at the top of the cliff. I was at those stables every single morning and every single evening for three full years… rain or shine, sickness or health - cleaning stalls, feeding my horses and riding them on the beach, and I never once wondered what life was like for the poor residents who lived in those trailers overlooking the barn. And now here I am living among them. How could I have been so wrapped up in my own world… and shame on me! And thank you Lord for giving me this opportunity to spend time with these people. Most of them are either disabled or on welfare, while many have drug or alcohol problems or are forced to live on a small social security or disability check. I'm actually glad that this is the only place I could afford; because this is the kind of place where the people really NEED to be reminded how much God loves them. These are the people Jesus took the time to seek out... and I'm going to do the same.

When I first drove Lucky into the trailer park a little after noon today, I left the engine running, (in case it wouldn't start again), while I hurriedly searched the entire property on foot looking for the manager. Finally I found a beat-up little travel trailer near the back of the park with a hand written sign on the door that said "manager". I knocked as loudly as I could, in case the person inside was elderly or hard of hearing, but no one answered.

So now, even more worried about Lucky's engine idling and over-heating, I literally ran up and down the half dozen or more streets lined with old, old, and older mobile homes and countless tiny beat up travel trailers, looking for someone... anyone, who could tell me where the manager was. But eventually I gave up and decided to pull into an empty space up close to the highway. I'd have to worry about finding the manager and checking in later - because I didn't dare leave Lucky idling any longer.

Naturally, I'd have much rather parked in the row that overlooked the ocean, but those spots were already taken by permanent single-wide trailers that looked like they'd been there forever - and the only RV parking spots were up front along Highway 101, the main street in Gold Beach.. But view or no view, it worked out for the best because I'll be walking everywhere I go... which means being close to the highway is a good thing. At least I can HEAR the ocean - and guess what? It still fills my heart with joy and wonder.

It took a while, but eventually I found the semi-crippled elderly lady who runs the place and after more than an hour spent visiting with her in her little trailer... and listening as the obviously lonely woman showed me dozens of her "treasures", from pretty rocks and agates to whimsical figurines, family pictures and doilies she had crocheted… she was so proud to show me her special possessions that even though I was eager to get settled in, there was **no way** I could take the joy of that time away from her.

But eventually, I managed to make a polite escape and headed back to the parking spot that will be my "home" for the next month. Since the rent was $180, that means I now have $70 left over. So… if I go light on the food, fill only one of my 30-gallon gas tanks when I leave town, (at $.99 per gallon), and fill my propane tanks, (which are absolutely vital to keep my refrigerator running), it looks like I won't have much left for making flyers or photocopies of the poetry I plan to give away at my show. But that's ok. I'm not the least bit worried because I know that **somehow** the Lord will provide; just as He did when He touched Dean's heart and a man known for NOT parting with his money gave me a hundred dollar bill. And guess what? I even have cable TV to watch on my little 12-inch television.

To some, it may seem like a drastic fall from a 4000 square foot home and shop on the ocean and riverfront, filled with comfortable furnishings, (not to mention my prized antique grand piano), but to me… it's plenty. After all, I'm rich in all the ways that matter!

I still can't believe I'm back in Gold Beach again… and starting tomorrow I'll start making arrangements for my first performance. Once a week we have a Soroptimist luncheon, so this week I'll walk to the meeting and share my plans with my Soroptimist Sisters. Not only will they be shocked to see me - as I had already hugged each and every one of them goodbye when I left town the first time, but I have no doubt that they'll let me use the meeting room for my show. Then, as soon as I've nailed down the exact time and place, I'll begin making the flyers and placing the ads. I'd also better get busy practicing my poetry and songs on the guitar because I haven't played my music, (other than the piano), or put on a poetry reading for more than seven years now… and I'm not sure how good my memory is. I don't believe in "poetry readings" because they're boring! I like to act out my poems - sometimes even using props and costumes, (since many of them are stories), and I refuse to read from a piece of paper unless it's absolutely necessary.

So it looks like I've got more than enough to keep me busy... and plenty to be grateful for! I am so blessed!

Finally made it, age 15.

chapter 10

October 2, 1998

Another gorgeous day at the beach - and ANOTHER MAJOR SURPRISE!

Last night I was taking a walk in the moonlight, (heading for the ocean of course), when I saw an all-too familiar figure entering the trailer next to mine. It was Jon, my ex-husband (or almost ex-husband - because our marriage wasn't legal because he neglected to divorce his first wife before he married me).

Even though I had known he might still be living in Gold Beach, I certainly didn't expect him to be only a few feet away from my front door. And yes, I was sincere when I said that I bear absolutely no grudge or animosity towards him, because he, too, is one of God's children. Just because he was still married to someone else, (unbeknownst to me), when I let his startlingly handsome good looks, charming manners and what appeared to be unending supply of energy and enthusiasm, fool me into thinking I had finally found the man of my dreams, doesn't changed that.

Actually, the fact that he already had a wife in Florida turned out to be yet another blessing, because before the honeymoon was even over, I discovered that marrying him had been a horrible mistake. Maybe it was because I'd been alone for so long, and that my dream project was almost ready to open for business. Maybe it was because my children were finally adults, so "good father material" was no longer a factor, and Jon treated me like a queen, which felt wonderful… but whatever the reason, I had been fooled - and had no one but myself to blame. But the single-most attractive thing about Jon **should** have raised a big red flag - but instead, it was the one thing that really clinched the deal for me. Yes, I'm gradually slowing down as the years go by, (thank goodness), but I'm still a bundle of energy and enthusiasm compared to most people, and Jon was the first man I'd ever met who could keep up with me… step for step.

It didn't matter if it was 2:00 in the morning, after a long day of working on the project, Jon was always happy to accompany me on a moonlight walk along the beach - even if I wanted to climb a tall and difficult cliff just to check out the view from as high up as possible. We talked, laughed and had fun together – and since I no longer needed a provider or a father figure for my children, I thought that having a companion I could simply enjoy myself with was enough. But within two weeks of our wedding day, I got a call from his wife in Florida, explaining that she had never actually filed the divorce papers Jon had signed before he left town, so he was still legally married to her. I suppose I should have been heartbroken, but instead… I felt relieved! I felt FREE.

In 1995, when he asked me to marry him, I said "yes", but insisted on a one year engagement period before the wedding. I was no spring chicken at 44 years old, and I wanted the "newness" to wear off so we could see what was beneath the goose bumps and butterflies before we actually said "I do". And I've got to give Jon a lot of credit, because he kept up the façade for one full year… until **after** the wedding, (actually it was on the honeymoon), when I found out some things that broke my heart; I found out **how** he could kept up with my boundless supply of energy and I found out **why** he liked to talk the night away with me. It was because he was doing drugs; (using methamphetamine), and shooting it up with a needle… which is why he never had a red or runny nose, usually a good indicator that someone is snorting something.

That also explained why the money kept disappearing, and why I would wake up in the middle of the night and his side of the bed was empty; he was either gambling at the Indian Casino about an hour south of Gold Beach, sleeping with another woman or simply too "wired" to sleep. (Of course he told me he had insomnia and took long walks on the beach so I wouldn't be bothered.) And to make matters even worse, I soon found out how he supported his gambling and drug habit; he was so drop-dead gorgeous that it was easy for him to trade either drugs or money for sex; and, in fact, it was one of the "older women" who *kept him in money* who finally came to see me - and told me what was going on.

And believe me, she didn't do it out of anger or revenge; in fact, she broke down in tears and literally **begged** me to let him keep seeing her - even while he was married to me. She said she couldn't live without him; and this from a woman who had been, (and was still), married to the same man for 30 years. Wow! Now there was a sister who desperately needed help... which is exactly what I tried to do when she told me. She was so miserable, and my heart went out to her. We talked, (and prayed together), for several hours that first day when she came over, and on several days following... until I finally convinced her not only to tell her own husband what she had done and ask for his forgiveness, but to come with me as I confronted Jon. There's no sense going into more detail, but it was heartbreaking to see how desperate she was - and just as sad to find out that Satan was using drugs and gambling to control a good, kind man like Jon. It's not a memory I care to dwell on, but I will say that I'll never forget the look of complete shock on Jon's face as she and I walked up to him - arm in arm. (You kind of had to be there!)

So I guess that explains why I felt such utter relief when I found out he already had a wife in Florida... and why I firmly believe that it was a gift from God; **my freedom.** I take my vows seriously - for better or for worse, in sickness and in health, and I would have felt bound by honor to stand by his side and try to heal him for as long as it took, as his wife. But now that I was off the marriage hook, (excuse the trite saying), anything

I did to help him was as a friend and as a Christian - rather than as his spouse. Even though he moved out of the house immediately, I became his mentor as well as his "cheerleader" as I did my best to help him beat the addictions of both drugs and gambling. He kept telling me that I was his **one last** connection with the good, clean side of the world, and we spent countless hours reading the Bible, praying and discussing his future. I tried to convince Jon that Satan must really be afraid of what he could do for God - if he was so determined to hold on to him, but I felt like I was in a battle with the devil himself... fighting the powers of evil for a lost brother. I gave it my very best, even though I was dealing with the aftermath of the flood, trying to sell the property, and healing from surgery that removed part of one breast. (All this, and much, much more, happened AFTER the flood and the miracle of the Bible.) Gee, I wonder who ELSE Satan was after?

As I drove away from Gold Beach on that hot August afternoon, I prayed that Jon finally had his demons under control. The night before I left, he assured me that he was moving somewhere else and starting a new life... far away from the circle of friends (?) that surrounded him in Gold Beach. That's also why I said earlier that he MIGHT still be in Gold Beach... because even though I was **hoping** he had done as he said he would - and I prayed that he was in some other town, making new friends, and starting a new life for himself, I still had my doubts. Satan has found a powerful tool with which to steal souls... even really good and kind hearted people like Jon, and that's "meth" or "crank" or whatever the street name is these days. It's cheap, easy to make and easy to hide from those around you. I prayed long and hard both **for** Jon and **with** Jon - but no matter what I said or did, it was HIS battle to fight – and I had my doubts that he would be able to stand on his own. When I saw him entering the trailer next door to mine, I had no doubt that my fears were well-founded.

At first I didn't even recognize him because he looked so horrible. The once extremely handsome Italian man, clean cut and well built, looked like he'd been living in a shopping cart under a bridge. His hair was long and matted, his face fully bearded and untrimmed, and his clothes were dirty and worn. When he walked, he was hunched over, like someone carrying the burden of true shame on his shoulders and was trying to move around without being seen. He probably wished he was invisible... and it made my heart ache to see him that way. What could have happened after I left?

When I saw him enter that trailer, (and he saw me at the same time), I held some small hope that he was merely visiting someone; at least I did... until about an hour later when he knocked at my door carrying a small bag filled with my favorite bakery treats, (maple bars). My first reaction was... I'll just be polite. I'll say "Hello. How are you, Jon?" But I won't invite him in.

But apparently the Lord had something else in mind... because I just couldn't do it. The words wouldn't come out of my mouth. He looked so sad and so lost that my heart went out to him. He was suffering; even if it was his own doing, and I, as a cheerleader for the people, can't pick and choose who I want to encourage. And besides that... maybe seeing him again was part of God's plan - and I should try to save him one more time.

"Hi Jon," I said as I opened the door with a big smile and genuine warmth. Normally, my next question would have been "How are you?" but the answer to that was already obvious and I didn't want to make him feel any worse than he already did... so I let it go – and instead I simply asked, (much to my own surprise), "Please, won't you come in?"

As he stepped inside, his head was still down and his eyes refused to meet mine. "I wasn't sure you'd let me in, but I was hoping you might. I rent that brown trailer right over there," he said as he pointed to the rundown trailer so close to mine, "so I guess we're neighbors."

And that was the beginning of a three hour conversation that focused on forgiveness and salvation through Jesus. I chose not to dwell on the "story of Jon" earlier when I said, "...and did I mention having major surgery and ending a marriage during that time?"That's because it's such a long and complicated story, and filled with so much pain and disappointment, that I refuse to give it any power. But now I think that Jon was part of my training, or perhaps a test of my willingness to put my own feelings aside and focus on what I can do for others. Whatever the reason, it was because of my experience with Jon; and the year I spent trying to help him fight the *beast*, that I can now understand and relate to others who find themselves in similar situations; and there are millions of them out there! We are ALL God's children and we must mourn, (not hate), those who have been beguiled by Satan; those who might never make it "home" to be with our Heavenly Father again. Each soul is a loss for ALL of us, and it makes me want to weep for their fate. I just wish I could do more.

The Lord works in mysterious ways, so perhaps living only a few feet away from Jon held TWO wonderful opportunities for me: One, I could try one last time to steer him on the right path, hopefully convincing him to turn to God for his comfort and joy - rather than drugs, women and gambling... and two, I could get rid of any lingering resentment (or feelings of inadequacy), that I might still be carrying deep inside my heart. After all, 'tis all vanity', as the Bible says, and I know it was my "ego" that suffered most when I found out about his *secret life*. I tried to deny it, but the truth was that I couldn't understand why **my** love, (and our life together), hadn't been enough to take the place of the drugs and gambling. Wasn't I worth it? Wasn't a life with me better than getting high, throwing away money at a casino or having sex with strange women?

But on the day after the flood, when I held that miracle Bible in my arms and felt so many emotional and earthly obstacles literally float away... those self-centered, egotistical feelings were among them - and seeing him now has reaffirmed that fact. It was never about me in the first place, and there was nothing more I could have done.

This is truly the beginning of my new life; (my REAL calling on Earth), and if I am to give myself completely to God, then I must be clean in both spirit and body- and **free** from any past regret or pain. I firmly believe that the Lord KNEW I still had some small part of me wondering "why", and now... as I pray for Jon and once again try to help him, it will be helping me as well. (More training...)

But I think the most surprising, (and wonderful), thing is how I **feel** about the situation. Deep in my most secret "heart of hearts", I don't feel the least bit angry or betrayed; I just feel sad that he is so lost and miserable. I don't feel jealous or inadequate because he slept with other women, (and exposed me to disease and possibly death); instead I feel relieved that the Lord has given me one more chance to get through to him. I am so thankful that I didn't get Aids or some other sexually trans-mitted disease during the short time I THOUGHT we were married, which easily could have happened since Jon admitted to sharing needles with who ever he happened to be with at the time. I truly am blessed to have come out of that horrible situation unscathed, completely healthy and a whole lot wiser. Poor Jon, he's the one who's still suffering... and I can only pray that as I counsel him, the Holy Spirit will put the words in my mouth that will somehow get through... and that eventually he will find his way back to God.

Now I have another problem. After dealing with something so pow-erful and heart wrenching, it's hard to get my mind back on the "nuts and bolts" of setting up my first performance. I've only got three weeks in which to prepare for and promote my first show... so it's time to put Jon out of my mind - and get back to work finishing my "poetry on the road" flyer and practicing my songs and poetry. I'm not worried about the stories - because they come without practice when you simply tell the truth, but the songs and poetry are going to take some work.

So... Id better get started.

chapter 11

October 14, 1998

ALMOST TWO WEEKS LATER

Oh no! It's only five days until my first performance at the Soroptimist Center and my throat is so sore I can't even talk, let alone sing. I've spent so many hours practicing my songs on the guitar that I sound like a frog – and the blisters on my fingertips from playing for the first time in so many years haven't had time to turn into calluses yet, so I don't know which hurts worse… my throat or my fingers.

But at least I got the flyers done and finished drawing the logo that I'll be using from now on; a picture of my RV towing a big book of poetry under a rainbow, (in honor of the rainbow the Lord placed over my head when I made my covenant with Him.). I'm not much of an artist, but it actually looks pretty good, if I do say so myself.

George, the printer we once used for our project, insisted on doing all my Poetry on the Road printing for free, so I made copies of the poems I'll be reciting in case anyone in the audience is touched by a particular poem and would like to take a copy home with them. At the Soroptimist luncheon I stood up and told everyone the whole story and that I had chosen Gold Beach as the beginning of my journey. Since Soroptimist Ladies are business-women, I kind of expected them to think I was nuts… taking off with no destination and no plans, but that wasn't the case at all. Of course they were surprised, but they were also enthused, and even asked me to do a poem for them while they ate. And guess what? They LOVED it! In fact, they were so enthusiastic and supportive that they're not only letting me use the meeting room, but at their suggestion, I'll be using it for **two** nights and putting on two shows, just in case it doesn't hold enough people. And to top it off, they've even volunteered to provide refreshments at both performances.

As you can image, I was on cloud nine after the meeting... blessed with the unbridled encouragement and enthusiasm of my Soroptimist Sisters and the generosity of George, the printer. And if that wasn't amazing enough, after the meeting, as I was gathering up my things for the walk back to the trailer park, one of the ladies came up to me and said, "I'm so sorry, but I'll be out of town next week so I can't attend your program. I just wanted to give you this before I left," she said with a smile as she handed me a $50 bill. Unbelievable!

"Thank you so very much," I said and gave her a big grateful hug.

"May the Lord bless you on your journey, my dear," she responded as she hugged me back. "I'm just honored to be able to help, and I'm sure you'll touch more hearts than you know," she added. I'm still dumbfounded. There are so many kind and loving people out there... and I am so very blessed to have been given the ability to inspire and encourage them. It's not me, you know... it's my Lord at work here - and He's been putting in some real overtime!

The way people have been reaching out to help me has been amazing, but I do have to admit that it's been pretty emotionally draining to be here in my little town again - especially when I counsel Jon or when I run into the couple that literally "stole" the project right out from under me after the flood. (Yet another story for another time.) I guess the Lord knows I need to practice "forgiveness", and running into them - and helping Jon again is giving me lots of time to work on it.

But right now, I need to focus **all** my attention on getting well before my first performance - and I've only got five days in which to do it. I fear that this is no ordinary sore throat because now I have a fever too. So, on that unpleasant note, I'm going to bed and pray that **if** it be **His** will, my Lord will heal me. I always pray that way, because as I've found out so many times in the past... sometimes suffering serves a purpose of its own. Sometimes it brings strength, or teaches empathy, or gives you the opportunity to show God that we're not a "good time Charley" - and can find joy amidst the pain... and praise Him no matter the circumstances.

So, green tea with honey and lemon - and some healing sleep; that what I need now.

Where the killer bees attacked.

chapter 12

October 21, 1998

Whew! I did it; two performances in two nights, with a cup of Theraflu sitting on the podium. My throat was on fire and I was running a pretty high fever, but I guess the audience must not have noticed - because there was a bigger crowd on the second night than on the first. And guess what? Not a single person got up and left! In fact, the show (or whatever you want to call it), was only supposed to last an hour but it went for over two because they wanted to hear more. I still can't believe it!

And on the second night, I did something completely unplanned, at the suggestion of one of my Soroptimist sisters. I placed a little yellow picnic basket on the table behind me where I laid out photocopies of my poetry. Then I taped a piece of notebook paper to the picnic basket that said, "If you would like a copy, please feel free to take one. If you would like to **help** keep this 'poetry on the road', your contribution would be appreciated."

I felt kind of strange doing that, but because the basket was on a table **behind** me, rather than by the entry or being passed around, I didn't feel like it would make anyone feel pressured to contribute… so I relented.

And then, when I had finished my final poem and thanked the audience for attending… something happened on both nights that I really caught me by surprise. After I finished my last poem and thanked the audience for coming, rather than getting up and leaving, most of them gathered in front of the table picking out copies of their favorite poems, (until there were no more left), and then lined up in front of the podium where I stood for almost an hour signing their copies. Here I was thinking they might laugh at me, or maybe even think I was crazy… and instead they told me over and over again how honored they were to have been there and how much they enjoyed both my art and my testimony. I was shocked beyond belief… and I must admit that I felt guilty for signing my name, even if it is only my "pen-name", when I know who SHOULD be getting the credit… as well as the standing ovation; and that's my Lord, (which is exactly what I told every single person who asked for an autograph).

On the second night, when I put my little picnic basket on the table, there were about 35 people in attendance, and as curious as I was, I couldn't peek into my picnic basket until everyone had left the room. When they finally did, I opened my basket and I couldn't believe my eyes! There was $250 in the basket… and it was because they **wanted** to put it there; not because they felt obligated. How could that have happened? I'm still in a state of shock because I didn't expect anything - let alone $250 from 35 people, most of whom where couples. Well, there's only one answer to why that money was in the basket; my Heavenly Father opened both their hearts and their wallets, and I couldn't be more grateful! Now I have enough money to fill both gas tanks, buy propane and refill my cupboards with some left over. What a relief – and thank you, Jesus!

One man who attended the first performance returned on the second night, this time bringing his teenage daughter with him, which was a real compliment. And even more surprising was that when my presentation was over, one of the ladies approached me and asked if I would recite some poems to her church group next weekend, so of course I accepted. And then another lady asked me to entertain during the lunch hour at the Senior Center and another one, who spends her winters in Sun City, Arizona, asked me if I would travel to her area and park at her house while I put on some shows there.

It's still so hard for me to believe… because when the Lord told me to use my gift for His work, I had absolutely no idea HOW. I was prepared to stand on the street corners or shout it from the rooftops, but here, at my first performance, I feel like He was showing me a path… a way that I could reach people. I know these little shows don't bear much of an impact, but at least now I know that people DO want to hear what I have to say; and THIS was supposed so be my toughest audience; my hometown. Now that I have actually seen how people respond, I know **will** listen and that they **will** be touched by hearing about the Lord's miracles… and that they **will** be comforted by my inspirational poems and songs. Even though I hadn't recited most of them for over 10 year - and wasn't sure I could remember all the words, they seemed to flow easily and directly from my heart, which means that the Holy Spirit was guiding me all the way. .

But to tell you the truth, I think it was a lousy performance. My voice was hoarse and I found myself having to look at the written pages every now and then, especially when the one hour turned into more than two. I missed numerous guitar chords, sang off key several times, and was constantly taking sips of Theraflu. I know I can do MUCH better once I get more practice, (and recover from this bug).

But now, performance number one and two are over… and two more are already scheduled. Today is the day I speak at the Senior Center luncheon and this weekend at one of the local churches. I just KNEW that if God wanted me to use my gift to serve Him, that He would provide a way… and tonight was a perfect example!

Yes, I'm still sick as a dog, (I wonder where that saying came from?), but I feel like I'm wrapped in the loving arms of my Father in Heaven. Now all I need is a few hours under the covers and lots of liquids, and I'm sure I'll be as good as new. And how blessed am I to even HAVE a bed with soft covers to lie in… and you can add a can of chicken soup to that list of blessings, too. So thank you Heavenly Father - for taking such good care of your daughter!

chapter 13

October 29, 1998

Wow! That's all I can say… and of course a great big "thank you"… not only to my Heavenly Father, but to all the kind and generous people who have touched my life during this past month in Gold Beach.

From the time I arrived, the wonders never ceased. After my two open shows at the Soroptimist Club, I spoke at the Lutheran Church at the request of one of the ladies at my second show and there I didn't put out my picnic basket - or fill a table with copies of my poems. This time I just walked up front when called and began by reciting a poem. The group was small, (it was the ladies bible study group – not the regular Sunday Service), but they were so eager to hear what I had to say that they asked question after question, which led to story after story, with a few poems in between. This appearance, (since it wasn't really a "show"), lasted no more than half an hour, and after it was over, I (and everyone else in the room), could feel the presence of the Holy Spirit so strongly that almost every eye was brimming with tears, both shed and unshed.

I can't tell you how honored I was… and yet how important it was to me that I DIDN'T take the credit. Every word I speak comes from my Lord - and I have to make SURE that **He** gets the glory. I literally cringe when they applaud, but I tell myself – it's the message they're clapping for; not me. And wouldn't you know it… as I was getting ready to leave, the ladies took up a collection, (in spite of my protests), and sent me back to my little trailer park with not only $65 in cash - but another request for me to speak at a lady's Garden Club meeting tomorrow.

And then there was the Senior Center luncheon; a group from which I absolutely refused to accept any money. But believe me, I was **more** than amply paid with hugs of gratitude, tears of joy and a feeling of love so thick in the room that you could almost touch it. The Senior Center is where the local elderly people who don't have much money go to eat a hot balanced meal every day… and so far, I think they're my favorite group to speak to. Most of the folks at the Senior Center were not only poor, but in pain and many of them were alone because their mates and many of their friends have already "been called Home", and you'd be surprised at how many of them have children who don't even bother to visit. I can look into their eyes and see the loneliness and the fear. And even though the majority of them are Christian, they now find themselves knocking on death's door… and suddenly their past mistakes and the regrets they feel can cast doubt upon their faith – just when they need it most.

And yes, once again, every single photocopy of the poetry I shared with them was quickly picked up off the table when I finished, (and I should have brought more), and once again, I had to sign each and every one of them.. But this time, there was no picnic basket for contributions because I went away RICH in the way that **really** counts; rich in spirit. I am so thankful that I was blessed to be of some small comfort to my elderly brothers and sisters. Their joy is my joy… and it's such an honor to be able to make them smile and comfort them in their time of loneliness and need.

So, only a couple more days and my month in Gold Beach will be over. I started this chapter with one word; "Wow"… and I'm going to end it the same way.

WOW!!!

OUR SAVIOR, JESUS CHRIST

Who makes the darkness bright again – when life seems so unfair?
Who makes the pain that strikes ALL men – an easy cross to bear?

Who knows me so completely – that there's nothing I can hide…
and yet he'll NEVER leave me – He's always at my side.

Whose love will bring me happiness… whose Word will make me wise?
There's only one so powerful – our Savior, Jesus Christ!

— Poem by Abigayle

chapter 14

November 1, 1998

At last – I'm on the road again… and my month in Gold Beach is one more cherished memory to add to my book of life. Besides putting on my shows and saying goodbye to old friends and neighbors, I also had many hours in which to counsel Jon. I'm not sure if anything I said helped because only God can take that burden off his back, but I did everything I could and I'm leaving without a single negative emotion regarding our past. Instead, I have only concern for his future. I'll continue to pray for him, but for now, I can do no more.

I feel so alive and full of joy right now I'm literally vibrating. It's like I'm on "sensory overload" but instead of feeling restless and impatient, I feel empowered… as though I've tapped into emotions that are new and exhilarating.

I have truly been reborn, as Abigayle the poet and servant of God. A new day is dawning in my life and I have absolutely **no** fear of what it might hold. The *visitation* and the miracle of the Bible have left me with **unshakable** faith and trust in God, and my joy is no longer based on where I live or what I own. It's all about how much joy and encouragement I can bring to others… and how much I can do to serve and glorify my Lord and it feels great! It's a whole new kind of "freedom", and I love it.

The kind citizens of Gold Beach were so unbelievably generous that when I left town a few hours ago I had 2 full tanks of gas, food in my cupboards and almost $500 in my pocket. Isn't that amazing? You know, there was a time when I paid $10,000 for a horse and didn't think twice, but those days are long gone… and believe it or not - I'm glad. I'm getting more joy out of this $500 than I ever got out of $10,000 when I had money. In fact, I'm hoping to find someone in the next town who can paint a rainbow on the back of Lucky and the words "poetry on the road." below it. Wouldn't that be great?

The one-month rent I paid at the trailer park in Gold Beach was up today, so this morning I emptied my black and grey water tanks, charged my interior battery with the battery charger my father gave me and left my beautiful little town for what could be the very last time. I did feel sad… but it wasn't nearly as traumatic as when I drove away from my family and friends in Portland. I think having my first few performances out of the way and seeing how someone as insignificant as me can inspire people, have lifted a big weight off my shoulders. I couldn't have imagined that people would be so touched by what little I have to give. So now, all I have to do now is figure out **where** I'm going - and what to do when I get there.

I sure did learn a good lesson about propane this morning though. My refrigerator only works on propane so it's important that I keep my two five gallon cans full. Unfortunately, there's no gauge, but I figured they must be nearly empty since it had been over a month since I had them filled when I left Portland. I must admit that I was pretty darn proud of my *mechanically challenged* self when I finally figured out how to unhook and remove the two cans from the side compartment in my RV. (I do think someone should kick the guy who decided to reverse the threads on propane containers though, because it took me quite awhile to figure that one out.) But as with any challenge, big or small, it really felt great when I finally overcame it and gathered up the 2 empty cans to walk 4 blocks to the gas station where I'd seen a "propane sold here" sign.

The gentleman who came out to help me had a rather odd look on his face when I walked up to his BIG propane tank carrying the two rusty-white containers, but I didn't think much about it at the time; not until he was finished filling them anyway - and I tried to pick them up again. Yikes! How can AIR be so darn heavy? I couldn't even lift **one** of them, let alone two, and I still had four long blocks to walk back to my motor home. Suddenly I knew why he asked me where my car was while he was filling the tanks. I told him I didn't have one, but that I would be fine because I only had a few blocks to go… which also explains why he then smiled and said, "I don't think you'll be walking anywhere carrying these tanks, young lady."

But once again, the kindness of others saved me from my own ignorance when a customer at the gas pumps saw me trying to lift the two heavy tanks and came over to see if he could help. So now I've learned **two** new things about propane; it smells like rotten eggs and it weighs a ton!

After a very busy day of stashing, stowing and saying goodbye to the numerous people who came to my RV to wish me well, it was rather late in the day by the time I was actually ready to drive away. That's why I decided to go only 15 miles down the coast - where I could spend one last night at my great-great grandfather's homestead, which is now a State Park. The Thunder Rock Cove pullout is just above the waterfall and I wanted to say farewell to the land both my great-great grandfather and I had come to love so deeply.

I brought my trusty video camera, but since it took me so long to get out of Gold Beach, the sun was already setting by the time I parked at Thunder Rock Cove. And what a gorgeous sunset it was! The path to the beach from the parking area is almost half a mile long, down a steep, winding and difficult dirt trail… so I hurried as fast as I possibly could, racing the fading sunset because it was already bright red and purple and I really wanted to get some pictures before it faded away. That's why I practically jogged down the rutted trail as it carved its way through the thick forest of pine and fir trees, carrying both my rather large shoulder mounted video camera and my little Nikon instamatic. The problem was; in my almost manic haste, I hadn't considered how I'd get back UP the trail once the sun set and it was completely dark. Uh-oh.

I'm actually kind of glad I didn't think about it though, because as I sat down to slide over the last 20 feet of slippery rocks bordering the beach, the only thing on my mind was how fast I could jog to the hidden caves, and whether there would be enough light left to get good pictures. Had I realized at the time that I had no flashlight and would be hiking back up the cliff in the dark, I might have chickened out and headed to Lucky right then, without my precious pictures. But as usual, everything turned out just fine and I carefully felt my way back up the almost pitch black, (but oh-so familiar), dirt trail by kneeling down and feeling the path with one hand and holding the cameras with the other. I can tell you one thing for sure; it took a whole lot longer to get **up** that hill then it did to get **down** it.

So here I am, parked at Thunder Rock Cover, writing by candle light at my dining table and trying to decide where I should go tomorrow. It seems so strange to have no schedule and no destination. Maybe I'll just head South down Highway 101 and decide where to stop when I get there. Crescent City, California is the next town of any size once I leave Oregon and it's been my home away from home for the last seven years. Maybe I'll stop there and find someone to paint a rainbow on Lucky.

This last month in Gold Beach has been anything but restful, (although I did manage to recover from the flu), so there's one thing I know for sure; I need some rest - both physically and emotionally. I need to find someplace to park where no one will knock on my door and I can read my Bible, pray, practice my poetry and songs, and surround myself with the beauty of nature.

Even though I truly love people, I've always found my *true* peace in the soul-calming quiet of the wilderness. How many 30-something year old women do YOU know who would hike 10 miles into a mountain wilderness, (or riding her horse), with nothing but a backpack - no tent, no ax, and usually alone. I've always relished the solitude, and I enjoyed taking my two small boys and my Labrador retriever on mountain retreats that sometimes lasted only a few days - and sometimes as long as a few months. To me, it's more like a spiritual pilgrimage… because the wilderness was the **one** place where I could get away from the constant stream of never-ending activity and ease the pain of a serious illness that it took the doctors 20 years to diagnose and cure. (That's the story I said I'd save for another time.)

I do have one funny short story though about one of my many pilgrimages into the wilderness. I must have been almost 19 because I had my first son when I was 20 and I had no children at the time. In fact, now that I think about it, it was when my husband was in basic training for six weeks so I decided to head for the mountains alone - where I could pretend that I was the only person on Earth.

I'm not sure how many miles I hiked into the beautiful Mt. Hood National Forest, but it was far enough that after driving 2 hours on dirt logging roads and then hiking for several hours at a pretty good pace, I was pretty sure I'd be alone. I happened upon the most beautiful spot to camp; right next to a flowing creek, as it tumbled and turned around the volcanic rocks and huge boulders covered with a soft carpet of green (and slippery) moss.

I've always been what you would call "extremely modest", both in dress and in undress. This was 1970, and during that era it was common for people to drop their clothes at outdoor concerts, public parks and even at parties. But even though I may have fit the "flower-child" picture as far as my traits of loving animals, nature, people, and music; that's where it ended. No free sex, no nudity and nothing but nice clean clothes for this flower-child of the early 70's.

So, even though I was sure I was completely alone, I spent the first three weeks bathing in the creek while wearing my swimming suit… just in case. Three whole weeks – and I hadn't seen even one other person, so finally - sometime during the fourth week, I decided I was being ridiculous and that there was no one out there but me… so why not take off my clothes and enjoy my FIRST skinny dip - which is exactly what I did. And I have to admit, as soon as I got over feeling uneasy about being naked and constantly looking both up and down the stream for anyone who might suddenly appear, I began to really enjoy myself. My long blond hair was blowing in the wind as I leaped from rock to rock, splashing in the cool water and dancing to the music of the wind in the trees.

And that's when it happened. Wouldn't you know it... nearly a month without seeing another soul and then, just when I least expected it, I glanced downstream and there was this young man sitting on a rock, grinning from ear to ear and watching me play. Oh my gosh! I was so embarrassed I could have died. I literally **ran** for my clothes and prayed that he wouldn't come to my camp site.

But of course he did. "Hi there," he said as he approached. "Do you mind if I join you for a little while? I promise I'm harmless," he assured me with what appeared to be a very sincere tone. He looked clean cut and seemed polite, or I would have been worried.

"Normally I'd say, sure... but I'm so embarrassed right now, I'm not sure I want to face you," I answered, looking down, rather than directly into his eyes and turning beet red.

"Why should you be embarrassed?" he asked. "You didn't expect anyone to be hiking up that stream - and to tell you the truth; I didn't expect to find a beautiful river nymph playing naked in the water either. I thought I was dreaming at first, so I apologize for watching... but what a wonderful scene it was. Please, dear lady, accept my apology... but it sounds to me like we were **both** surprised, and I assure you, I am a gentleman and will behave as such."

So, that was the first time, (and the last time), I ever went skinny dipping... even in the middle of nowhere, and yes; he did turn out to be a gentleman who visited for a few hours and them headed on up the mountain.

So many memories, I could spend the rest of my life looking back on them – and so many more yet to make. I'm obviously not planning to drive Lucky into the wilderness, but I **am** hoping to find a place to park for a few days where I can look out my window and see nothing but God's handiwork. With no telephone or television, and no neighbors (or ex's) to knock on my door), I can be completely alone, even if I'm surrounded by people. THAT sounds like a plan... but where?

But one thing I **am** sure of; God knows what I need more than I do – so if such a place exists, He will guide me. Tomorrow morning I'll just start Lucky's engine, head south and see where I end up.

chapter 15

November 2, 1998

What a beautiful Indian summer morning and how wonderful waking up on my couch/bed to the sound of the crashing waves and the birds singing. I am so blessed! I have it better than the Queens of old, (meaning the Bible days, of course), because all I had to do was walk over to my little propane stove, light a burner... and before I knew it, I had a cup of sweet herbal tea to top off an already wonderful start to my first day back on the road.

I decided to step outside and enjoy my tea, but as I opened the door and went to put my foot on the first step, there was a paper bag with a note stapled to it. Being the only vehicle parked in the scenic highway pullout, I had no idea where it had come from, but my curiosity was put to rest when I opened the bag and saw three maple bars and a letter from Jon.

The letter wasn't long; just long enough to thank me for not judging him and for trying to help when he had expected nothing but hatred. It was the frosting on an already magnificent cake, because now I knew for sure that even if he **is** far from the point where his addictions will no longer have a hold on him, he DOES appreciate, (rather than resent), the things I said to him. Jesus loves us... bad or good, lost or faithful, and wants nothing more than to see us happy and back at home with the great I AM. I used my time with Jon to show him that true Christianity doesn't judge or bear hatred; it prays for those who are lost and shares the pain of those who are suffering. Perhaps just by setting an example, someday it will help him overcome his demons. I can only pray that will be the case.

So it was goodbye to my great-great grandfather's land grant and the State of Oregon, (my family's home for 7 generations), and hello Crescent City, California. On Highway 101, it was only 35 miles south of where I spent the night, and I thought that since I had so much money now, I'd see if I could find a sign-painting company who would paint a rainbow and the words "poetry on the road" on the back of Lucky, (cheap).

But I'm beginning to wonder if I'll EVER be able to turn off the engine without worrying about whether it will start again - because this morning, I had to use the little jumper cables my father made me to get it started... so I avoid turning off the engine until I absolutely **have** to.

After I drove through the town of Brookings, the last town in Oregon before crossing the border into California, I heard a noise that sounded like something had fallen off my RV and was bouncing along the highway behind me. I looked in my side view mirror and there was a big dark spot on the driver's side of my RV where the compartment cover to the hot water heater used to be. Un-oh. Because Lucky's so old, (1977), it's not easy to find parts - so I had no choice but to stop and try to find the missing cover.

I love Indian summers, but it was already hot outside and as usual... my motor was overheated. I was afraid to turn the engine off for two reasons; one, it would get hotter without the fan running and two; I wasn't sure I'd gone far enough to recharge my batteries and was afraid there wouldn't be enough power to start again — even using both batteries. The only thing I could do was to leave Lucky idling on the side of the Highway while I ran up and down both sides - searching for my missing compartment cover. I'm sure the people driving by must have wondered what I was doing, peeking in bushes, and moving so fast you'd have thought someone was chasing me.

And since I'd already learned my lesson from the tow truck driver who pinched my bottom, I was wearing sweat pants and sweat shirt, rather than the shorts and sleeveless top that would have been far more comfortable in the heat, so I was dripping wet by the time, (thank you, Jesus), I actually found my missing part. Hip-hip-hooray! It was scratched and bent, but not so badly that I couldn't use my trusty duct tape to reattach it to the side of the RV. I LOVE duct tape! In fact, I think I could probably survive in the wilderness with no more than duct tape, super glue and WD 40.

As I climbed back into the cab with the motor still running, I was disappointed to see that the engine was even hotter and I was holding my breath and praying all the way to Crescent City where I could stop for a few hours and let it cool down.

So now I'm at the sign painter's shop, (engine shut down and getting cooler, I hope), but the owner says he's not sure he can fit me in today... but **maybe** tomorrow. Hmmm... Should I stay? I don't think so. He could be just as busy tomorrow and I'd have waited for nothing, and the fact is, things always seem to have a way of working out for the best. Maybe I **shouldn't** be spending any of my $500 on sign painting when I never know what emergency might lie ahead. I'm in the God's hands... so if this man doesn't have time to paint my sign, I'll take that as a hint.

This probably isn't the best time for me to spend money getting a sign painted anyway, but at least I can stay here in the parking lot for a couple of hours and eat lunch while Lucky cools down. And then, off I'll go... hoping to find my little "piece of peace". (Oh how funny!)

So now I'll just make some lunch - and take a nice nap. Isn't life rough!

chapter 16

Still November 2, 1998

What a beautiful place the Lord has led me to. There I was, driving yet another steep and winding section of Highway 101, South of Crescent City and through the giant redwood forest, (praying that my engine didn't burn up as I climbed the 45 degree slope on the shoulder of the road at 25 miles an hour), when I rounded what I hoped would be the last tight corner…and there it was; the mighty blue Pacific Ocean stretched out as far as the eye could see in front of me; so close to the road that the shoulder became sand… and the shoreline was lined with parked RVs. I couldn't believe my eyes. I had found the perfect place to park, plan and rest… and I hadn't even known that it existed. I'm so glad I didn't give up and stop before I found this little piece of RV Heaven!

I had to drive nearly a mile along the parked RVs before I found an open spot and when I finally did, I moved carefully back and forth, a few feet at a time, searching for a level spot. My sons gave me three level bubbles, one for the dash, one for the kitchen counter and one for the bed in the rear of the RV. They said my refrigerator wouldn't work if I wasn't level and I sure didn't want to lose any of the food I had so carefully purchased before leaving Gold Beach. Back and forth, check the levels… back and forth, check the levels - again and again.

Finally, after about my 10th try, an elderly gentleman climbed out of a 5th wheel parked directly in front of me and approached my RV. I have a feeling he couldn't stand watching me struggle any longer without offering to help. People are so nice!

"Hello Miss," he said as he approached my driver's side window. "Is there something I can do to give you a hand?"

"Thanks for offering," I answered, "but I don't think so. I'm just trying to find a level spot so my refrigerator will work," I explained.

"Well, my dear," he said with a chuckle. "I think you're just fine right where you are. You don't have to be perfectly level, you know... just close to it."

"Really? My sons told me I had to be level... and if I turn my engine off, it probably won't start again so I thought I'd better get it right the first time."

"Believe me, dear, you're good right where you are. I take it you must be a green pea?"

"I don't know," I asked. "What's a green pea?"

"Someone who's new at driving an RV," he answered with a smile. "And that's not an insult – because we ALL started out as green peas," he said with a chuckle.

"Well then, I reckon I must be just about as green as they come, sir," I laughed. "I sure do appreciate your help though... and no, I'm not insulted. It's a good day when I learn something new, and you, my friend, have just made an already great day even better. Thanks for the advice," I said as I gratefully shut down the red-hot engine and my new neighbor waved and walked back to his trailer, smiling and shaking his head all the way.

And was I ever happy to be stopped. My shoulders ached from gripping the steering as I negotiated the tight corners and trying to stay on the shoulder of the road as much as possible so other drivers could get around me, and my back was screaming for me to get out of the driver's seat. What a relief it was to turn off the engine and take my first look at my new home; nothing but sand and ocean. Hip-Hip-Horray! The weather is perfect, and the smell of the salt air has already revived me!

What a wonderful place to rest my body and my soul… and best of all – it's free! I think I'll take my guitar out to that big old log by the water and put my joy and gratitude into song.

Thank you, Jesus!

chapter 17

November 5, 1998

Where does the time go? I've been parked here at the beach for three whole days already... and I wish I could stay forever; but I can't. Why? Because this place is "all about me" and something, (the Holy Spirit?), is driving me to get on with whatever it is I must do.

There are no words to describe how restful and pleasant these last three days have been. I spent a good portion of each day reading my miracle Bible and praying for guidance. I took long walks on the beach searching for pretty rocks and shells, and when I got tired of doing that, I'd write in my journal, practice my poems, (or write new ones), and play my guitar on what has so quickly become my "favorite log".

Then there were the hours I spent walking up and down the mile-long trail of RVs... sojourning with my brothers and sisters. Each and every one of them has a story to tell and it's helping me to understand what people need most, or at least what I might be able to do or say to encourage and comfort them. Of course I shared my poetry and songs around many a campfire, along with telling the story of the flood and the visitation, but I spent even more time just listening their stories. I was surprised at how happy it made them to have someone show an interest in their lives. Of course my response was always spiritual, giving them encouragement and reminding them of the "big picture", but it seemed to bring them great joy just to know that someone cared enough to listen – and since **their** joy is **my** joy, it's been great!

I have no television to watch and nothing but candlelight to brighten the dark nights so I sat alone in my RV thinking… and the solitude was just what I needed to recharge my OWN batteries. With a hundred RV's parked along this one particular stretch of road, it wasn't exactly what you'd call solitude, but all I had to do was close my curtains… and I was alone.

And although I've used this time well; studying the Bible, praying for guidance and expressing gratitude to my Lord and master… something overpoweringly strong has been filling my heart, and it's the last thing on earth I would have expected. I'm being literally "driven" to find and spend time with my birth mother. I've only seen her two or three times since I was seven years old, and when I did, I'm ashamed to admit how it made me feel. It wasn't anything she said or did that made my stomach spin… it was just the fact that when I saw her, I once again became that motherless little girl.

Fortunately, my younger brother Ronnie kept in touch with her over the years, (which is how I know she lives in Sacramento, California), but for some reason I just couldn't do it. Why? Maybe it's because I was three years older than he was - so my memories of those early years are clearer, or maybe it was just because I was too weak and selfish. But whatever the reason, I've always felt guilty about putting the woman who brought me into this world out of my mind and out of my life.

Perhaps I wasn't ready to deal with the painful memories of my early childhood yet. It certainly wasn't **her** fault, because she was only 16 years old when she gave birth to me and she never had the spiritual or financial advantages that my father's side of the family took for granted. As a young girl, she watched as her brother shot and killed her father, and then, still a child herself, she took over as surrogate mother to her two younger sisters as HER mother wasn't capable of doing so. She was born into a completely different world than my father was, and he, at the tender age of 18, wanted to rescue her in the only way he could; by marrying her.

I know how hard she tried to fit into my father's "Leave it to Beaver" world, but having been raised in the clutches of alcohol, drugs and promiscuity, it had to have been nearly impossible. She had no self-esteem whatsoever and no guidance or support, and when you add that to no education; (having dropped out of school to take care of her siblings at age 13), she never felt *good enough,* and turned to prescription drugs for her solace. In the 1950's there was no such thing as "Rehab Centers" so she was put in the Oregon State Mental Hospital - which is why my father was given custody of my brother and I... a rare occurrence in the 1950's.

As I look back, I realize now that losing her two children must have broken her heart. In fact, when she was released from the institution, she spirited my brother and I away in the middle of the night, and we were on the run for months before my father finally found us. During that time, many things happened... things I don't wish to remember, and things that weren't her fault. I remember one time when she left us with one of her male "friends" for a quick trip to the store and got into an automobile accident. If course, Ronnie and I didn't know why she didn't come back, and the man she left us with (and his four teenage sons) was the epitome of evil. After some period of time, (I'm not sure how long because thankfully... my young mind blocked much of it out), I made my way to a neighbor's house for help and the police called my father, who immediately set out from Oregon to California to rescue us. It was a child's nightmare... and yet, it wasn't her fault. She was in a hospital, unable to stop what was happening - but my 7 year old mind didn't understand that at the time.

And yet, according to my brother, she has somehow managed to overcome all odds and after traveling a long and much more difficult road than I can possibly imagine, she has made her way back to God. I am in awe of how strong she must be to have overcome such obstacles and become a devoted Christian woman. Who knows how **I** would have turned out if I had walked in her shoes? I guess that's why we leave all the judging to God.

According to my brother, my mother's been teaching Sunday school for almost 20 years now, and that she doesn't drink or smoke and hasn't had even a single man in her life for many years. Jesus is the only love of her life – and she lives for him. I can feel the tears welling in my eyes as I think about how much she must have suffered; both as a child and as a young woman… trying so hard to live in a world she'd never been exposed to before and never feeling good enough. Now it's time for me to put my arms around her and tell her how proud I am of her, and that I love her. I feel the Holy Spirit literally driving me to do so… so perhaps HER prayers are being answered through me.

I'm really ashamed of how selfish I've been. There's no adequate defense for my inability to re-establish our mother/daughter relationship before now, but I have to admit that the hole in my heart where her love should have been, is a wound that never completely healed… at least not until the day I held that miracle Bible in my arms after the flood; until that moment when the Lord emptied my soul of all earthly desires and healed my heart completely. It was truly a gift… but before that day, on the few occasions I did see her while I was growing up – it was painful; like old wounds were being reopened, and I was once again that heartbroken little girl who missed her mother. It took me many years to get over what happened to me during those months on the road; years of counseling by both family and professionals, but I'm still ashamed of myself. Instead of facing what had happened, (like I should have done), I just buried my pain in the deepest recesses of my mind and pretty much pretended that it, (and she), didn't exist.

But now - all that is over, and Jesus has healed my heart so completely that I can't wait to throw my arms around her and tell her how sorry I am, and that I love her. It's time… way past time!

And now, as always, I see that those early, (and painful), years were yet another blessing in disguise. How could I possibly hope to comfort someone who has been sexually abused or deserted by a parent if I "hadn't walked in their shoes?" And I have… so I can. Thank you, my Lord, for giving me yet another way to encourage and comfort others.

But even now, I don't get the credit for putting that trauma behind me... because, like with Jon, only God could do that. The Holy Spirit is moving me so strongly right now that it's like I don't have any choice but to obey. And since I trust Him completely... and know that He **always** has my best interest at heart; He must have a very good reason for sending me to her. But, (and here comes the best part), I don't **need** to know what those reasons are. How can I, (a mere human being), ever hope to grasp the reasoning of one so powerful and magnificent that He who created worlds without number? I can't... which is what makes my path so easy; all I need is **faith**. The "whys" and the "wherefores" no longer concern me because I know that the Lord has a plan... and He loves me; so if I'm obedient... and have unshakable trust in Him, it will be as He said when he spoke to me - "everything will be fine."

Oh, by the way, my birthday is only two days away and since she lives in Sacramento, if I leave this morning, I can be at her house in time to celebrate it with her. I still can't believe this is happening... as it was the **last** thing on my mind when I drove away from Gold Beach - and where are the butterflies that used to fill my stomach every time I thought about her? I'll tell you where they are – they're gone! And now my heart literally yearns to tell her I love her and to thank her for bring me into this world.

I've spent the past three days and nights praying for my Heavenly Father to show me the path He would have me take... and now I have my answer. It's strange how the Holy Spirit works - seldom anything as dramatic as a "burning bush", or a "voice", (like after the flood), but sometimes it's just a thought that refuses to leave your mind until you listen. And that's what happened to me during the last few days... and that's how I know that Sacramento is where the Lord wants me to go.

So, first stop; a payphone to get her telephone number from my brother, and then a phone call to her to let her know that I'm coming. If you could see my face right now, you'd see that I am actually laughing out loud; filled with joy and anticipation, as tears of relief roll down my cheeks. The pain is gone! First, it was revisiting my beloved town of Gold Beach, where I rid myself of any lingering sadness at losing my home and dream business – and then it was Jon, where the Lord healed me of any leftover wounds or unanswered questions and helped me learn to love him as a brother, without judgment or regret, and now… MY MOTHER!

Thank you Jesus – and look out Sacramento… here I come! (Let's just hope Lucky starts!)

II Timothy 1:7,9

7) For God hath not given us the spirit of fear;
but of power, and of love, and of sound mind.
9) Who hath saved us and called us with an holy calling,
not according to our works, but according to his own purpose and grace,
which was given us in Christ Jesus before the world began.

chapter 18

November 6, 1998

Drat! It looks like I won't make it to my mother's house today after all. Lucky broke down again… and this time I can't get it repaired until tomorrow morning. Here's what happened.

I drove all day yesterday, (after getting a jump start from one of my new friends in the string of RV's parked along the ocean), and then I decided to park for the night in a Sentry grocery store parking lot near the base of the coastal mountains in Northern California. Of course I asked the manager for permission first, and he kindly said "Sure, just don't open your door to any strangers."

As anxious as I was to get to my mother's house before my birthday (which is tomorrow), I decided to stop and sleep last night because I didn't want to drive the steep, winding coastal mountain highway at night with Lucky's engine still overheating every time I climb even the smallest of hills. That's why I thought it would be safer to travel during the day; so I could find help if something happened.

Sacramento's a pretty big city, but I carefully wrote down the instructions my mother was so thrilled to give me over the phone, (you should have heard the joy in her voice, in fact, I think she was crying), so I don't think I'll have any problem finding the gated trailer park community where she lives. As it turns out, she has an RV parking space on her lot right next to her mobile home. She usually rents it out to supplement her disability income, but wouldn't you know it; the people who've been renting it just moved their RV last week - which means it's empty... and waiting for me. If all goes well, I'll be driving up to her house sometime tomorrow afternoon. How exciting is that?!

So I left my little spot at the Sentry Market early in this morning, and after many long and tense hours climbing the steep hills of the Northern California coastal mountains, (and watching my temperature gauge soar to new and dangerous heights), I finally reached the downhill side of the mountain and was literally whooping with joy as I crested that last big incline. "From here on," I thought to myself, "it's all downhill!"

And what a relief that was... because no matter how hot the engine gets climbing **up** the hill, it always gets cool again on the downhill side. But what I **didn't** expect was that halfway down the first big hill, (just as I was celebrating the temperature gauge's gradual return to "normal"), a bright red *brake warning* light begin to blink on my dash. "Uh-Oh, this can't be good," I thought to myself as a chill raced up my spine. I don't know much about engines, but I DO know that the brakes are nothing to fool around with, especially since Lucky's so big and heavy. Even with *good* brakes, it's hard to stop this much weight, and on these steep hills, (so steep they have escape ramps for trucks that lose their brakes), I was really worried, (to put it mildly).

And then, as if the big red blinking light on my dash wasn't unsettling enough, coasting down the steep descent increased my speed and I realized that I was going dangerously fast. I quickly pumped the brake pedal a couple of times and guess what? My brakes weren't working. For just a moment in time, I was in a complete state of panic as I hurriedly continued to pump the pedal again and again. Eventually, after numerous clear to the floor pumps, I got a little bit of resistance and was able to slow down, but only by putting all my weight into it and pushing as hard as I possibly could. As you can imagine, I was praying fervently, asking God to help me make it to the nearest town.

But unfortunately, there weren't any towns on that particular stretch of mountain highway… and so mile after mile I watched for a sign, any sign at all, which could mean that civilization was near. I suppose I should have been more cautious and pulled over immediately, town or no town, but I didn't…. because I figured that as long as I had enough braking power to keep it under control… and as long as I kept Lucky in low gear, I could make it. I'm only allowed two tows a year on my Triple A card and since I've already used one, I wanted to save the last one for another time, since it was becoming more than obvious that I'd need it.

So, prudent or not, that's why I chose to go on – and that's also why I found myself in for the *drive* of my life. Every time I started down another hill, Lucky kept going faster and faster… and I kept pressing harder and harder on the brake pedal. Pumping it didn't seem to help anymore, so I finally put **both** feet on the pedal and pushed as hard as I could, constantly praying that a town would be just around the next corner.

And then, when I thought I couldn't last another minute, (with my legs literally shaking from the constant strain of pressing on the pedal), I reached the bottom of an especially long and dangerous incline and there it was - a town. Thank you, Jesus! Repair shop or no repair shop, it was time to get off the highway. But even that was no simple task, as I pushed as hard as I could on the pedal… trying to slow down enough to make the tight turn onto the exit road. And then, with one last gargantuan effort, (and with Lucky tipping dangerously to one side), I made the turn… and I was safe!

As you can imagine, my heart was racing… as the adrenalin pumped through my veins and I hooted and hollered and yelled my thanks to God at the top of my lungs. And wouldn't you know it; there, just a few blocks away, was an auto repair shop that looked to me like an oasis in the desert. When I pulled into the parking lot and turned off the engine, it was such a relief that I just sat there for a few minutes letting the tears flow. I am a lifelong rollercoaster fanatic and have searched dozens of amusement parks all over the country for the scariest rides possible, but I honestly can't ever remember being so frightened as I had been racing down those huge hills … and my tears were those of pure gratitude that I hadn't tipped over as I exited or gone sailing over the guardrail down some deadly mountain cliff.

As soon as I composed myself, I walked inside the repair shop office and was informed that they were already full for today but would try to fit me in tomorrow morning. The man I spoke to was nice enough to recommend a nearby RV Park, (the only one in town), and even though I hated to waste money on a place to sleep, I decided it would be worth it because I could empty my holding tanks and recharge my battery before arriving at my mother's house tomorrow. It continually amazes me, but things always have a way of working out for the best. It happens so often that I don't know why I ever bother to worry in the first place, (which is easier said than done).

And I have more good news; Sacramento's only three hours away… so if they fix Lucky in the morning, I can still make it to my mother's house in time to see her on my birthday. It will be the first birthday I've spent with her since I was 7 years old and I can't wait! And it's a good thing I didn't spend any money getting that rainbow painted on Lucky, because I don't have any idea how much the repairs are going to cost tomorrow. I still have the $500 I left Gold Beach with, (minus $15.00 for staying here at the RV Park tonight), so after filling my gas and propane tanks again, I can only hope I'll have enough left to fix whatever's wrong with my brakes.

So thank you generous citizens of Gold Beach… because tomorrow morning the money you so kindly gave me will be put to very good use. And if I'm lucky, (Gee, I'm just queen of the bad puns lately), I might just have enough left over for some groceries.

Sometimes I can't believe how blessed I am. Before this journey started, I could never have imagined the joy I could get from having $20 to buy food. For most of my life, I took things for granted that I have now learned to appreciate (and squeeze every drop of joy from). I'd always thought I was in control; earning the money, washing the clothes, paying the bills, raising the kids, doing the laundry… but now I know better. I'm never really the one in the pilot's seat, because I have been quite firmly reminded since the flood that without God's grace, I'd have absolutely nothing. So thank you my Lord, for getting me through this most difficult and dangerous day, and thank you for the money for repairs, food and gas... and thank you for sending me to see my mother. I'm so excited I can barely stand it!

So, here I sit... at the only RV park in town; so over-crowded that I had no choice but to maneuver myself into a space so small I didn't think it was possible to get in. But here I am, sitting in the lap of luxury... as I plugged in my little black and white television, filled up my half-bathtub, and try to imagine what it will be like to see my mother tomorrow. Isn't life amazing?!

chapter 19

November 7, 1998

"Happy Birthday to me".

It was almost noon before the mechanics finished working on Lucky and they told me that both reservoirs in the master cylinder were completely dry, which explains why my brakes weren't working. But for some strange reason, (here we go again), they can't seem to find a leak. So where did all the brake fluid go? Oh well, at least they didn't have to replace my brakes… but I'd still feel better if I knew WHY the reservoirs were empty. But looking on the bright side - now I know where the master cylinder is, and it's almost impossible to reach - hidden under the driver's seat; one more victim of poor design.

I was so happy when they finished… and then so disappointed when I drove away only to discover that my brake light was still flashing. Of course, I immediately turned around and drove back to the repair shop and had the mechanics take another look.

This is beginning to sound all too familiar, but once again they can't figure out why the brake warning light is still on. So off I go - red light still blinking… but brakes working fine. At least Sacramento's only three hours from here and the steep hills are a thing of the past, so I'm sure I'll make it. But now I'm getting such a late start, I'll be hitting rush hour traffic in Sacramento… which will REALLY put my brakes to the test. Is there never a dull moment?

It's a good thing that I finally figured out that there's no sense worrying about things that might not happen – so instead, I'll just focus on the good things; like how my holding tanks are empty, my batteries are charged, the sky is blue and I'm about to spend my first birthday with my mother in almost 40 years. And guess what? After refilling both gasoline and propane and paying the repair bill, I still have almost $200 left! I think that's more than enough reason to celebrate!

So off I go! Wish me luck!

chapter 20

November 8, 1998

My mother's directions were perfect, so after changing freeways twice and driving right through the center of Sacramento in bumper-to-bumper traffic, I found the entrance to her mobile home park. My brakes were working fine… but the warning light was still flashing and it really makes me nervous - so I think I'll get it checked out again before I leave Sacramento. I only plan to stay for a few days, (maybe a week), but since "man proposes – but the Lord disposes," we'll see what happens.

As I drove into my mother's mobile home community, I was pleasantly surprised at how nice it was, with brick fencing, beautiful trimmed hedges and green lawns. It's a "gated community" so I had to stop at the entry and dial the number she gave me on the *gate-phone*. I could hear the excitement in her voice as she told me how to get to her lot and promised to be waiting for me outside so I wouldn't miss it. I wasn't too thrilled about the twelve **extra tall** speed bumps between her place and the front gate, but at least I had no trouble finding her double-wide trailer. There she was… standing right out in the road, waving and beaming with joy as she pointed to the RV parking space next to her house.

Geesh! I couldn't believe it when I saw how narrow the parking space was. I thought the one at the RV Park last night was bad… but this one was going to take a miracle. There was a cyclone fence on one side and two metal storage sheds on the other - and the space in-between them was so narrow that I didn't think Lucky could possibly fit. And just to make matters worse, it was situated on a 90 degree corner… so I couldn't approach it directly from the front, which meant going back and forth, back and forth, back and forth, gradually straightening Lucky's 27 feet until I was parallel to the spot and could pull directly into the narrow space. Once again, my "if there's a will – there's a way" attitude prevailed and I eventually got Lucky parked, with 12 inches between the driver's door and the wire fence and even less than that between the passenger side and the two sheds. Fortunately, I was able to open my main door because it was positioned right between the two sheds, or I've have been parked – but trapped inside. It was a challenge, but I think I'm getting better at maneuvering this home on wheels.

The parking spot is perfect because I'm close enough to her patio that with an extension cord and a long water hose, I'll have both electricity and running water. And if I use the extra long cable television cord that my sons made for me to use at Alan's house, I'll even have television. Yes, those are little things; things I don't need…. but they still bring me joy. But the best joy of all was seeing my mother again.

And how do I describe her? It only takes one look to know that she's young in both spirit and heart. The first thing you notice, even before her thick almost waist length red hair, are her bright blue eyes that twinkle with energy and enthusiasm. It was strange looking into eyes that are almost a reflection of my own, since my father's are more of a blue/grey – where hers are almost turquoise, like mine. Compared to my long and lean 5'7" inch frame, she's very petite… maybe 5'1" and not as slender, but a whole lot more buxom, than I am. (Hmmm. How did I miss out on that?) All in all, for her 64 years, she's quite attractive and I can only hope that I'll age as gracefully as she has.

"Hi mom," I said as I first stepped out of Lucky and she ran into my open arms.

"I can't believe you're here," she gushed with emotion as she returned my hug almost ferociously. "The Lord has answered my prayers! I've been praying every single day that I'd see my daughter again and for 10 years now I've been putting your name in the prayer book at the Temple... and every day I've begged the Lord for another chance to be the mother I've always wanted to be - and here you are! Thank you, Jesus," she said, as tears ran down both of our cheeks.

So that was how it started... and from that very first moment, I knew exactly why the Lord had led me here; He was answering HER prayers. She came from such difficult beginnings that I can only imagine what her life must have been like, and one thing was soon apparent; her self-esteem had suffered greatly. She explained to me that she never felt like she could measure up to my father's family, although she tried as hard as she could. It only made things worse when she tried to soothe her sadness and feelings of inadequacy with prescription drugs and alcohol and my heart truly aches for what she must have gone through, and I am so glad that my visit is bringing her some much deserved happiness.

And I'm so proud of her! She not only fought her way out of the addictions that once controlled her life, but she has become one of the most devoted and sincere Christians I've ever met. For 15 years now, she hasn't drunk alcohol, smoked cigarettes or been with a man. She explains the change in three simple words; *I found Jesus* - and from that moment on, she was reborn. "**He's** the only man in my life now," she explained... and at last, I could see that she was truly content. She attends church every Sunday and has taught Sunday school for 11 years now. According to her, in spite of her many health problems that keep her on disability, there was only one thing missing from her life - and that was her daughter.

I could just cry when I think of how going to visit her never once crossed my mind, and that unless the Holy Spirit had literally LED me here, (through the grace of God), her dream might not have come true. This time, it isn't just HER joy that I'm feeling; this time my heart is filled with my OWN joy as well. I have a mother – and I not only love her but I'm proud of her!

As you can imagine, we spent that afternoon, (my birthday), in hours of deep discussion and true confessions. Yes, I was raised by my three wonderful aunts and my grandparents, as well as my father and Roma, but for the first time I could actually see where so many of MY own traits from; both the good and the bad. She's enthusiastic, extremely animated, and constantly smiling … with piercing blue eyes twinkling and direct. And she's brimming with love; love for everything from plants and animals to people. She's independent and strong, yet so sweet that it makes you want to put your arms around her and squeeze. And as for the bad, yes… we're both impatient, have lousy eating habits and tend to be loners, to name just a few. I can't describe how deeply the emotions ran as we just kept just looking at each other… sometimes in silence, with our eyes saying everything. Thank you, Lord for leading me to do what I should have done so long ago!

And last night, she threw me a birthday celebration, complete with cake, ice cream and a whole slew of relatives I haven't seen since I was a little girl. I've never really enjoyed parties, (and neither does she), but when my mother explained to me how many years she suffered… as the only one of her relatives with no children to show off at the family gatherings, (and how sad it made her), there was no way I could deny her this long overdue bit of pleasure as she finally got the chance to show off HER daughter. Oh boy… So, whether I liked big family get-togethers or not, I just did like I've done all my life with my father's side of the family (which is HUGE) and put my own discomfort aside and concentrated on making sure everyone else had a good time. I wouldn't ever want anyone to think I didn't love them - nor would I want them to think that I thought I was too good for them. I'm just not comfortable in crowds - which makes it pretty ironic that the Lord has called me to speak to every group I can manage to gather together. Fortunately, my discomfort never shows; in fact everyone thinks I LOVE big gatherings, so this time was no different.

Now I just wish I could do something to erase the sadness and the regret I can still see behind her smile; the obvious guilt she still carries deep in her heart over not being there for my brother and me when we were growing up.

And hopefully, I can; because this is the woman who brought me into the world; the woman who as a child of only 16 years old… fed me, changed my diapers and held me close to her heart. But even though I am sincerely grateful and love her with all my heart, I'm not sure what we'll have to talk about once we've caught up on the events of the past 30 years. I don't want to make her sad by bringing up ANY of the difficulties or the pain I experienced at not having her in my life, nor do I want her to know what happened when she was in the hospital and Ronnie and I had to stay with that awful man. I also don't want to make her feel sad because of all the wonderful things she missed, like my first horse show and winning the State Championship at the Oregon State Fair, or the Senior Prom as they crowned me queen… or watching me in the plays or cheerleading. The fact is; I'm not sure WHAT to say that will bring her joy without reminding her of all the things she missed. That's why I think I'll only stay here for about a week (at the most) and then "on the road again".

But the truth is, after being here for 24 hours now, I'm still in a bit of shock. I can't believe I'm actually here – at my mother's house. And you can bet I wouldn't be, if it hadn't been for her prayers… and for God seeing fit to answer them. As I said before, God called me – and He has a plan, usually with reasons I can't possibly understand. But this time that's not the case - because this time I don't have to rely entirely on my faith and trust in Him to lead me without question… because this time, I understand why.

It's a gift; a gift to both of us. I'm getting to know my mother and she's getting to know me. I'm learning all about my family history and she's being assured that she'll never be out of my life again. I have my mother back – and she has her daughter back. Thank you, Lord… this is wonderful!

PSALM 84: 11, 12

11) For the Lord God is the sun and shield;
the Lord will give grace and glory;
no good thing will he withhold
from them that walk uprightly.
12) O Lord of Hosts, blessed is the man
that trusteth in thee.

chapter 21

December 7, 1998

ONE MONTH LATER

The Lord certainly does work in mysterious ways, which is something every Christian already knows… and while I was at my mother's house this past month, I was once again blessed with the opportunity to experience it first hand.

There I was, one week after I arrived, packing up my things and getting ready to drive away early the next morning, when suddenly I came down with the most horrible case of the flu I've ever had. I spent the next seven days flat on my back in bed; complete with raging fever, chills and not even enough strength to make it to the bathroom to throw up. (Thank goodness for my mom's garbage pail!) The second week, I started feeling a little better – which meant I could now get to the restroom by myself, and even keep down a few swallows of chicken broth and sips of 7Up, but I was still bed-ridden; too weak to even read or watch television, (let alone visit with my mother). By the third week, I began to feel more like myself again, so I moved from my bed in Lucky to my mother's couch, where together, we watched television and talked, and talked, and then talked some more. And now, here I am; week four… 10 pounds lighter – and finally strong enough to think about hitting the road again.

I've always believed that there's a silver lining in every cloud, and this extremely painful case of the flu was no exception. Because I couldn't leave after the first week as I had planned, my mother and I were given a precious four more weeks of unplanned time together. Apparently, the Lord knew what we **both** needed... and that was time to bond.

So that's how a severe case of the flu turned out to be a life-changing blessing in disguise. I must admit that this is the first time I've ever been grateful for getting the flu; but the fact that it literally forced me into spending an additional month here in Sacramento was truly a blessing. For the first time in as long as I can remember, I was given the chance to be tenderly nursed and unconditionally loved by the one person in the world who thinks I'm beautiful - even when I'm throwing up; my mother. She spent hours every day sitting by my bed, bathing my brow with cold cloths and even spoon feeding me, spoonful by loving spoonful. Yes, I was miserable... but I was also pampered and loved by the one person who had been missing from my life ... and it was a time we will both cherish forever.

According to my mother, even though she hated to see me suffer, it was an experience that she, too, knows was an answer to her prayers. After all these years apart, because of my sickness, she finally got a chance to take care of me - as a mother would care for a small child, rather than as the full grown adult woman I have become. All the talking in the world could never have meant as much as the fact that for three weeks - when I really NEEDED her... she was there.

So thank you dear Heavenly Father. I am truly in awe of your grace and your love. What a tremendous weight is lifted off our weak earthly shoulders when we understand that no matter what happens; no matter how bad it seems at the time... You always have our best interests at heart. And what a relief it is to completely trust in the fact that every single tribulation is simply one more step on the ladder that will eventually lead us Home, (as well as an opportunity to praise You under adverse circumstances). After all, it's easy to be trusting and grateful when you're happy and healthy, but when things are difficult and painful, that's when we're given the chance to show You that we love and trust You always, even in the worst of times.

Back in the days of Jesus, (and still yet in other parts of the world), people were thrown into dungeons (like John the Baptist, and Paul and so many others) for simply believing in Christ. Others were tortured or had their families killed because they refused to deny their faith. People have had their heads cut off, been crucified, and too many other horrors for me to even imagine. And yet we, who have roofs over our heads, food in our stomachs and are not threatened for our faith - dare to complain because we are unhealthy or lose a loved one, or need a new car, or whatever.. I know that pain and loss is difficult, even in this day and age – and I don't mean to make light of those human feelings… but I look at our times of suffering as a *wonderful opportunity* to show our Lord that we know that the true rewards are in Heaven and life in Earth is a blink of the eye in eternal time and a test of our faith. That's why I, (who have lost so little and never had to suffer because of my faith in Christ), look upon the worst case of the flu I've ever had, as a wonderful blessing.

Even though I'm still as weak as a "premature kitten" right now, I feel absolutely euphoric at the realization that I am in your loving hands. Now it's up to me to be worthy of that love by being humble, charitable and obedient, (to mention just a few) and by continuing to study your Word, the Holy Bible, every day. Yes, I went to Sunday school and learned all the stories, but until the flood, when you saved that precious miracle Bible from the black and stinking waters, I didn't realize the importance of actually studying it – and turning to it for at least a few minutes every day for my inspiration and guidance. It's like the Lord has given us a roadmap, and yet so few (myself included – before the flood) realize how IMPORTANT it is to make it a part of our everyday lives.

And there was yet another wonderful thing that came out of my well-timed case of the flu. This past week, as I rested and regained my strength, I had plenty of time in which to think about "poetry on the road" and how I could use my poems and lyrics to reach more people. Wouldn't it be great if I had some business cards printed up that showed Lucky driving under the rainbow - towing a book of poetry, like on my flyer? And wouldn't it be wonderful if I had a little hand-held tape recorder so that I could speak into as I travel - and then send the finished tapes to my mother. That way it would be like she was joining me on the road... something she has said numerous times she wished she could do. I also feel inspired to write a book about my adventures someday... and those tapes, (which I'll have my mother save for me), will guide my hand as I write it; taking me right back to the actual events and the feelings as I experienced them, rather than trusting in my faulty memory. Yes, I do keep daily written journals, but I'd have to write all day long to capture everything, so the tapes would be a wonderful addition; both for my mother and for all those who will read the book someday.

And I was also thinking that I should have my brakes checked, since that bright red flashing light on the dashboard still makes me nervous. I hadn't mentioned any of these things to my mom, not wanting her to feel bad because she was unable to help, but one night while we were sitting in her living room watching television and enjoying each others company, she suddenly got up from her recliner and said, "Follow me, dear."

And that's what I did... as she led me out onto her patio and inside one of her little storage sheds next to my RV. Once inside, she picked up a clay flower pot and took something out of it; a plain white envelope... filled with $20 bills.

Before I tell you the rest of this story, I have to give you some background on my mother's living situation. Because she had no opportunity for schooling past the 8th grade, she'd always found herself relegated to laborious jobs, like cleaning houses or serving food. She loves caring for people and her lifelong dream was to become a nurse. She worked very hard to get her GED - and then found a way to attend nursing school, which she loved. But as she was attending the classes, bunions on her feet got so painful she had trouble standing, which is why she went to a doctor to have them removed. But he didn't think that was enough – and decided that the only way to stop the bunions from returning was to break all ten of her toes, claiming that would prevent them from curling under and new bunions from forming. Not only was it extremely painful, but they never healed correctly… and she became so unable to stand that the nursing school dropped her, not because of her grades, (which were excellent), but because of her inability to stand, and that was the end of her dream of becoming a nurse. Even now, many years later, she finds it very difficult (and painful) to walk, and can't stay on her feet for any length of time.

Apparently that misguided doctor, (and I'm giving him the benefit of the doubt), made more than his share of medical blunders and some enterprising attorney filed a lawsuit on behalf of dozens of his patients. At that time, my mother knew nothing about any court case, but the attorneys must have subpoenaed his files and uncovered her story because they approached her and asked if she would be interested in joining the class action lawsuit. She doesn't know anything about the legal system, but after he assured her that it wouldn't cost her anything, she agreed.

It took a couple of years, but eventually, they won the lawsuit, and after the attorney took his lion's share of the proceeds, there was still enough left for my mother to make a down payment on this mobile home and the lot on which it sits. It still hurts her to walk, and her feet are terribly deformed, (which is why she lives on disability), but at least she was able to move out of the tiny little "motel room sized" apartment she had called home for more than 10 years and now she, (and the bank) owns her double-wide trailer in this nice, safe gated-community.

That's why I was so shocked when my mom picked up that fat little envelope and turned to me with the biggest and brightest smile I'd ever seen on her face and said, "Honey, the Lord has blessed me, and even after tithing, I've been able to put $20 a month in this envelope… and believe it or now, I've saved a thousand dollars. Please dear, I want you to have it. It would mean **so much** to me if you'd let me help you on your journey, please take it," she begged me with her words AND her eyes, as she held out the well-worn envelope.

I didn't know what to say... One thing was for sure; no matter how much I could use the money, there was absolutely NO WAY I would take it from her... which is why I answered, "Thank you so much, mom, but I just can't take your money. And the truth is - I don't **need** it. The Lord provides for me, no matter what happens... and I know that everything will be fine because He told me it would," I explained as I reached out and hugged her, still refusing to touch the envelope. "Mom,", I said as I backed up just enough so we could be face to face and she could see my love and sincerity, "just the fact that you WANTED me to have it is so unbelievably generous, that I will never forget it... and I have no doubt that the Lord will continue to bless you for your generosity, even though I won't take the money."

But did I mention how stubborn my mother is? Of course, she insisted... and insisted, and insisted. She refused to give up, and finally, she won me over with two well-made arguments. "But honey, you're doing everything YOU can do to help others... and now you've got to give me a chance to do the same. I can't go with you, but this is MY way of being a part of all the good I know you'll be doing. Please don't take that chance away from me!"

As good as that argument was, it still didn't work... so she followed it up with argument number two; "Honey," she continued to plead, "I missed watching you grow up. I missed buying your prom dress and helping you set up your first apartment. I missed so much... and now there's no way I can ever get those years back. But if you'll let me help you now, it would mean the world to me! Please, accept this gift from my heart - and don't take away my chance to make a difference in YOUR life."

What could I say to that? As much as I hated to, something in her eyes told me that I **needed** to accept the money, for **her** as well as for me and my work... and then use it in such a way that her gift would continue to grow and multiply, making her a part of the team.. Now that we've been reunited as mother and daughter, I have absolutely no doubt that some-day I **will** return this money to her… many times over.

So thanks to my mom, I now have enough money to buy that tape recorder and get some business cards printed. I can even have my brakes checked and leave Sacramento with money for repairs in case, (I should say "when"), Lucky breaks down again. Will the blessings never stop rain-ing down upon my head? I think not… and once again I am amazed by the path my Lord has set for me.

And as if that wasn't enough to leave me completely humbled and unbelievably grateful, she did something else that would make my trav-els more pleasant. While I was sick and she spent countless hours sitting next to my bed in Lucky nursing me, she noticed that I had a big plas-tic bucket in the bathroom under the roof vent. That's because it leaks, which I didn't think was a big enough problem to worry about because, after all, I have a bucket… and I can empty it whenever I need to. I meant it when I said I was thankful just to have a bed to sleep in and a roof over my head – but I never said that the roof didn't leak.

Well, apparently my mother was bothered by that bucket, and on the first day that I was well enough to venture outside, she asked if I would accompany her on a shopping trip. Of course I agreed; wanting to spend as much time with her as I could before I left, and I assumed that she meant the grocery store. Imagine my surprise when instead, we pulled into an RV Repair and Parts Shop. I asked her what she was up to this time… and she said, "I'm buying you an early Christmas gift – and don't you dare say a word about it!"

Twenty minutes later, we left the store with a new roof vent, still in the box, (hopefully with lots of easy to follow instructions), and my mother was smiling from ear to ear as we walked arm and arm back to her car. She was so proud… and I was so scared; afraid that my complete lack of mechanical ability would leave me unable to install the new vent that meant so much to her. I don't know which side of the brain is in charge of mechanical things, but I think I must be handicapped in that area because my two boys had to put together the "easy to assemble" toys they found in their cereal boxes by the time they were two, and now here I was - trying to install a new roof vent in Lucky... all by myself? Yes, I would do it... because there was no way I could let my mother down!

And boy-oh-boy... was it ever a battle! Apparently the previous owners had tried to stop the leaking vent many times before - because when I climbed up the ladder and stepped onto the roof, (for the very first time, I might add), it looked like a solid mound of what was once white (but now dirty brown and cracked) layer after layer of caulking, which completely surrounded the vent. I had carefully read the instructions, (I'm big on reading instructions and following them to the letter), which explained how to install the new vent - and it sounded pretty straightforward. But how was I going to get the old one off without ruining the roof, which had probably been waterlogged and rotting for years now.

Well, time to ask the Lord for His help again... so together my mother and I prayed for His assistance and then she stood (or sat in a lawn chair when it became too painful) right next to the RV for the eight solid hours it took me just to remove the **old** caulking; handing me tools and providing me with both encouragement and water to drink as the sweat poured off my face from the intense labor of hammering and chiseling. She was so proud of me that she took pictures as I worked and some of her neighbors even gathered when they saw me working, which gave her a chance to introduce (and brag about) her daughter. I wasn't exactly thrilled about all the attention – but the joy that lit up my mother's face was well worth it.

And we did it! Eight hours of pounding and chiseling; eight hours of wondering how hard and how deep I could go without damaging the roof itself... and it actually worked! I got the new roof vent installed, then borrowed my mother's caulking gun, (greatly surprised that she even had one – and even more surprised when I figured out how to use it), and if I do say so myself... it looks pretty good. And best of all - IT DOESN'T LEAK! Thank you, Jesus... and thank you, mom, because now I don't have to worry about that bucket tipping over or sliding across the floor when I turn a corner. Could things get any better?

And that's how I've been spending this last week; getting everything ready to go, designing and picking up my new business cards and buying a hand-held tape recorder so I can send my mother tapes as I travel. I even bought one of those "battery boosters" so I could jump start my engine whenever I need to. Just a few more days, and I'll be on the road again!

And guess what? I've decided on my next destination; Sun City, Arizona. Remember the elderly lady (her name was Elaine) at my performance at the Senior Center in Gold Beach? She was the one who invited me to park at her house and put on some shows in her area. Well, I called her today... and she was absolutely thrilled to hear that I was coming and wants to start scheduling appearances as soon as I have a more definite arrival date. But considering how unpredictable my trip has been so far, and the distance between Sacramento and Sun City, Arizona, I told her I couldn't possibly be sure when I'd arrive, but hopefully, it would be before Christmas and I would keep her posted.

So... one day at time, the path is being laid out for me, and once again I shall trust my Lord and follow it gladly - and with a heart filled with love and gratitude, (as well as a new and wonderful relationship with my mother)!

chapter 22

December 12, 1998

This is only the second time I've shed tears of anything but joy or relief since the flood. The first time was when I drove away from my sons and grandchildren in Portland and now again... as I said goodbye to my mother and watched her smiling through her tears and waving emphatically as I drove away from her loving arms. The seven year old little girl who lost her mother so long ago has found her again... and the only price I had to pay was the pain of saying goodbye.

It should have been so easy... because I have absolutely no doubt whatsoever that God will not only lead me – but will use me as He sees fit... and that someday we'll all be together again. But for that first hour, as I found my way onto Interstate #5 and headed south, I cried until my eyes were so swollen I couldn't see through the tears and decided to exit at a rest stop and ask the Lord for help.

"Dear Lord," I prayed. *"I belong to you... and you know that I love you and trust you completely. You have given us your greatest possession, your Son, our savior, Jesus Christ, and I can't possibly imagine how much it must have hurt you to see Him suffer and die for OUR sins. And here I am, clothed, fed, and almost completely healthy ... and yet my heart still aches. Please, my Lord, help me remove this burden from my soul. Help me use the gifts you have granted me*

to comfort and encourage everyone I meet and to glorify You. Help me be worthy of your forgiveness and your protection… and help me follow whatever path it is you would have me follow… without tears and without fear. I need you, my Lord… I need you so much. You are my rod and my staff. You are the master of all, and I will gladly devote the rest of my life to serving You, but I need your strength. I miss my family so much; please help me bear the sorrow - and learn once again to focus on the joy. "Thy will be done, Lord, on earth as it is in Heaven", so if you find this humble woman, naught but a rib taken from Adam, a sinner and no holder of the Priesthood… if you find me worthy of thy comfort and instruction; worthy of influencing and inspiring others, I would be so very grateful. Thank you, Jehovah, the great "**I Am**"…and only in the name of thy beloved son, Jesus Christ, would I even dare to approach you. Thank you, Jesus, in your beloved name I pray, always… amen."

And then, as I rose from my knees with the tears still streaming down my cheeks, this time they were different; these were the tears that come to my eyes almost every time I speak so directly and earnestly to God; they were tears of love and joy. I sat back down in the driver's seat, looking back on all that had happened since the flood in Gold Beach, when a pick-up truck pulling a trailer pulled in and parked right next to me. As I watched, an elderly gentleman and his wife got out of the vehicle and headed for the restrooms.

It's hard to find the words for what happened next, but something changed inside me when I looked at them. Suddenly, I LOVED them! It wasn't the kind of love I've always had for my brothers and sisters on this planet; it was the kind of love I feel for the mother, my father, my sons and my grandchildren. It was so strong that I wanted to get out of my RV and throw my arms around them and tell them how much I loved them. I couldn't believe it… but there it was. Yes, I was leaving love behind… but at the sight of these two people, and then the next two and the next one, I was given that same familial love for each and every person; the same love I felt for my earth family. I knew right then and there that the Lord had answered my prayer by filling the void in my heart with HIS kind of love...love for everyone - and I knew that he had lifted the burden of loss from my shoulders.

I have no idea why the Lord would think me worthy of such protection and guidance, but I do know that whenever more is given − more is expected... which means I'd better start focusing on what I can do for Him right now − rather than about how I'm feeling. "Ask not what Jesus can do for you − but ask what you can do for Jesus." I've never heard it said exactly like that before, (although John F. Kennedy was close, if you change "Jesus" to "your country"), but from now on − that will be my new motto!

Well, that certainly helped. Some things just can't be handled without God and now that I've been blessed with these new and more powerful feelings of love and contentment - it's time to get back on the road to Sun City, Arizona. I'm heading south on I-5 because according to the map, I can change over to Interstate 10 in mid-town Los Angeles and then take that all the way to Phoenix. I think I've timed it just right so that my passage through the heart of Los Angeles will take place during the middle of the night... which should allow me to avoid the madhouse of the legendary LA traffic.

And sitting right here on the seat right next to me is the hand-held tape recorder I bought before I left Sacramento. I've been speaking into it just as though I were talking directly to my mother, sharing both the scenery and my innermost thoughts. I'm hoping to have the first tape (both front and back side), finished before Christmas so it can be my gift to her. I have a feeling she'll like it.

So, time to get "On the road again"!

chapter 23

December 13, 1998

Last night, just before midnight, I was 90 miles north of Los Angeles; almost at the base of a stretch of highway they call the "grapevine" – well named because it's not only steep, but twists and turns, much like grape-bearing vines. Lucky was running like a top - but the fog was so thick that I couldn't see even two broken yellow lines in front of me. Driving in the fog has always been one of my worst nightmares, (that and white-out snowstorms), so I desperately searched for a place to pull over. But unfortunately, the exits were few and far between in the wide open farmlands of Central California - so I had no choice but to keep driving.

My one and only salvation was the steady procession of big semi-trucks that didn't seem to be bothered by the fog, and I struggled to stay close behind each one as it passed me, letting their taillights serve as my guide. But they were going so much faster than I could that it wasn't long before they'd leave me behind, frustrated and once again leaning forward over the steering wheel, gripping it with white knuckles and straining to see the road through the blinding whiteness. And as if that wasn't enough of a challenge, my windshield wipers don't work, which made it nearly impossible to see anything. The month I spent in Portland was in the summer time, so I didn't realize they weren't working or I would have had my sons see what the problem was. But now that I needed them, when I turned the knob... nothing happened. It wasn't exactly raining, but the fog was so moist that the windshield was covered with rivulets of water, and no matter how hard I pushed, pulled and twisted that wiper control knob, they refused to work.

And then, just when my eyes began to blur with the constant strain and I thought I couldn't possibly go on any longer... the engine died. There was no noise, no sputtering and no warning of any kind - and it happened so fast, I didn't even have time to pull completely onto the shoulder of the freeway before rolling to a stop. (Not this again!)

Naturally I tried to re-start the engine several times, but it wouldn't turn over, not even with the groan of a nearly dead battery. My heart sank and my first thought was, "Oh no, what could be wrong this time?" But then my second thought was, "What a blessing that I'm in a motor home. At least I've got a bed and a toilet."

It took me awhile, but I finally located the hazard lights and turned them on, somehow feeling comforted by the steady click, click, click... as they blinked their warning to the other drivers, who I could only **hope** were able to see them through the dense fog. Since it was almost midnight, I was on schedule to drive through downtown LA in the early morning hours, but apparently, that wasn't going to happen.

And then, as I sat there in the driver's seat wondering what I should do next, I noticed that the fog was lifting. In a matter of only a few minutes, the night air was once again perfectly clear and even without my head-lights - the moon was bright enough for me to see far into the distance. Unfortunately, there wasn't much to see; not a single exit and no apparent sign of civilization. "Oh well," I thought. "There's bound to be something within walking distance," so I grabbed my coat and stepped outside the motor home, planning to hike to the nearest exit.

But that's when I got my third surprise of the evening as I realized why the fog had so suddenly disappeared; it was being blown away by a driv-ing wind. It was so powerful that I could barely stand up and had to hold onto the door handle of the RV to keep from being lifted off my feet. I stood there for a minute, clutching the handle like a lifeline and hoping that it was merely a gust and would soon fade so I could find help. But it didn't let up… and I had no choice but to climb back into the motor home and wait for the morning light. No repair shops would be open at midnight anyway, so I might as well make myself comfortable, I thought. And things weren't so bad, because I had everything I needed right here, and thanks to my mother's generosity, I even had the money to get whatever was wrong with Lucky fixed.

After my long, stressful drive and then my battle with the wind, my heart was racing so I sat down on my couch to take a few deep breaths and try to calm down, (hoping I might catch a couple of hours of sleep before morning)… but as it turned out, that too would be impossible. The wind became even more powerful; so strong that it violently rocked the RV from side to side. I thought for sure that Lucky would be blown over, so I decided to stand up and brace myself by placing one hand on each set of the cupboards that line the center aisle of the motor home. I even went so far as to scan the RV, searching for just the right place to stand where I'd be safe from falling debris if Lucky tipped over.

But after one very long and miserable hour of such paranoid silliness, I began to relax; realizing that if it hadn't happened by now, it probably wouldn't. And that's when I had to laugh at the picture I must have made… standing there in the center aisle, bracing myself and ready to tumble over with the next gust of wind. "I guess I'm **still** a green pea", I chuckled to myself as I finally sat down to give my legs a much needed rest. I'd just spent three hours driving in blinding whiteness, and then another hour standing in the aisle - tensed and ready for the worst that might happen, so it felt absolutely wonderful to sit down and relax. But apparently… this night of adventure wasn't over yet.

The weak and aged batteries that came with Lucky had used up what little power they had left, and with one last feeble flash, the hazard lights quit blinking. That wouldn't have been so bad except that the wind had suddenly died down just as quickly as it had started and once again, the fog was back. Since I didn't have enough time to make it fully onto the shoulder before rolling to a stop, each passing truck sounded like a tornado as it bore down on me, then saw Lucky at the last minute and swerved to avoid a collision, causing the RV to rock wildly from side to side in its passing wake. I guess that wind was a blessing after all!

As you can well imagine, there was no way I could possibly sleep with truck after truck coming so close I thought for sure the next one would hit me... so I just sat there on the couch praying; asking God not only to protect me, but asking Him how someone as insignificant as me could possibly make a difference in this world. What did He expect me to do? I'm no preacher, nor am I a missionary. I'm just a poet... and there are so many people in this world more righteous than I, (and stronger than I)... why did He call me? What possible difference can my little gift of words make in a world so fraught with confusion and pain?

And that's when it happened. Suddenly, I no longer heard the sound of passing trucks and it became eerily silent... so silent that the beating of my heart seemed loud - yet at the same time, it was somehow soothing. Then, without warning... it felt like the door of the RV had blown open and the wind had come inside, lifting me up off the couch with the sheer strength of it. "This can't be happening," I thought to myself... but it was - and now I was floating through the air, surrounded by nothing but an empty sea of blackness.

Trying to remain calm and in control, I thought to myself, "This must be a dream. I must have fallen asleep, so if I just open my eyes - it won't be dark anymore and I'll be back in Lucky." But no matter how hard I tried to open them... nothing happened. It was as though I no longer had a body and my futile efforts faded as I gave in to the cold, silent blackness.

And believe me - I was afraid; afraid because my logical mind couldn't accept the fact that I was moving through a cold and empty darkness when I knew that I was really sitting on the couch in my RV. And then... just when a feeling of panic threatened to consume me, it began to get lighter and warmer, and the fear vanished. In fact, it felt warm and pleasant and I was actually enjoying it.

After a short period of time, (I have no idea how long it actually was), the fear was not only gone, but it had been replaced by a powerful feeling of warmth and contentment. I felt so safe and so loved; it was as though I was being hugged by someone who meant more to me than life itself. And then... I was there; I was beyond the veil. I was *Home.*

Don't ask me how I knew it - because there is no logical explanation; I just *felt* it with every fiber of my being. I could see people running to greet me, and they weren't family members, or people I had known on Earth, but people I had never seen before... and there were so many of them, (a zillion is an understatement). I can remember thinking, "I didn't know that this many people had ever existed." And then came the best part of all.

As the people drew closer and I was able to look into their faces... I realized that I loved each and every one of them with a love so deep and so strong that it put to shame the love I felt for my newborn son when I first held him in my arms and he gripped my finger with his perfect little hand. It was a love so all-consuming, and much more powerful than anything we are capable of here on Earth, that I literally laughed out loud from the pure wonder of it. Oh my goodness... It felt like my life on earth had been nothing but a dream, and now that I was awake, I was *"home"*.

And what was even more amazing was that I KNEW every single one of those people. I knew what they were thinking and how they felt. I knew everything that had happened to them during their life on Earth. Somehow, I was sharing their experiences - as if we were all spiritually connected. Without having lived it myself, I suddenly knew what it was like to be a ship's captain or an Indian maiden. There was no doubt in my mind that we were all somehow joined together; and I can only describe it as "a single golden thread" that bound us all - not only to each other, but to God, who was the center of everything.

Perhaps that's why so many people think they have memories of previous lives and believe in reincarnation. Could they have somehow tapped into this sharing of minds… and be mistaking their own memories for those who have gone before us?

And no, I didn't see a throne, or the great Jehovah – but I FELT Him, everywhere… and it was such a glorious feeling that I wanted to shout and praise Him at the top of my lungs, and even now, I can find no words to describe how it felt; other than *euphoria*.

Somewhere… deep inside my soul, I knew beyond a shadow of a doubt that I was at Home, and it was such a wonderful relief that it never even crossed my mind to wonder if I was dead. It's like when you're in your bed asleep and have a dream so long and detailed that when you wake up, you're surprised to discover that it was only a dream –because it had all seemed so real! But this time, it was "life on Earth" that was the dream, and I was awake again – and back where I belonged. That's when a flood of memories from "before" life on Earth washed over me. **This** was reality, and as much as I love beautiful planet Earth, I was so thrilled to be in the glorious presence of my Lord and master that I wanted nothing more than to stay right there - and to revel in His love for eternity.

But then I heard a voice say, "*It is not yet your time. You have much to do.*" I don't know where the voice came from, or who was speaking, because, (just like after the flood), I didn't hear it with my ears; it was just *there*, inside me, coming from everywhere at once. And just like before, it was that **same** voice; the one I was so familiar with; the one I recognized and loved with all my heart.

"No, please" I begged, "I don't want to go back. This is where I belong. Please let me stay!"

But again the words repeated, "*It is not yet your time. You have much to do,*" and while the voice was still speaking, the light began to fade… and I felt myself once again moving. I wanted to cry; to plead with the voice to let me stay - but then I heard the words, "*watch and understand.*"

The warm and soothing light continued to fade, and the warmth and love that I had so joyously reveled in just moments before faded with it… and in its place was that cold never-ending sea of blackness. Overpowering fear enveloped me - and I began to shake from somewhere deep inside, like the teeth-chattering chill that accompanies a high fever. And then I heard it… a sound I shall never forget for as long as I live… ***the wailing.***

When I was 14 years old, our beloved pet Cocker Spaniel named CoCo was trapped in my horse barn as it burned to the ground. My little brother and I stood there helplessly watching the flames - and crying hysterically as our beloved best friend screamed in pain and terror, again and again. My father shot his rifle directly into the fire, desperately trying to put her out of her misery, but he didn't know exactly where she was, so even though he fired in the general direction of the wailing, she continued to scream… and scream… and scream. My brother, who was 12 at the time, was so hysterical that he tried to run into the flames to save her and the firemen had to physically restrain him; eventually calling an ambulance and taking him to the hospital. I will never forget that heart wrenching sound – and how it felt to stand there listening to her WAIL, and yet to be powerless to do anything to stop it. And believe me, this sound was much, much worse.

And then, floating, (as if it had no body), suspended in that sea of empty blackness, a human face appeared before me… tears streaming down her cheeks and soundlessly mouthing the words "help me – please help me." I tried to reach out, but when I did the face contorted and changed, until it was no longer that of a human being. It had gradually turned into one that, (for lack of a better description), I can only describe as the face of a demon. It was monstrously inhuman and beyond earthly imagination … all but the eyes, and they were so horrific, I will never forget them. They were flame red, frighteningly intense and radiated pure evil… and they were so filled with hatred that I had to turn away as I felt the stomach bile rise into my throat. The most realistic horror movie I've ever seen couldn't hold a candle to the evil in that face, (if you could call it a "face"), and it was laughing at me… reveling in its power to strike fear and revulsion in my heart, and flaunting it's ability to posses the poor wailing soul I had seen just moments before.

And then the demon face began to contort… as it gradually faded and the human face reappeared. It was as though that poor human spirit was struggling; struggling to fight its way back to the surface… desperately trying to escape the torment. "Please help me," it wailed again and again - but there was nothing I could do… and before long, the demon face returned, once again smiling and victorious; savoring its power over this mere weakling of a human being. The creature was pure evil; I could feel it – and yet it never said a single word. It didn't need to… because it was obvious that it took great joy in showing me the sheer pleasure it took in tormenting its human captive.

And then another face appeared, and the same thing happened, and the wailing never stopped. Over and over again, that heart wrenching scene repeated - with so many different faces, both men and women, that eventually I lost count and could do nothing but weep, both for their suffering and for my inability to do anything about it. I was completely powerless to help them - because it was already too late…. "Oh my dear God", I prayed, "Please help them!"

Somehow I knew that these were people I once knew and loved – people who were lost and never found their way back to God. And now it's too late. If only they had known that they could have spent eternity wrapped in His glorious love. If only they had realized how short life on Earth is and that NOTHING could **possibly** be worth the horrific fate to which they have been eternally condemned. No amount of money, or power or even physical suffering would be worth even the possibility of such a fate! And if only those who DID know; those who accept Jesus as their savior and realize that life on earth is but a blink of God's eye, could somehow help these lost souls find their way home… before it's too late.

But all I could do now was sob… almost hysterically for their pain and their loss - as much as if it were my own, because it was! Their loss is a loss for ALL of us, because that golden thread that binds us all to God has been broken - and someday, we will **all** mourn the loss of each and every soul who'll never again be in the presence of the great *I Am*.

And then I felt myself moving again… uncontrollably and almost hysterically weeping, with great gut-wrenching sobs, over the suffering I had just witnessed, and still trembling with indescribable fear. Was that Hell, I wondered? I had always heard it described as fire and brimstone, but that's not what I saw. Could HELL be eternal darkness and never-ending torment? Or was this some place in between? I had no way of knowing; I only knew that it was a fate worse than anything I had ever imagined and the worst part of all was knowing that they would never again feel the all-encompassing love of God, but would spend eternity being tortured, not only by the demons I saw, but with the pain and regret for the choices they made while here on Earth. If only I could help them! If only I could do something! And then I understood; I knew why I had been given the opportunity to see this horrific torment.

Never again would I doubt the ability of one single person to make a difference in this world. From this day forward, I will eagerly devote the rest of my life to encouraging just one person to find their way back to God. So what if I'm only a poet. Look at the evil Hitler did with his words. Could I not use mine to tell people everything that I had seen and to encourage others to put life on Earth in the proper perspective? People need to see what I have seen. They need to realize that our life here is nothing but a moment in time -and that there isn't anything on this planet worth the price of such eternal torture.

At the very instant when I understood "why" I was being shown this horrific torment… the wailing suddenly stopped… and it was once again eerily silent and completely black. There were no more faces - and I continued floating through the darkness, wondering what would happen next. Suddenly a bright picture appeared in the black emptiness… much like a large movie screen in a dark theater, and on it was playing scenes from my own earthly life; as a young adult, a teenager, a child and even when I was a baby; the years I was too young to remember. I watched in amazement as all the events that had already occurred in my life played like a movie on the screen. But now I was even more confused, because the events as I saw them on the screen weren't exactly as I remembered them. They were somewhat close, but not quite right - and I became worried. Could I have been seeing my life as I WANTED to see it - rather than as it really was? Oh no, I thought as the full impact of that realization dawned on me. I have to be much more careful! From now on, I must try to see things from God's point of view, rather than from my own. How could I have been so ignorant?

And then it dawned on me what Jesus meant when He (and others) said in the Bible, "Fear the wrath of God," because I felt that soul-shaking fear; fear that I have been living my life for ME rather than for HIM; fear that I have disappointed my Lord and Master; and fear that I may never be worthy of spending eternity with Him.

And then suddenly, I was back on the couch in my RV; wide awake and shaking from head to toe. I was covered with perspiration and the tears were streaming down my cheeks. My stomach was spinning and I ran to the bathroom to throw up, again and again, until there was nothing left but bile that left my mouth burning. How could one vision be so amazingly wonderful and filled with love and peace - and then become so frightening and evil. It was Heaven and Hell... all rolled up into one. Apparently, as I heard the voice so clearly say, "It's not yet my time and I have much to do", so never again will I wonder whether I'm trying to accomplish the impossible, or if there is anything one simple poet and sinner can do. How can anything be a "waste of time" if it's what our Lord and Master wants? My question had been answered... and I'd gladly give the rest of my life to save just ONE single person from the clutches of evil.

I looked at my watch and was shocked to see that only 5 minutes had passed. To me, it had felt like hours, if not days or even weeks. I guess time really is subjective; yesterday, today and tomorrow; all wrapped up into one neat package.

There was so much to think about... and that's what I've been doing; sitting here trying to gather my thoughts for the past hour. I feel paralyzed by the scenes still whirling around in my head - and I'm struggling to bring myself back into my life here on Earth.

How ignorant could I have been? It doesn't matter if I'm broken down on the side of the road. It doesn't matter if people laugh at my weak attempts to share what I know to be true. It doesn't matter if I have a headache or nice clothes to wear. What matters is that as many of us as possible find our way "Home" and that I use my gift of words and my ability to influence and encourage people to share what the Lord has shown me with all who will listen.

No matter how hard I tried, I couldn't quit shaking, and I still wanted to vomit. One minute, I felt like I had awoken from the short, dreamlike existence of life here on Earth and was at home with my Lord - and then I was traumatized by the pain and suffering of people I couldn't help, and now, I'm back here in Lucky sitting on the couch... and I know that it's not "reality". How can I deal with this knowledge? How can I go on as if nothing has happened; as if nothing has changed? I think it's time to get down on my knees and pray, because without God's help, I can't.

AN HOUR LATER...

I'm back...and although I'm feeling a little better, I'm still having a hard time dealing with being back on Earth. It's like part of me is still "there"... and it's hard to focus on what must be done "today", (the nuts and bolts of life) here on Earth. It doesn't seem real anymore because this still feels like the dream... and I want to wake up and be home again. But like Paul said when he was in the dungeon; that he'd much rather be with his Lord. But if he was needed here - if that was the Lord's will, he would do whatever he could. I understand that now – and I agree. I'm happy to be of whatever service I am capable of, but my heart still aches to be "home"... and I knew I needed help. So I pulled out my big white miracle Bible and began to read... thirsting to recapture the feeling of being connected to God. Jesus must have seen how difficult life on Earth was for us, which is why the great Jehovah allowed His precious son to come down here and walk among us. He knew that without the help of our Savior, most of us would **never** find our way Home again. We're too weak and too self-involved; too greedy and too carnal Jesus atoned for our sins - which gave us a fighting chance. He gave us **hope,** and He showed us the way... and now it's up to *us* what we do with it.

"Thank you, Jesus. Thank you so very much," I sobbed. "You suffered and bled so that we could be saved from our own weakness. What a glorious gift! Thank you; thank you, thank you!"

And now, as I look out my window, I see that the new day is dawning... and even though I'm still trembling and having trouble accepting life on Earth as "reality", I'm also eager to make even the smallest difference I can in the life of the next (and every) person I meet. The sky is turning light orange and red, and every day is a new beginning... so I guess I'd better start walking to the nearest exit and see if I can find some help. There just might be someone at the RV repair shop (or even a tow truck driver) who needs to hear what I have to say. First I think I'll take a picture of where I'm parked right now, half-on and half-off the freeway, and the place where I left the old Abigayle behind - and began seeing life from God's point of view.

Lucky broken down on I-5 in the fog.

chapter 24

December 13, 1998

As soon as it was light enough, my early morning walk to the nearest exit turned out to be less than a mile, but the ride in the tow truck was a long and slow 25 miles. But at least *this* time the driver was a kind and courteous young man who even had a picture of his wife and two young daughters riding proudly on the dash. After last night, I wasn't about to waste an opportunity to plant a seed, so we spent the whole time talking about why I was on the road, and what it was I wanted to share with everyone. I recited a couple of my poems and he liked them so much, he asked for signed copies; which I just happened to have left over from my last show. You'd think a young man, wrapped up in caring for a family with small children wouldn't be touched by my poetry – or even my stories, but he was… and when we arrived at our destination he hugged me and thanked me, and asked if there was any way he could follow my journey. I told him there wasn't, but I'd see him in the hereafter… and we parted ways.

The little mountain town he towed me to was just that – little. There was only one service station, two restaurants and one auto repair shop. It's a good thing we got there early in the morning, because they were able to fit me in right away, but I do have to admit that I was a little concerned when I was introduced to the mechanic who would be doing the work on Lucky.

The best way I can describe him is that he was "simple". I don't mean he was mentally retarded, because he wasn't, but his face was wide and round, his speech slow and halting and his body language shy and diminutive. And he was a big man…not fat, but soft and round like a huggable teddy bear, and when the manager introduced me to him, he nervously shuffled his feet and met my eyes for only one brief moment. But in that single moment, I was touched by a feeling of such warmth and kindness that I immediately recognized this "simple" man as one of God's special spirits.

Unfortunately, I still had vivid memories of my last breakdown - when a team of three supposedly *expert* RV mechanics couldn't find anything wrong with Lucky and then, only 100 miles later, (if it hadn't been for Alan showing up when he did), I'd have been left stranded in the coastal mountains) so I had good cause to be wary. But for some unexplainable reason, this time I wasn't. Somehow I instinctively knew that I was in capable and trustworthy hands.

It couldn't have been more than 20 minutes later when the gentle young man walked into the waiting room where I was passing the time writing in my journal, and said, "Excuse me, ma'am but there's something you ought'a see."

I followed him into the noisy shop, and then inside my RV, where he'd obviously been working on Lucky's engine. He pointed down into the maize of greasy parts and picked up a small rubber hose. "This here's your fuel line," he explained, looking up at me with the patience of a kindly teacher instructing a rather slow student. "The gas goes right here, through this hose and into your carburetor; that's this thing right here," he said as he pointed to what looked to me like just another of many greasy parts in an engine I knew very little about. "Look at this here," he said as he crooked his finger, beckoning for me to come closer to where he carefully held the hose in his huge oil stained fingers.

"See this crack in the line?" he explained as he bent the rubber hose so I could see the rather large opening. "It's a big one, but it didn't break all the way through. This piece right here's holding it together - but most of the gas never made it to the carburetor; it got pumped right out'a this big crack. I just thought you ought'a know," he said as his face lit up with pride at his discovery, "cuz it's some kind'a miracle that you didn't catch on fire. The leak's right over the manifold, and it gets mighty hot, so you could'a had a fire last night."

It was the first time I'd seen his face glow with enthusiasm and confidence as he expressed his wonder at what *hadn't* happened. It was obvious to me that simple or not, engines were this young man's world... and one in which he not only excelled but felt at home. He was "on his own turf" now, and I stood watching as he deftly, and almost lovingly, removed the cracked hose and replace it with a new section. When he was finished, he put the engine cover back on with such precision and care that he might have been a surgeon and the engine was his patient. It warmed my heart to see someone who'd probably been teased and laughed at for much of his life show such skill and pride in his work. Then he carefully, (and almost lovingly), checked more of the fuel line for cracks as his eyebrows furrowed in deep concentration. "She should run just fine now, ma'am," he announced with a smile.

"Thank you so much," I said, making sure that my deep appreciation for his skill was obvious. "I wonder if you'd mind giving Lucky a check-up. She's been running really hot ever since I got her and it worries me. You seem to know so much about engines that I'd feel a lot better if you'd take a look and see if you can find anything else about to go wrong. I'm especially worried about the alternator, because my batteries keep going dead."

"I'd be pleased ta', ma'am," he said with a nod and a smile. "You wait inside and I'll come get ya' when I'm done."

I knew that it would cost extra money for the once-over, but I also figured it would be money well spent if I could avoid another breakdown. About 30 minutes later, my mechanic friend reappeared in the waiting room and said, "S'cuse me ma'am, but I'm done checkin' out your rig. That engines in real fine shape, and I oughta know cuz my truck's got a Dodge 440 and I do all the work on it myself. They tend to run pretty hot, but as far as I can tell, yours is hardly broken in, so if you take good care of her, she'll last for a long time. Even the alternator is working jus' fine."

"Thank you so much! That's just what I was hoping to hear," I said as I smiled and shook his hand.

He handed me a piece of paper and I went inside to pay the bill, where the manager grinned knowingly and said, "I don't who designs these things, but we tow in several burnt out RVs every single month. They run that fuel line right over the manifold, which doesn't make much sense to me because those big old Dodge 440s really heat up, so if there's a break in the fuel line, the gas rolls right out onto that hot manifold, and well… you've got yourself a fire. Catching on fire's bad enough, but then they put the propone cans just a few feet away and before you know it… BOOM, and then you got a **real** tragedy in the making," he said throwing both hands in the air to emphasize the word "BOOM". "The way I see it, you're one lucky lady."

Although I happily agreed with his assessment, I knew that it wasn't merely LUCK that the engine had quit running when it did… because once again I'd been saved from what could have been a major catastrophe. As he handed me my bill, I noticed that I'd been charged for the "one-hour minimum" even though the repairs had only taken 50 minutes. "Excuse me, Sir," I said to the man behind the counter. "I wonder if I could ask your mechanic to use that extra 10 minutes to take a look at my windshield wipers. They weren't working last night and I'd sure like to know why."

"No problem," he answered as he picked up the phone to call the kindly mechanic who'd already returned to work in the garage. And it took him no more than the extra 10 minutes to make a diagnosis. "Sorry ma'am," he said. "I was hope'n it was just a fuse or a loose wire but it's not. Your motor's burnt up. We don't carry those in stock cuz' it's a 1977 and we don't get much call um'. You could prob'ly get one at a junkyard and I'd be happy to put it in for you," he kindly offered.

"Thank you," I said, "but I think I'd better just keep going and get it fixed later. By the way, do you have any of that stuff they put on windshields that makes the rain run right off,' I asked?

"Sure do. It's right over here," he said as he led me down one of the narrow aisles crowded with auto parts and supplies. He pointed to a bottle of RainX, which I happily bought and then, because I'm ignorant about such things (and spoiled because my two sons always handled anything and everything to do with cars), I carefully read the directions to see exactly how to apply it. The manager said I could use a corner of their parking lot where there was a water hose, so I moved Lucky and then got to work. I followed the written instructions to the letter, first cleaning the window with soap and water and then allowing it to dry before applying the first coat.

It took me more than an hour… as I stood on the front bumper and stretched and strained to reach every corner of that huge windshield, and by the time I finished, I was literally dripping with sweat. The instructions said to apply the solution to the clean dry window, let it set until it turned white and then use a dry soft cloth to buff it until the white wax disappeared and the window was clear and shiny… and then start all over again. Geesh, what a lot of hot work that was… but I figured it was well worth it if I could see the road next time I got caught in the rain.

So this is the *second* time my engine has quit running and it turned out to be a blessing. I guess next time it happens, I'll just say "thank you"… instead of worrying about it.

By the time I'd finished waxing the windshield and refilling my gas and propane tanks, it was almost noon… which meant my plan to drive through Los Angeles during the off-traffic hours wasn't going to happen. Oh well, I thought, "how bad can it be?" But I still had one last thing to do before hitting the road again. I asked my new mechanic friend to pose for a picture in front of Lucky and gave him a big thank you hug as I whispered into his ear, "Thank you, my friend, for being my guardian angel today." He looked so happy and so proud that I could feel tears welling up in my eyes as he stood there waving at me when I drove away. Another person I love just as much as my family, I thought; another brother-in-Christ.

The city of Los Angeles proper was still 75 miles away, and when I asked myself "how bad can it be," I didn't have any idea how *bad* that really was. It was worse than anything I could have imagined. First I had to drive the stretch of highway they call the "grapevine" which was nearly 50 miles of steep hills and sharp corners with 6 full lanes of bumper-to-bumper traffic. And to make matters worse, within minutes of leaving the repair shop, Lucky did what he always does and overheated, so I looked for a place to pull over and let the engine cool down. You'd think they'd have a rest area on a highway with so much traffic, I thought... but they didn't, so I continued driving until the temperature gauge was at the very top of the red zone and it began to smell like something was burning.

That's when I had no choice but to pull over at the only place available; a wide spot on the shoulder where a freeway entrance provided an extra lane for the entering cars to get up to speed. Not the safest spot, I thought, but it will have to do or Lucky will catch on fire. I thought I'd fix some lunch and read for an hour or two while the engine cooled off, and then get started again.

But things never seem to work out according to plan (not MY plans anyway), and as soon as the engine was cool enough to drive, I turned the key and guess what; the battery was dead. "Oh well, that's no problem," I thought to myself with a smile. I'd just use the "quick start" battery booster I bought with the money from my mother. It cost me a hundred dollars but since even the new battery Alan had given me was now dead, I thought it might be better to spend the money on the booster rather than on another new battery, at least until I could figure out why they weren't recharging.

Since the friendly repairman who checked Lucky out this morning told me that the alternator was working fine, my boys were probably right when they said that something was wrong with the charging system. Well, whatever the problem is, until I get it fixed, at least with the battery booster I'll be able to give myself a jump-start whenever I need it, and now it was time to see if my hundred dollars had been well-spent.

I took the "quick start" battery pac out of the box it came in and carefully read the instructions. "Attach the red cable to the positive battery post and the black cable to the frame of the vehicle," it said. Well, that sounded easy enough… until I discovered that the cables attached to the battery pack were much too short to reach from the battery to the frame. I guess they were talking about cars – not RV's, so now what? I was completely stumped… and reluctant to experiment with something that could explode, like a battery.

I tried everything I could think of, like attaching it to the grill or to the brace that holds the batteries in place… but nothing worked so eventually I gave up and decided to walk to one of those emergency telephone boxes the State of California puts along the highway and ask for help. The phones ring directly through to the California Highway Patrol so maybe I could ask one of them where I should hook the negative cable. I told the woman who answered the phone what my problem was and she replied… with obvious irritation, "Sorry, lady, but the California Highway Patrol aren't mechanics."

"But I don't need a mechanic," I argued. "I just need to know if there's some other place I can hook the negative jumper cable so my battery doesn't explode," I pleaded with her. Unfortunately, my call for help fell on deaf ears, because she not-so-politely refused to offer any advice or even direct me to someone who could. Finally, in complete frustration, I had no choice but to walk back to the RV and turn to my Heavenly Father for help. "Please, Lord… This ignorant servant of yours is in trouble again. I hate to keep bothering you, but I really need your help."

The traffic was getting heavier by the minute as rush hour approached and the noise was so loud I could hardly hear myself think – and then I spotted a police car in one of the inside lanes. I frantically began waving my arms, hoping to get his attention, and just as he was about to pass me, he looked over and saw Lucky. I was amazed at how quickly he was able to cross four lanes of traffic, which he did... just in time to pull up in front of me.

I guess they must have a lot of trouble around here, because I was dumbfounded when he didn't get out of his vehicle... but instead used his loudspeaker to order me to "stay where I was and keep my hands where he could see them", as he slowly and warily approached, circling my RV and looking in the back window before asking me if I was alone.

I assured him that I was, at which point he finally relaxed and asked what my problem was. I must have sounded like an idiot... because when I told him about the battery cable he began to laugh. "Miss, all you've got to do is attach it to the negative pole on your battery. It just needs to be grounded."

I was stunned by the simplicity of the answer. "Well then, why didn't the instructions just say that?" I asked as he quickly hooked the black handled jumper cable to the negative post on my battery.

"I really couldn't tell you, ma'am. Maybe they just assume you already know. There, that should do it," he said. "Why don't you get in and give it a try. This is a dangerous place to park so you need to get moving right away."

Well, I guess the $100 I spent for the battery jumper was well worth it because the engine started right up. The kindly officer then removed the cables and handed me the power-pac through my passenger window. I waved a very grateful goodbye as the policeman forced the traffic to part and I carefully pulled out into the bumper-to-bumper rush hour mania. I have no doubt that I'd have **never** gotten into that steady stream of impatient drivers if it hadn't been for the kindly policeman... but with him standing there, everyone suddenly became courteous and patient as they made room for my entrance onto the busy freeway.

So how about that! I learned something new today, and now I know how to hook up my new battery booster. Those ridiculous instructions still irritated me though ...but there was no time for frustration, or even for reveling in my new-found knowledge because it took all my concentration just to drive in this madhouse they call a freeway in Los Angeles. I still had a long way to go before I could leave the LA traffic behind and I was looking forward to driving on the peaceful open road again.

The next few hours were no better, in fact it seemed to get worse; six lanes of bumper-to-bumper traffic - all going at *least* 75 miles an hour. How do they do that? Lucky won't even GO 75 miles an hour. And besides that, I've always believed in leaving enough room between me and the vehicle in front of me to stop in case of an emergency, which in a 27 foot RV is quite a bit farther than in a car. The problem was, every time I left even ONE car length open in front of me, someone pulled into it – again and again and again until it felt like I was going backwards. It was awful! People were honking and yelling at me. "Why is everyone in such a big hurry around here," I wondered?

And just to make matters worse, I couldn't drive in the far right hand lane; the one usually designated for slower or exiting drivers. The freeways are different down here and you never know when another freeway will split off two or more of the lanes… and sometimes it's the LEFT two lanes you need to be in. There was no way I could change lanes that quickly in Lucky, so I had no choice but to stay in the center and hope that I'd see the sign for Interstate 10 in time to be in the correct lane to make the exit. I was already exhausted from zero sleep last night, (and a vision that left me still weak and trembling), and my shoulders and neck were burning from the strain of hunching over the too-tightly gripped steering wheel (not to mention the labor of Rain-X'ing my windshield). Just when I was beginning to think I'd somehow missed my exit and was wondering what I should do, I saw the "Interstate 10" sign. I was so happy and so relieved… because I thought that meant I was almost out of this never-ending traffic jam, and I certainly didn't want to be stuck driving this nightmare of a freeway with a million headlights blinding me - and insane drivers pushing me to go faster and faster.

But no such luck… and after two **more** hours of mayhem on Interstate 10, I was really beginning to wonder if this nightmare would ever end - and then I saw it; a sign that said, "Truck stop, next exit."

Hip-hip-horray! I could get gas **and** park for the night. I'd never thought of a truck stop as an oasis in the desert before, but that's what it looked like to me right then as I drove up to the gas pumps and shut down my very over-heated engine. While the gas tank was filling, I asked the attendant where I could park for the night and he informed me that they had a gated yard where you had to pay $5.00 to sleep. No problem, I assured him. I'd be happy to pay $5.00 for a chance to close my eyes and relax, but I still couldn't believe it when my gas bill came to $150. Gas was $1.10 a gallon and I'd only driven 200 miles, so how could I have used that much gas? When I paid the attendant and expressed my dismay, he said "ma'am, you're bucking a 40 mile an hour headwind, so I'm not surprised."

Wouldn't you know it; at this rate, I'll be out of money again long before I make it to Sun City, Arizona… and I was hoping to have enough left over to buy a new battery and see what was wrong with my converter.

Oh well, right now, I had something much more immediate to worry about. I wasn't sure if it was that fact that I hadn't slept in 48 hours, or if it was because I was still weak from my vision last night, but I had a feeling that the horrible case of the flu my mother had nursed me through was about to grab me again. Even though I was completely recovered when I left her house, I was still weak, and if I had a relapse now - I'd be completely alone. Just thinking about how she took care of me made me miss her, so I put it out of my mind and concentrated on how wonderful it would be to get a full night's sleep - and pray that my Heavenly Father would heal me.

When I finished paying for the gasoline, and handed an extra $5.00 to the clerk so I could park in the "sleeping area", (surprise-surprise), he wouldn't accept it. Instead he said, "You probably need that money more than the truck stop does," as he smiled and handed me a ticket with instructions to put on my windshield. People are so nice!

But when I walked back to the pumps to start Lucky, looking so forward to laying down and resting my aching muscles, I discovered that my battery was dead AGAIN - and this time there wasn't enough power left in the "quick start" battery to get it started. I'd already used it once today, so

I guess that means I'll need to recharge it between every use. Oh well, at least I had the small cables my father made me, so I connected the interior battery to the start-up battery and thank goodness… it started! What a day! What a day! What a day! And now I need some sleep, which is where I am right now… tightly tucked between two big and very noisy semi-trucks (with their generators running) and hoping I won't be sick tomorrow.

I'm too weak to even think about eating, and I can't decide whether I'm too hot or too cold because it changes from moment to moment ,so maybe I'll just lie down, close my eyes and see if my head will quit pounding long enough to fall asleep. I'm sure everything will be fine, even if I do get sick again, but I'd better have a long talk with my Heavenly Father and ask Him to help me. Without Him, I can do nothing… but with Him, everything is possible!

December 14, 1998

"Happy days are here again!!!"

I had a wonderful night of much needed rest; both body and soul. The constant drone of diesel trucks and refrigeration units actually lulled me to sleep and before I knew it, the new day had dawned and it was time to get back on the road. I got up really early, hoping to beat the morning commuter traffic, but no such luck. Apparently, everyone else had the same idea - and I began to wonder if the traffic in Los Angeles **ever** dies down. Imagine what it would be like to live in a place where the open road was nothing but wishful thinking. I shuddered at the thought, and even though it was only 6:00 in the morning, I was dismayed to see that the highway was already bumper-to-bumper with cars and trucks and that the air smelled like gasoline and exhaust fumes.

But on a lighter note, guess what? I woke up completely well! I'm feeling fit as a fiddle; no fever, no headache, just one big lump in my throat when I think of how blessed I am. Traffic or no traffic, the Lord has given me another new day and I'm eager to see what it holds. In fact, I'm so filled with the Holy Spirit right now, I feel like my heart could burst with joy. Last night when I was afraid I was getting sick again, I prayed for the Lord to heal me… and He did! Thank you, Jesus!

I passed beautiful Palm Springs and then Indio before the traffic finally began to fade. But wouldn't you know it, another challenge took its place; more big mountains to climb. I've gotten pretty used to Lucky's temperature gauge riding in the red zone, but when you're in the middle of nowhere, (in the desert), with many long and empty miles between exits, and the hot sun beating directly down on you without so much as a single tree to offer respite from its glare… being stranded on the side of the road raises a whole new set of fears. Now my prayer was; "please Lord, just get me over one more hill."

Somehow I slowly (and miraculously) made my way to the top of what appeared to be an insurmountably long and steep incline, (passing numerous less fortunate trucks and RVs parked on the shoulder of the highway with steam spouting from their radiators), and I actually cheered out loud when I made it to the crest of what I was **sure** must be the summit. But then, just as I reached the top, where I'd hoped to see a nice easy downhill slope so I could coast and allow my engine to cool, there it was… stretched out in front of me as far as the eye could see; another even longer and steeper hill to climb.

"OK, Lord, just one more hill," I asked again and again, and again. "Surely *this* must be the last one." And that's how I spent the entire morning; praying and cheering and then seeing another, (usually greater) challenge lying directly in my path. "I guess it's like *life*," I thought to myself; "a constant succession of challenges, one after another, each one waiting to be conquered so another one can take its place."

Eventually the road leveled out and the mountains were behind me. It wasn't long after that when I saw a big green freeway sign that said "Blythe, California – next three exits." It was still pretty early in the day, but I was already so tired that all I could think of was how wonderful it would be to stop driving. I could empty my tanks, make something to eat, and since I'd be plugged into electricity, I could recharge my "battery pac", hook the battery charger to my start-up battery and even watch some television on my little TV. I'd have absolutely nothing to worry about, and after the last few days, to me… that sounded like Heaven. So when I saw the second little green sign that said "RV Park, next exit" the decision was made - and I cheerfully exited the freeway.

I continued following those little green "RV Park" signs all the way through Blythe and eventually found the Park they led me to, but for some reason… it just didn't feel right. Lucky's thermostat was in the "red" zone so I really needed to stop, but I couldn't. I found myself consumed by an overpowering urge to leave - rather than to park. Since I couldn't shake the feeling, I kept right on driving; in one side and out the other. I had no idea why I felt so driven to leave that particular RV Park, but the feeling was strong… and I've learned to listen when the Holy Spirit guides me. Lucky's engine was getting hotter by the minute as I drove slowly through the little one main street town of Blythe, so I knew that I didn't dare spend much time looking for another RV Park. Apparently, Lucky needed rest as badly as I did… and that's when I saw it; a sign that said "Blythe Mobile and RV Park".

I sighed with relief as I turned into the driveway… and although it didn't look much different then the first RV Park, this one *felt* different. I can't explain it - but instead of a sense of foreboding, I felt welcome, which is why that's where I'm parked right now; at my new "home for the night"; Blythe Mobile and RV Park. This is only my second night in an RV Park since I left Gold Beach in August, so even though I don't like wasting the money, I feel like I've earned it. I need time to reflect on that unbelievable vision and to prepare for my shows in Sun City. With the sun shinning and 75 degree weather in the middle of December, this looks like the perfect place in which to do it.

When I first entered Blythe Mobile and RV Park, I drove up and down each of the four rows, searching for just the right spot… and then I found it. There was a beautiful little baby palm tree, with branches hanging so low that they spread out over the cement pad - so if you didn't park just right, you couldn't open your door. I knew right then and there that this was MY SPOT, and now I even had my very own palm tree!

I can't believe how happy I am right now. It's as though the vision, as well as all the adversity I've been through, has given me a new appreciation for the simple things; things like that beautiful baby palm tree and how the breeze makes the branches rustle and wave at me… things like the fact that I have dinner in my cupboard and a soft couch to sit on. And I love my very first palm tree. They don't grow in Oregon, so it makes me feel like I'm vacationing in the tropics. It's so wonderful I think I'll take some pictures and capture the beauty of this special moment forever… on film.

After I fixed myself a meal (blessing after blessing), I used the knowledge I gained yesterday from the policeman about battery cables to hook up the battery charger and plugged in my battery pac to recharge so it'll be ready when I need it again. (Notice, I said "when", and not "if".) Then I called Elaine, the lady in Sun City, and told her that barring unforeseen circumstances, I should be arriving some time tomorrow afternoon and she really sounded excited. She's 86 years old and lives alone, so I'm sure she's looking forward to having company for Christmas, which is only 10 days away. Where does the time go?

And speaking of time - it's time to get some rest now so I'll be ready for whatever adventures come my way tomorrow. Elaine's directions to Sun City sounded a bit confusing and Phoenix is a pretty big city… so I think I'd better get an early start

What a wonderful day this has been!

chapter 26

December 15, 1998

LATE THE NEXT EVENING...

I had planned to leave for Phoenix (Sun City), early this morning, but surprise – surprise... I'm still at the RV Park in Blythe and so much has happened, I don't even know where to begin.

I got up early this morning, full of energy and eager to be on my way to Elaine's house in Sun City, but apparently, Lucky had other ideas. I left the battery charger hooked up overnight, so this morning when I turned the key - the engine started right up... and then promptly died. I started it a second time, and again it sputtered and died.

The owner of the RV Park drove by, and when he saw that I was having trouble, he offered to help. He was a tall, slim young man, (in his mid-thirties), which made me wonder how he had come to own a large trailer and RV park at such a young age in a small town like Blythe). He said that he wasn't very good with engines but that he had a friend who was... so he'd call him and see if he could come right over. He explained that his friend was an unemployed mechanic who had a family to support, so he really needed the money... which gave me high hopes that if he hurried right over, I'd still be able to make it to Sun City later today.

Within the hour, he arrived… but after two long hours of tinkering with everything he could think of, he still had absolutely no idea what the problem was, and gave up. Once again, Lucky just refused to move. I paid him for his time, even though Lucky still wasn't running, and I could see that he felt uncomfortable taking it from me. But the way I see it, he tried… and I'm sure he needed the money even more than I do.

By that time, (after so many attempted starts), both batteries were completely drained, so I resigned myself to spending another night here at the RV Park, (hooked up to electricity so I could recharge both batteries, as well as my "battery pac"), and then try to figure out why the engine kept starting and then promptly dying. Once that decision had been made, I walked to the payphone and called Elaine in Sun City to fill her in on my latest unforeseen delay, (and apologize), assuring her that I would keep her posted and that I still planned to get there before Christmas. She sounded so disappointed… and I hated to let her down, but there was nothing else I could do. So now what? Should I call a tow truck and have Lucky towed to an RV repair shop?

As I was hooking up the battery charger, a rather tall, robust and well-dressed middle-aged man walked up and introduced himself. "Hi there, young lady," he greeted me with a warm and almost familiar smile. "My name is John, and my wife Mary and I are parked in that coach right over there," he said as he pointed to a beautiful diesel bus converted into an RV no more than 50 feet away from where I was parked.

"Wow… now that's the way to travel," I replied, complimenting him on his coach. "My name is Abigayle, and it's nice to meet you," I said as I extended my hand for a hearty handshake. He took one look at my battery charger, shook his head and said, "I'll go get mine." Since he didn't pause long enough for me to either protest or ask why, (because the one my father gave me was working fine), I figured he must have a good reason; one which I discovered a few minutes later when he returned with his lovely wife Mary and a nice, new, and much bigger battery charger.

And then it began to rain... so with a sheet of plastic and careful place-ment of the charger, it didn't take long before it was all hooked up and doing its duty. That's when he turned to me and said, "Since it appears you're going to have to wait for this to charge, do you mind if Mary and I have a little chat with you?"

Of course I'm always happy to meet new people, in fact — I've never met a stranger, but there was something in his voice... a note of authority and purpose that I couldn't quite put my finger on. "Sure," I answered. "There's not a lot of room inside, but you're more than welcome. Please, come in and I'll make us some tea."

After I made the tea, we sat down to visit and I must admit, they seemed much more than normally curious about what I was doing on the road - and where I was going from here. That's why as we sat at my dining room table, I told them the entire story, from beginning to end. They listened with such intensity and asked me so many questions that I was beginning to wonder who they were - and why it felt like I was being interviewed.

But then they explained... and as John spoke, he held his wife's hand across the table and looked at her every few seconds, as if for confirma-tion, and she would smile and nod as he continued with his story.

"We didn't want to mention anything until we found out more about you, but when you pulled in yesterday - we were looking out our win-dow. As we watched you hooking up, a strong feeling came over both of us at the exact same time. Since this has never happened to us before, we talked about it for quite a while, and then we prayed about it last night and again this morning... and in the end, we both agreed. We feel very strongly that the Lord has put it on our hearts to watch over you. We're not sure why — or for how long - and we certainly can't explain it... but we have no doubt that God is working through us to protect and prepare you for something," he said as he put his arm around Mary and squeezed, and she once again nodded her sweet, loving face in agreement."

Needless to say, I was stunned. So far, I thought I'd been doing pretty well... at least I haven't felt like I was in danger, (other than engine problems), but this was so strange and so unexpected that I didn't know what to think. But then I remembered how uncomfortable I felt when I drove through that first RV Park... and how I drove up and down every street in this one before I felt drawn to this particular spot. Could it be merely coincidence that the site I selected was so close to John and Mary? And how about the fact that I got up before they did this morning, so if Lucky hadn't refused to run, I'd have been gone long before we got a chance to meet. Could that ALSO have been a coincidence? I didn't think so... especially since the mechanic couldn't find anything wrong with Lucky.

I don't understand what's happening any more than they do, but something is telling me to pay attention... so I've decided to accept it without question. They're such a warm and loving couple; devout Christians who are obviously blessed both spiritually and financially, and so far, my Father in Heaven has led me and watched over me every step of the way... so there was no way I could question the strange and unexplainable events that led to our meeting.

And another thing; since Blythe is only two hours away from Phoenix (maybe 3 hours from Sun City), even the fact that I felt driven to stop for the night here in Blythe, rather than continuing on to Elaine's house yesterday, now seems to have all been part of the plan; the plan for me to meet John and Mary. Yes, my Lord, you truly are the pilot... and I am merely the co-pilot, and I trust you completely. So it appears that now I have two new friends, (as well as guardians), and I haven't the slightest idea why.

Even though none of us needed any more convincing, as we sat there at my little dining room table, the presence of the Holy Spirit was so strong that we felt bathed in the glow of His presence. It was so powerful that we didn't even try to put it into words or discuss it. We just looked in each other's eyes and smiled... knowing that it was obvious to all three of us that something very special was happening; something ordained by

God. It was one of those moments I will never forget… and all I could say was "Thank you," and "What do you say we join hands in prayer?"

So there we were; three people who didn't even know each other yesterday – and yet today… we were family. I was suddenly reminded of that "single golden thread that bound us all to God" in my vision… because I was experiencing that same deep feeling of love, (and respect), for John and Mary as we held hands and prayed. All three of us thanked the Lord for bringing us together – and asked him to guide and bless us, as we carried out His will, whatever that might be.

I explained to John and Mary that I was on my way to Sun City and that someone was waiting for me to put on some shows there - and they suggested that I stay here in Blythe for just a few more days so we could get better acquainted while John tried to figure out what was wrong with Lucky's engine. Since I wasn't on a tight schedule, (still 6 days before Christmas), (and they insisted on paying my space rent), I finally agreed.

I had used some of the money my mother gave me to buy business cards, the tape recorder and the "battery 'pac" before I even left Sacramento… and then I spent even more for engine repairs at the bottom of the 'grapevine'. And the fact that I'm only getting 5 miles to the gallon, means that I can't count the number of times I've had to fill my tanks between Sacramento and Blythe, (on the Arizona border)… so already the money is nearly gone- and I still have to drive to Phoenix, as well as eat and buy propane while I'm there. According to John, the steep hills I've already climbed are **nothing** compared to those that lie between here and Phoenix, so I don't dare leave Blythe without figuring out what's wrong with Lucky. I'm still planning to make it to Sun City in time to spend Christmas with Elaine, so I happily agreed - but insisted, (to no avail), that I pay for the RV space.

So the decision was made, and we all hugged and chattered on… acting more like old friends enjoying a reunion than people who had never met before. Mary suggested that the three of us go out for a nice steak dinner (their treat, of course), so I had my first meal in a restaurant since I left Gold Beach in August. During our delicious dinner, I discovered that John is a retired police Sergeant and that he and Mary own a small ranch in Northern California, but spend every winter traveling in their coach. I guess they're the exact opposite of a "green pea" (like me) so I'm sure they have a lot to teach me. I know this is silly, but I can't help but laugh and wonder if my guardian angel got tired of having to constantly pull me out of the fire... and opted for some reinforcements! (Just kidding...)

After dinner, I went to the RV Park office to speak to the owner about staying a few more days and he said that since I'd already paid him for one night, he'd let me stay the rest of the week for $50.00. I couldn't believe it. What a deal! I wonder if he, too, is a part of the plan to keep me here in Blythe. It sure looks like this is where the Lord wants me right now... so I gratefully accepted his offer, gave him a big "thank you" hug and then returned the rest of the money John and Mary had given me, (expecting the cost to be more than $50.00), and even John was shocked at the price. I know Elaine will be disappointed by my further delay... and that makes me sad, but it will be so wonderful NOT have to think about driving anywhere for five whole days - and I DO need to know what's going on with Lucky. And besides, I can still make it to Sun City before Christmas Eve, so once again, *"everything will be fine."*

And that explains why I'm still in here in Blythe, almost out of money, and with Lucky broken down AGAIN! At dinner tonight, I discovered that John's scheduled for surgery on his shoulder next week and since the doctors have already tried everything they can think of short of surgery, he's pretty discouraged about it. Maybe this is **my** opportunity to do something for him, rather than the other way around.

We spent the rest of the evening at John and Mary's coach and boy-oh-boy was it ever nice. They have solar panels on the roof for power and an interior that looks like a high-end apartment. I guess John bought a big diesel bus and did the entire conversion by himself - so he must be pretty handy. This time we sat at THEIR table and this time I shared some of my poetry with them. By the time we finished our two hour "chat", John said he was feeling much better about his surgery; in fact almost eager to see what the doctors could do for him, and no longer worried about what would happen if they weren't successful. I don't know what I said or did to make a difference - but he thanked me several times and said, "Obviously the Lord knew what he was doing when he called you as an *encourager*."

Before I went back to Lucky, the three of us prayed for his healing... and I feel very strongly that the Lord will reward his faith, generosity and obedience. If the doctors are unable to help him - well, perhaps there's something the Lord wants him to learn that he can only learn through suffering. Or perhaps there is another reason... one he can't (and doesn't need to) understand. But what he *can* do is accept whatever lies ahead with grace and courage and look at it as another wonderful opportunity to show his Lord and Master that he's not a "good-time Charlie".

John agreed wholeheartedly... and is now looking at his upcoming surgery in a new and more positive light - while I, on the other hand, feel blessed to have been given the chance to do something for my new friends... even if it was just a little bit of encouragement.

It's been a long but lovely day... and I'm looking forward to sleeping again to the sound of the palm branches brushing against my roof.

Good night!

chapter 27

December 16, 1998

Yesterday morning, while the unsuccessful mechanic worked on Lucky, a neighbor who lived in one of the permanent trailers in the park stopped by to see what was going on. His name was Jim, and as we talked I told him that I wrote poetry and songs and he told me that he played in a band and loved music. He was a young man, maybe 35 years old... who was not only nice looking but seemed full of energy and enthusiasm. After a little while, he said goodbye and added, "Maybe I'll see you again sometime."

And even though I replied, "Sure, I'd like that," I was caught completely by surprise when he knocked on my door a little after midnight last night... and even though it was late and I was ready to call it a day, I'm actually glad that he did. Obviously, he needed something... and I would never turn anyone away whom I could possibly help.

The sad part was that it didn't take more than a few minutes before I realized that he was using drugs; specifically "crank", otherwise known as methamphetamine, (and the one that had possessed the soul of Jon in Gold Beach). As we talked, he fidgeted and ground his jaw relentlessly, babbling on about nothing and losing his train of thought - often mid-sentence. It made my heart ache for him, because here was a really nice, polite young man with great potential, who was obviously under the spell of that horrid and soul-stealing drug.

And it's effects on his reasoning were obvious, because there it was, after midnight, and he saw nothing at all wrong with dropping in on a complete stranger, and a woman at that… and believe me, if I'd have allowed it, he would have talked non-stop until the morning light. Unfortunately, I've seen first-hand what meth can do to otherwise good and productive people, and now I knew why the Lord had brought him to my door.

And yes… I called him on the fact that I could tell he was obviously "wired". He seemed surprised that I knew, and he even defended himself by saying that the drug helped him play his music. I wanted so much to say or do something that would make a difference, but I'm afraid there's not much you can do in a single two hour discussion, especially when the person you're trying to convince is "high". That's why I told him he was welcome to drop by again tomorrow evening, (but earlier this time, and NOT high on drugs) and we'd play some music together and continue with our conversation. He seemed to be listening to what I had to say… but it's hard to tell when their under the influence, so **if** he comes back, I'll know I didn't push him too hard and that he truly is crying out for help.

Satan has found the perfect tool of corruption in meth. At least cocaine was expensive and usually drove people to bankruptcy before it killed them, but methamphetamine is cheap and easy to make so there's no need to import it. In fact, it's being cooked in every single city in the America, and unlike alcohol), which you can smell on someone's breath), meth is odorless and all too often undetectable. You'd be shocked at how many people from ALL walks of life are being driven into the pits of despair by this evil drug, and besides prayer… I'm not sure that I have any power over it. But at least I can try!

When I was young, there was a short period of my life in the early 1970's when I experimented with drugs, but fortunately I was blessed with a non-addictive personality so I never become dependant upon them. But at the same time, I saw what it did to some of my friends who weren't so fortunate. During those years, I lost several people who I loved and respected, but there was nothing I could do but watch helplessly as drugs completely destroyed their lives.

And now, when I look back on those years, I'm actually glad that I had those experiences... because if I hadn't, how would I be able to counsel and help those who are caught in its evil grasp now? Because I have firsthand experience, I understand what it is that attracts people to it, and "users" seem to feel more comfortable talking with someone who has actually walked in their shoes. "Crank" (or "meth") is definitely the Devil's tool, the worst drug yet... and HE, (Satan), doesn't play fair. He finds a weak spot and then pounces on it, without pity or conscience.

During my vision of the "other side"... when I found myself at "home" and was so happy that I didn't want to leave, I felt different than I do here on Earth. There was no such thing as being tired or depressed and I felt strong and capable of absolutely anything. Our weak earthly bodies aren't wired for the power and intensity that filled my soul when I was on the *other side* of the veil, and there's nothing on Earth that can compare to those feelings. But "Crank" is the one drug whose effects are the closest to duplicating it. The users get a feeling of complete and limitless euphoria. When people are under its effects, they feel invincible. Those who are tired - feel strong, and those who are sad - feel happy. Those who are ill... no longer have pain - and those who are shy, suddenly feel aggressive and powerful. It's not even CLOSE to the way we'll feel when we're at "home" with our Lord again, but it's just a tiny, tiny taste... just enough to reach some hidden corner of our subconscious mind that *almost* remembers – and craves to feel like that again.

And **Shame on Satan** for preying on peoples' confusion and pain; shame on him for exploiting the loneliness and depression, pain and loss that so many people here on Earth are experiencing. I don't know whether there's anything I can do to help Jim, but I'm sure going to give it my best. I just wish I had more time.

Well, that's enough for today. John and Mary are taking me on a tour of the area in a little while, and I'm looking forward to seeing a lot more of this breathtakingly beautiful desert scenery and enjoying the company of my new-found friends.

chapter 28

December 21, 1998

8:00 P.M.

This has been just one more day, (one last day), in a string of wonderful days spent writing, studying my bible, talking with Jim, (not sure if it's helping), and delving deeply into spiritual matters with John and Mary.

John checked and rechecked Lucky, and he couldn't find anything wrong with the motor. Except for that first morning, every time the batteries are charged, the engine starts right up and keeps on running. Of course, that's when it's sitting and idling... so who knows what will happen when I'm climbing the steep mountains between here and Phoenix, but I'm not worried. How could I be - when the Lord has been taking such good care me?

I've also done more than my share of walking, because with Lucky parked, it's my only means of getting to the grocery store or anywhere else I need to go, without asking John and Mary for a ride. Of course, the exception to that rule was when I asked them to help me refill my two 5 gallon propane cans, but that's only because I learned my lesson well in Gold Beach and I'll never try to carry them by myself again.

It's not that I don't enjoy all the walking, even when I'm carrying groceries and gallons of drinking water, but when I begin putting on shows again, it will be tough to get to all the places I need to go, especially carrying my guitar and hundreds of copies of poems. I'm hoping that as soon as I have some extra money, I'll be able to buy a bicycle; maybe even an old-fashioned one with a basket. Wouldn't that be great?

So… early tomorrow morning, I leave for Elaine's house in Sun City, Arizona, which is why I hooked up the battery charger tonight - hoping that Lucky will start in the morning.

John and Mary asked me to return to Blythe as soon as I'm finished in Sun City so they can tag along with me for awhile. Where we're going, I'm not sure… but they said they have some parking places in the desert they want to show me… and I'm game for anything!

Sounds like a plan…

chapter 29

December 22, 1999

10:00 A.M.

I thought it would be fun to give you a "direct quote" from the tape I'm making for my mother. I plan to mail it when I get to Sun City, so unfortunately it will be a little late for Christmas, but this is the last entry, and it shows how I'm talking directly to her — just as if she was traveling with me.

"Hi mom. It's just me… your wandering daughter, driving across the Arizona desert on Interstate 10 in this noisy RV, (as you can hear), heading for Phoenix and talking into the tape recorder and wishing you were sitting here in the passenger seat next to me."

"And what a morning this has been! I was planning on leaving for Sun City by 7:30 A.M., (while it was still cool outside), but after I was all packed up, unhooked and ready to go, (on schedule I might add), I had to go searching for the man who owns the RV Park so I could let him know I was leaving, thank him for his generosity and tell him that I was coming back as soon as I finish my trip to Sun City. But wouldn't you know it; he was nowhere to be found."

"After walking up and down row and row of trailers, I finally found him at one of the older and more beat-up permanent mobile homes in the park, where he was doing some remodeling. He said that he was sorry to see me leave, but would look forward to my return and offered to make me the same deal; $50 a week for as *long as I'd like to stay — which will depend upon John and Mary, my new friends I told you about. By then, it was almost 8:30 and I was anxious to get started so I hurried back to Lucky and tried to start the engine. But lo and behold… nothing happened. I even tried my trusty battery pac and still nothing happened."*

"But like always, my guardian angel must have been watching out for me because John and Mary looked out their window and saw my predicament, so John came over and gave me a jump-start with his Mercedes."

"And it worked; Lucky started right up. But before I drove away, John warned me not to shut down the engine again until I'm safely parked in Sun City, because there's a good chance that it won't start. That would be fine with me… except for one thing; I'm almost out of gas so I have no choice but to leave the engine running at the gas station while I fill up. Oh well…I'll just ignore that big sign that says 'turn off engine before filling', and hope for the best."

"So at last, I was on the road again …first stop; the gas station / mini market just a few miles east of Blythe, where I pulled up next to the pumps, left Lucky's already overheated engine running, and ran inside to ask the lady clerk to turn on the pump. The place was packed with customers so I had to stand in line for what seemed like forever, but eventually she turned the pump on and I hurried back outside to a now even MORE overheated Lucky".

"And wouldn't you know it… nothing ever seems to be simple. When I tried to pump the gas into the tank, the nozzle shut right off. I pressed the handle again and "click"… it shut off again. I was beginning to wonder if I had the right tank, because during my week at the RV Park in Blythe, it was the general consensus of all the kind people who tried to help me figure out why Lucky wouldn't run, that I either had water or bad gas in one of my two tanks. John finally switched over to the tank that was empty and then brought me 5 gallons of gas in a can, and wouldn't you know it… the engine ran perfectly. That's why I've decided to use only the one tank and forget about the other one until I get it checked out, (although it's a real shame because it's holding 30 gallons of valuable gasoline that it sure would be nice to have)."

But now that the tank I thought was empty was refusing to take any gas, I began to wonder… "Uh-oh…do I have the wrong tank? I decided to find out for *sure and switched over to the other tank - but the same thing happened; it kept shutting off. I was so darn frustrated... all I could do was run back inside and ask if someone could help me. Apparently, the lady clerk was the only person on duty at the time... and she said she'd get to me as soon as she could - but with so many people waiting in line, it seemed like an eternity..., especially with Lucky still idling and getting hotter and hotter by the minute."*

"Eventually she came outside to see what the problem was, but by then Lucky's engine was so hot there was a flood on the pavement underneath my radiator, hopefully from the emergency overflow, and nothing worse. I hated to hurry her, since she was being nice enough to help me in the first place, but I definitely needed to get moving again as quickly as possible so the engine could cool down."

"Just as I expected, she had the same problem I did, so she explained that the gas pumps are pressure sensitive, which is why you can't leave the engine running while you fill the tank. Great! So now what could I do"?

*"When I explained that I **couldn't** shut the engine off because it wouldn't start up again, I don't think she was too happy about the prospect of me blocking the busy gas pumps so she tried to force some gas into the tank. But every time she'd get about a gallon in, the tank "burped" and the gasoline shot back out of the tank and all over both her and the ground. Then she'd take the nozzle out for just a moment or two... and then put it back in and pump another gallon... until it burped again.*

"She had so many customers impatiently waiting that she handed me the gas hose and told me to continuing doing what she did, over and over...until I got 20 gallons of gas, but Lucky was so darn hot by then that even though I needed more gas than that to get me the 187 miles to Phoenix, I decided that stopping a couple more times, (and getting a only a few gallons each time), would be better than burning the engine up right there at the service station."

"When I went inside to pay, I thanked her for her kindness and then raced outside to get Lucky back on the road, and hopefully cooling down. Usually the engine cools down when I drive fast, (unless it's uphill), so I was looking forward to a few miles of flat open freeway; hoping that Lucky would cool down before any real damage was done. But that didn't happen because there was another problem;

the wind here is unbelievable! It's coming at me head on - so it's like I'm driving uphill even when I'm not... and I'm having a heck of a time keeping Lucky in one lane - let alone going fast enough to cool the engine down. Now you can see why I said this has been a **crazy morning**!"

"And even now, as I'm sitting here driving and talking to you, the temperature gauge is at the very top of the red zone and my biggest challenge yet is about to begin. For as far as I can see ahead of me, there's a really big mountain to climb. Who knew there were mountains between California and Phoenix? Oh boy... I'm sitting here watching this long steep incline ahead of me, doing 40 miles an hour, (which is as fast as I can go with the wind blowing directly at me and the accelerator all the way to the floor), and knowing that if I stop to let it cool down, it won't start again and I'll be stuck."

"So golly-gee-will'ickers, mom, it looks like I'm in a bit of a pickle! Maybe it's a good thing you couldn't travel with me because I'm not sure your blood pressure could take all this excitement. Well... there's only one thing left to do and that's send up a prayer for help to my Father in Heaven. Only HE can get me through this day!"

"I think I can, I think I can, I think I can..." Now I'm doing 20 miles an hour in second gear... but I can see the summit coming and I'm almost there! I hope my voice doesn't sound too panicked, mom, because I'm really not. After all, no matter where Lucky stops, I've still got a roof over my head... but it sure would be nice if it wasn't on a mountain in the middle of nowhere in this desert heat and wind. Come on Lucky, you can do it! You can do it! Please Lord, just get me up this hill."

"We did it! We did it, mom! We're at the top and there's a long down hill stretch ahead. Hip-hip-horray! The engine's already getting cooler. Thank you, Jesus... Thank you! See mom, I didn't have anything to worry about after all.

"Uh-oh... I just went around a corner and you won't believe what I'm looking at; it's **another** mountain — and this one's even taller than the last one. Oh my gosh! I guess we're not out of the woods yet, mom. I'm so nervous right now I'm probably babbling... which is exactly what I'd be doing if you were sitting here in the passenger seat. The people passing me, (of which there are man,y since I'm on the shoulder doing 15 miles an hour in first gear now) must think I'm nuts with this tape recorder held up to my mouth... just chatting away."

"Oh gosh… we've almost made it… just a few more yards and I'll have survived another huge hill. How many more can there possibly be? And could this wind get any stronger?"

*"Oh no… I've been so focused on the wind and my overheated engine that I forgot all about needing gas. As ;you already know, from when I was at your house in Sacramento, my gas gauge isn't working, so I set my trip-meter and figure out how much gas I've used according to the mileage I should be getting. But in this wind, I'll be lucky to get 4 miles a gallon, so it's already way **past** time to get gas. Drat… and once again, I'll have to keep this overheated engine running while I force in as many gallons as possible, one at a time. Will this morning never end?"*

"I'll talk to you later, mom but right now it's time to focus on finding an exit that says "fuel". Wish me luck – and I love you!"

When I thank my dear Lord for my blessings,
the list is so long… I'm in awe.
But you, my dear mom - are the TOP of my list…
right after my Savior and God.

So no matter what trials life brings us,
our LOVE is a gift without end;
Because YOU are much more than my mother….
You're also my VERY BEST FRIEND!!

— Poem by Abigayle

chapter 30

December 23, 1998

I did it! I actually did it! I made it to Elaine's house in Sun City… and believe me - it wasn't easy!

Yesterday, driving from Blythe to Sun City, I was a nervous wreck. I've never left the motor running while I got gas before, and it really worried me because all the signs say "turn off engine before filling"… but I didn't have a choice. And unfortunately, even that didn't work very well because I couldn't get more than a few gallons at a time, which meant several stops for gas, and an engine that was practically glowing red by the time I got here. Luckily, (no pun intended), I had a bottle of water with me and I poured it on my right leg, (the one next to the "dog house") because so much heat was radiating through the carpeted covering that my leg was turning red and hurting like crazy.

And talk about big, long stretches of mountains to climb. I spent the entire time praying for God to help me make it up the next hill and I didn't dare pull over to cool the engine down because I knew it wouldn't start again. All I could do was pray and hope for the best.

But eventually I made it; after three gas stops… and four more stops to ask directions between Phoenix and Elaine's house in Sun City. Lucky's engine was HOT, HOT, HOT and so was I, but since I got an early start this morning, I made it to Sun City at about 2:30 this afternoon. Whew! What a relief it was to pull up in front of Elaine's house and turn off the engine. It was beginning to smell like burning rubber inside so I can't tell you how wonderful it felt to not have to worry about it anymore; at least for a little while.

Elaine was so happy to see me that she ran outside and greeted me with a big hug... chattering on and on about all the places she wanted to take me. It seemed to mean so much to her, that I tried not to let her know how tired I was as I joined in the "plan-making" with what I hope sounded like real enthusiasm.

It took three extension cords to reach her house from where I was parked on the street (because her driveway was too small), but eventually the mission was accomplished and we sat down for a nice visit. That's when she told me that I would have to move Lucky every other day because the zoning laws in Sun City don't allow RVs to park on the street for more than 24 hours at a time. Great, I thought. I sure hope Lucky starts... and that I can find somewhere else to park. I sure wish I had the money for two new batteries, but I don't. But then, as my step-mother Roma always used to say, "If wishes were fishes – we'd have some to fry."

Oh well, never a dull moment... and before I even had time to catch my breath, Elaine wanted to take me out to dinner. Apparently, she has a "2 for 1" coupon for the "early-bird special" at a local restaurant... so off we went. I wasn't even slightly hungry, but she was so excited by my arrival, I couldn't possibly disappoint her.

When we got home, I agreed to play cards for awhile... before I could politely make my excuses and head out to the RV for a much needed night of sleep.

Tomorrow, we're going to the Senior Center for lunch, where Elaine has arranged for me to put on a little show while they eat. I'm really looking forward to that, but not as much as I'm looking forward to a good nights sleep tonight.

Yes, I'm dog tired… but never too tired to be profoundly grateful that my Heavenly Father saw fit to bring me here safely. And in three more days, it's Christmas; the day we have chosen to celebrate the birth of our Savior. So thank you Jesus; for without you… none of us would have had a chance of making it home again!

10 MINUTES LATER

Unbelievable! Amazing! I'm stunned… and so grateful that I can't stop the tears of joy from falling. Guess what happened? Oh never mind… because you'd never guess.

For some reason, and I don't know why, when I finished writing tonight's entry in my journal, I looked at the oven door and felt the sudden urge to open it. I've never once used that oven, (or even opened it), mostly because I was saving what little propane I can carry for the refrigerator, but also because I've never used a gas oven in my life - and the thought of lighting the pilot light, (when I don't even know where it is or how to light it), gives me the willies', so I can't imagine what possessed me to open it right then… but I did; and you won't **believe** what I found inside; $140 in crisp twenty dollar bills!

Do you believe it? It's enough for a new heavy duty battery, (maybe even two) AND a night at an RV park next week so I can empty my tanks. How could I possibly be more blessed? And I have a feeling I know where the money came from. Not that it would be more than a small miracle for the Lord to have put it there, but I think it's more likely that John and Mary, who came over to visit last night, stuck it in there when I went to the bathroom. Hmmm. The Lord certainly does use people to carry out His wishes… and Jon and Mary knew that I wouldn't accept the cash from them; not after they'd already done so much for me.

Well, I'll certainly sleep better tonight! As soon as I have time, I'll buy a battery (or two) for Lucky and have it (or them) installed. Wow! Will wonders never cease! Merry Christmas to me - and thank you, Jesus!

chapter 31

December 24, 1998

CHRISTMAS EVE!!!

I just got home from my Christmas Eve poetry reading at another Senior Center luncheon, and it was absolutely wonderful. So many of the people in the audience were physically handicapped, (some in wheelchairs and others struggling just to walk), that it filled my heart with joy to put smiles on their faces.

Because I was merely the *meal-time entertainment*, I didn't put a table behind me with copies of my poems, nor did I set out my contribution basket. These were low income seniors, so I took special care not to do anything that might make them feel obligated to donate money - because the fact is; most of them need it far more than I do.

After an hour of sharing my poetry and telling stories from the road, (at extremely high volume because there were so many "hard of hearing" people in the audience, I was immediately inundated by enthusiastic seniors; some asking for copies of poems -while others just wanted to tell me their own poems and stories. I spent two hours listening, loving and encouraging… and I can't tell you what an honor it was! If I was able to bring even a small amount of joy to my elderly brothers and sisters, it was the **perfect** way to spend my Christmas Eve.

I don't know why, but for some reason I'm still exhausted. There wasn't much physical effort involved today, so I don't understand why, but I suppose it could be that my long and stressful drive to Sun City is finally catching up with me. That's why when we got home a few minutes ago, I begged off another game of cards with Elaine, complimenting her on her seemingly boundless energy and telling her that I need to walk back to my motor home and take a much needed nap.

So that's what I'd better do now... if I want to keep up with 86 year old Elaine anyway. I had to move Lucky this morning (the 24 hour RV parking rule), so I drove a few blocks to a 24-hour grocery store parking lot, where I spent the night. She's scheduled an appearance for me at the Arizona Council of the Arts meeting next week as well as a couple of the local nursing homes and assisted care living facilities. I'm eager – but tired... and since I barely got Lucky started this morning, even after being plugged into electricity all night, I don't expect the engine to start when I try to leave the store parking lot and return to Elaine's house tomorrow morning, Christmas Day. But no matter what it takes, somehow everything will be fine and Ill get back to Elaine's house where together we will celebrate Christmas Day. After we attend her church service, we'll spend the rest of the time just resting, talking and, (because she loves it so much), probably playing more gin rummy.

I can't wait to use the money I found in the oven to get a new battery (maybe even two?), because constantly worrying about whether Lucky will start or not is getting old... fast! Oh well, at least it should be easy to find some kind person to give me a jump-start on Christmas morning, and next time I have to move, I'll drive directly to a battery store. Hip-Hip-Hooray!

Happy Birthday, Jesus

I stand in awe that the "King of all Kings", our Lord and Savior Jesus Christ,

loves us so much that he suffered and died that we might be saved.

Surely, there is no greater love!

I stand amazed that all we have to do is admit our sins

and ask our Father in Heaven in humble sincerity to forgive us - and all shall be forgiven.

Surely, there is no greater gift!

I stand in wonder at his Promise that if we love Him and obey His commandments,

we shall be blessed with eternal life - and joy beyond our comprehension.

Surely, there is no greater miracle!

— Poem by Abigayle

chapter 32

December 25, 1998

Happy Birthday, Jesus

Dear Father in Heaven,

What a glorious Christmas day you have blessed me with! Thank you for every breath I take and every sight I see. Thank you for food, shelter and clothing. Thank you for my health - and for my family who loves me. And thank you for the love I feel for ALL my brothers-and-sisters in Christ! But most of all, thank you for sending us your SON; our Savior Jesus Christ. He walked among us, and then suffered and bore our sins on His back. He showed us the path to righteousness and the way to everlasting life with You.

Father, you are taking such good care of me, that I want for absolutely nothing … except to help others find the same peace and contentment my faith and trust in YOU has given me. But I need thy guidance… as I struggle to use my gift of words to uplift and encourage others during these times of confusion and sorrow. I'm no one special, my Father, so it is only through You… as **your** love shines through me - that I am able to be of some small service and glorify your name to all I meet.

But I need you to lead me, Father… and chastise me when I am wrong - so that I might learn how to be more righteous and more pleasing unto thee.

And I thank you, my most wondrous Father in Heaven, on this beautiful Christmas Day, for taking care of my family in Oregon as I sojourn among my brothers and sisters. I also ask thee for wisdom and understanding, that I might use it to spread both thy glory and thy Word to all who will listen.

I love thee so much… and I honor thee with all my heart and soul… and in the name of thy most beloved son, Jesus Christ, who I can never **possibly** thank enough for what He has done for us, I kneel humbly before thee… in unceasing gratitude and unbridled joy!

Amen

chapter 33

December 26, 1998

9:00 A.M.

W hy do I even bother to worry? Perhaps I shall learn that lesson some-day... because once again, my Lord has come through and removed two more burdens from my back.

Yesterday, Elaine gave me $300 for Christmas. When I objected, knowing that she lives on a fixed income, she insisted that because I refused to take any money at any of the shows she scheduled for me, she wanted to help; to thank me for coming to her neighborhood and spreading the message of joy and the peace. Isn't that wonderful?

Yes, I was hoping to have enough money to buy two batteries, (and now I do), but I hadn't considered the money I'll need to get back to Blythe and pay for the RV spot while I sojourn with John and Mary. As much as I appreciate the unexpected $300 Christmas gift, (especially when all I gave Elaine was a poem I wrote especially for her), I've discovered that money doesn't last long when you're on the road getting 5 miles to the gallon; even when all you buy are the absolute necessities. That's why I've decided to use my own physical labor to "earn" some more money before I leave Sun City and return to Blythe. Elaine told me about a local newspaper that comes out once a week where I could place an ad offering my labors, and then use her telephone number to answer the calls I hope it will bring. That's a great idea and I'm already planning how to word it.

I haven't spoken to my sons, (or any other relatives), since I left Portland in August, (except for the tape to my mother), so I wrote each of my boys, (even at age 25 and 27, I still think of them as my "boys"… and probably always will), a very personal and heartfelt Christmas letter; one I hope they will cherish forever. It doesn't seem like much of a Christmas present, but I'm hoping they will value my love for them more than anything I could buy at the store. So, Christmas was wonderful… and I am truly blessed.

But right now, it's time to move Lucky before Elaine gets a ticket… and I know exactly where I'm going. Just three blocks from her house, there's a shopping mall with an auto repair shop. I'll drive Lucky there, get two new batteries installed and then ask them if I could use a far corner of their parking lot in which to park every other night while I'm here. It's so nice to have a plan!

So, off I go… wish me luck.

NOON:

Talk about prayers being answered! The blessings just keep on raining down…

Right now I'm at United Car Care, the auto shop I mentioned this morning, where they will install my new batteries as soon as they have time. When I first got here, the lady at the counter, (the wife of the owner), asked me what brought me all the way from Oregon, (since Lucky has Oregon license plates), so I told her a VERY abbreviated story; explaining that I'm an inspirational poet and that I travel the country looking for people with whom to share my art and bear my testimony. She asked for a sample, so right here, in the auto shop's cramped little office, I recited a couple of poems and she was so enthused that she immediately got on the phone and called her husband and a friend, insisting that they hurry right down to the shop and meet me.

While I waited for them, (and for Lucky to be fitted into the shop's already busy schedule), I asked her about parking on their property and she said not only can I park in their lot, but to forget about the "far corner" because they'll be closed from tomorrow until January 2nd so I can park in the shade of their carport-type structure right next to the building - and even plug into their electricity. Right now she's writing me a "letter of permission" in case the local police come by and wonder what I'm doing here.

Wow! See what I mean about blessings? And I've got two more things to tell you. The service man just came to talk to me and it turns out that I don't **need** two new batteries. When they tested the interior battery, it checked out just fine. That means I can afford to buy the heaviest duty start-up battery they have… and it's being installed right now. Do you believe it? Now I'll have enough money left over for a night at an RV Park, (if I can find one), more propane and even some groceries.

Opps – looks like they're finished with Lucky.

LATER THAT NIGHT…

The owner and a friend arrived so I recited a couple of my poems for them and now they've asked me if I would attend a dinner at their house day after tomorrow and put on a poetry reading for their dinner guests. They're devout Christians… and they feel sure that it was the Lord who led me to their shop.

Can there be any doubt?

Just think; I won't have to move every other day, (at least for the next week), and I can easily walk the three blocks back and forth to Elaine's house. What a relief that is! Plus I've got the wording for my ad in the local newspaper:

"Have energy – will work! No job too small or too dirty - for $8.00 an hour. Please call XXX." (which is where I'll put Elaine's telephone number.)

Who knows – with the Lord's help and some hard work, I might even make enough money to buy a second-hand bicycle! That would be so wonderful, and…once again

I am so blessed!!!

chapter 34

December 31, 1998

It's New Years Eve already... where does the time go? Elaine found quite a few places for me to share my poetry this past week and we spent the rest of the time playing cards and playing tourist. It's been wonderful and I especially enjoyed feeding two loaves of bread to the ducks at a local pond, which brought back memories of my life in Gold Beach often referred to as the "duck lady".

I also did the reading at the owner of the auto shop's house for about a dozen of their friends. One of them was a minister who has a Christian radio show on one of the local radio stations. He asked me to read a poem or two and tell my story on his radio program, so of course, I happily agreed. So far - so good, and I couldn't be more amazed as the Lord continues to lead me from one opportunity to another.

And now here it is - New Year's Eve already. This particular holiday has always been a special time of reflection for me, looking both forward and backward, and taking stock of the events that brought me to where I am on that day... and this year is no different.

It's funny, but even though I love my family with all my heart, I haven't spent a single minute in sadness over leaving them. The Lord filled that void in my heart, and I have left them in His loving and capable hands. Actually,

I don't DARE to think of them, or I'd be sad… and that would accomplish nothing. No amount of time or distance can ever take away the love we have for each other, so I've put all those thoughts in the far corner of my mind and am concentrating on the present (and the future) instead.

But one thing I do really miss, (and was reminded of when we fed the ducks yesterday), was my animals! I've raised Siamese Cats, (selling purebred kittens), and Labrador Retrievers, (selling both black and yellow puppies), for at least 20 years… and I really miss them. I've had every pet imaginable, from giant parrots to fish, from monkeys to ducks and geese… but most of all - I miss my horses.

After the flood, as my family did everything we could to avoid corporate bankruptcy, I had to sell my horses, crying like a baby as I said goodbye… and not daring to think of them again, knowing that I'd start crying; which once again would do nothing - but leave me with red, swollen eyes.

But in the interest of celebrating the coming of a new year, I'm going to allow my mind to look back - and thank God for the wonderful memories that will always be a part of me, as well as a myriad of stories to tell. In fact, I think I'll take a few minutes right now and share two special memories about my horses. Number one; how I got my first horse, Prince.

My family who raised me, (all of them, from parents to aunts and uncles, and even my grandparents), all lived in the City and not a single one of them owned livestock, especially not a horse. But for some reason, I was BORN with the love of horses so deep in my heart that I drove everyone around me crazy. By the time I was two, I whinnied rather than talked half the time and I galloped instead of walking. In kindergarten and first grade, I went to school with a small rope around my neck, hoping to convince someone (anyone) to rein me during recess, so I could gallop around the playground like a horse.

By the third grade, I'd read every book in the school library about horses, and even went to the public library to find more. Since I'd taught myself to read before I was 4, it didn't take long to exhaust the supply of "horse books" at each school I attended. I remember one particular teacher at one of the grade schools I went to who put up a chart up on the wall and every time one of the students read a book, we were asked to give an oral report on it - and then stick a gold star next to our name. The idea was to see who could get the most stars, using competition as an incentive for reading, but for me, that wasn't necessary. I read for the sheer joy of reading... and I'll never forget the day that the teacher asked me to stay after class so she could speak to me.

Although I was concerned that perhaps I had done something wrong, she quickly assured me that that wasn't the case, and instead told me that I had so many stars already that they would have to put up a new chart just for me – and there simply wasn't enough room. She then asked me if I would mind "not" giving any more book reports, and assured me that I already had an A in reading, so not to worry. But I wasn't worried; I was disappointed... disappointed because I loved sharing the books I'd read, (sometimes two or more each day), with my fellow students, but I guess there just wasn't enough time - or space on the chart.

So even though I didn't actually own a horse, I learned to ride by reading... and imagining, and I just knew that the first time I sat on a horse, I'd take off at a gallop, wind blowing my hair and the horses mane tickling my face, while people watched in wonder as my beautiful steed and I raced by. Every time I went anywhere (with anyone), I spent the entire time in the car looking for horses and yelling "HORSE – HORSE – There's a HORSE until every adult around me was sick to death of it, (except my little brother Ronnie who happily played along.)

Finally, my father got so tired of my constantly going on and on and on about horses, acting like a horse, sounding like a horse, walking like a horse and yelling every single time I saw one, that he made me a deal; a deal he thought would be IMPOSSIBLE for me to keep, which is I'm sure the only reason he made it.

When I was 8 years old, he announced one day while we were traveling in the car, (and I was yelling "HORSE – HORSE – I SEE A HORSE), that if I could go one whole month without whinnying , galloping, or even saying the word "horse", he would buy me one for my birthday.

OH BOY – did he ever make a mistake! He figured that little miss "couldn't possibly be quiet for more than two seconds", couldn't do it… but he was wrong. Not only did I jump on that "vow of silence" deal, but I even put tape over my mouth every time we got in the car so I wouldn't get excited and forget; the one thing he was counting on.

Needless to say, I did it! A whole month went by and you'd have thought I was blind and mute when it came to horses, unless you saw the tape covering my mouth and the ear-to-ear grin on my face. I was ecstatic because the dream of actually owning my own horse loomed in my future… and there was no way I would give that up.

And then it was my birthday… one month after we made our deal and when I woke up that morning, my father said, "Happy birthday, honey. I think you'd better come outside and say hello to your birthday present."

I can't possibly describe the explosion of joy that sent me racing outside, where tied to the fence I found Prince, all saddled up and ready to go. I screamed, jumped up and down, and hugged my father until he cried "enough - enough"… before mounting up on my new horse and taking off for parts unknown. And I was right; I DID know how to ride. I was either born with it - or I had read so many books and imagined it so many times that I actually knew how to do it, but whatever the reason, I felt like a lifelong cowgirl and Prince and I spent the entire day together, me in pure Heaven, and him (an older and very tame horse), probably wondering where we were going and who this silly girl was on his back.

This most wonderful event happened on my eighth birthday, and because we lived in the city, my father was forced to rent a pasture (not far away) in which to keep Prince. There were six other horses in the pasture, a couple of which were owned by other young girls who were members of a 4-H Horse Club. I was in awe… because they got to go to horse shows, have trail rides and even got together for 'play days', which included barrel racing, pole bending, keyhole and other fun horseback games. I wanted to join 4-H more than anything, but my father insisted that we didn't have enough money for a horse trailer (which would be needed to get me to the horse shows), or money for the entry fees and proper equipment.

I guess you could say I was a very bad girl… because I refused to take "no" for an answer. I asked one of my new riding friends when their next "play day" was, and if I could sign up, and she said, "Sure. They have some papers your parents have to fill out and a $25.00 entrance fee, but here's the address."

That was all I needed to hear, and I was ON MY WAY! Since I spent every waking moment (except school hours) at the pasture while my father worked, no one would know if I **rode** Prince to the address she had given me, (rather than bringing him in a horse trailer like the other kids), and I could earn the $25.00 fee by milking the neighbor's cows, putting on little circuses, (more like trained dog shows) around the neighborhood with my two dogs, and collecting refundable pop bottles from every house for miles around; which is exactly what I did. And as wrong as my rebellion was, I was so determined to join 4-H that I even forged my dad's name to the permission papers and lied about my age, because you had to be 9 years old before you could join the 4-H Club, and I was only eight at the time. (Shame on me…)

So, for almost a whole year, (which was the longest I lived in one place during those early years), I regularly rode Prince to the County Fairgrounds for horse shows… and I rode to whatever ranch the "play days" were being held at, even though sometimes that meant riding right through the middle of downtown Medford, through traffic lights, next to train tracks and putting myself in all sorts of dangerous situations. But I was undeterred and undaunted, and continued to keep my membership a secret from my dad.

Eventually, I got caught… but it took an injured finger that had become so swollen and infected that I got blood poisoning, and literally passed out and fell off my horse in the middle of the show ring at the

Jackson County Fairgrounds. Naturally, they called my father, who was not only shocked that I was being taken to the hospital – but just as shocked that I belonged to a 4-H horse club and was riding in a horse show when I fell.

Now that I'm an adult and have raised two sons of my own, it scares me to wonder how many things THEY got away with that I wasn't aware of. I'll admit that it was pretty sneaky, (and that I was wrong for lying and forging my father's name), but in my own defense, I did it out of pure love... and no one, (but my finger, that is), ever got hurt. In fact, when my father raced to the hospital where the ambulance had taken me, he was so worried about me dying from blood poisoning that the error of my ways went far less severely punished than I had expected... and in fact, I think somewhere in his eyes, I actually saw some small amount of respect. How had I managed to ride so far all alone, to all those meetings, play days and horse shows, he wondered, and how had I learned enough to at least attempt to keep up with the other girls in the club; kids whose families were involved and owned all the proper equipment.

Prince was the horse that inspired my childhood dream of the horse motel in Gold Beach, and even though he was already considered an "older" horse when I got him, (tame enough for kids to climb around on), he wasn't even close to the quality of the horses that the other girls road in the shows. I can remember trying to get him to gallop when the ringmaster said "lope your horses", and I'd kick and kick and kick... barely nudging him into moving any faster than the already slow trot he considered to be far too much work.

That's why, when I moved back to my father's house in Medford, (after living with my aunt and uncle in Salem for almost a year), I noticed a new and beautiful horse in the big pasture we rented; a horse that no one ever came to visit, or groom, or even ride. After a whole month, I'd never once seen the owner, but the horse was absolutely gorgeous; a dappled Appaloosa who pranced like a royal steed and ran like the wind. I loved Prince, but by then, he thought even a trot was too much work,

so I began catching and riding this beautiful (and to my young heart...
abandoned and unloved) horse rather than my own. I named her Dusty
and together we set up jumps, learned to change leads, side pass, pivot
and race across the field like I'd always imagined in my dreams; something
Prince would never do.

I was 11 years old by that time, and had been riding Dusty for nearly a
year, when one night a strange man stopped by our apartment. He wanted to talk to my father, but of course, since it was such a small apartment,
I listened from the other room, figuring it HAD to be about me because
the man was wearing cowboy boots, a leather vest and even a cowboy hat.
Uh-oh... I wondered. What was I in trouble for this time?

"I understand your daughter has a horse staying in the same pasture
where I keep one of mine," he said to my father, "and I think there's
something you ought'a know."

Now I was really worried, as my dad replied, "Yes, she keeps her horse
there. Has she done something wrong," he asked?

"Well, I don't know what you consider wrong, but I drove over there
the other day; hadn't been there for quite some time... being so busy and
all - and I saw her riding my Appaloosa mare. Now that alone wouldn't
a' been so bad. I'd a' just told her to get off my horse and never to get
back on... but I just couldn't bring myself to do it," he explained, as he
fidgeted with the cowboy hat that he now held in his hands.

"Why not," my father asked? "She shouldn't be riding your horse when
she's got one of her own, and I'll make sure that it never happens again,"
he assured the grandfather-aged cowboy standing in the middle of our
tiny living room.

"Well, sir," the cowboy drawled as he grinned and shook his head at
the same time. "There's a reason I couldn't do it. See, I've had that horse
for five years now and she's a purebred with mighty fine blood lines, not
to mention pretty as a picture, so I can see why your daughter would like
her, but the problem is, that horse was so darn wild that no one could
ride her. Oh, I suppose if I'd brought her home and spent some serious

time breaking her, it could'a been done, but it could'a broke her spirit too, which is why I didn't have the heart, which is why I just let her run free in that field with the other horses. Then I drove up there the other day, and there was your little girl - not just ridin' her but jumping jumps and doing tricks like nothing I've ever seen before. I wouldn't a' believed it if I hadn't seen it with my own eyes."

"You're kidding," my father shook his head, not sure whether to be angry or proud. "She actually trained a wild horse?"

"Yup," he answered, "and she did a mighty fine job, too. That's why when I took a look at that old nag she was supposed to be riding, no offense meant sir, I could see why she'd rather be riding my mare, and I reckon she's earned it."

"Yes, but it's YOUR horse," my father insisted, "and I'm sorry if she stepped out of line."

"Well, sir," the cowman went on, "the way I see it, your girl's got a natural way with horses, so I'd sure hate to break her spirit - just like I didn't want to break that mare's. I was thinkin' maybe you and I could work out some sort'a deal, and if I made the price right, maybe you could buy that mare for your daughter. I think she deserves it, and if you could see the way she rides… well, I think you'd agree."

Although I was hiding in the bedroom, I literally had to cover my mouth with my hand to keep from squealing as I heard the conversation, but I also knew that we lived in this little one bedroom apartment because my father didn't make a lot of money, so I didn't dare get my hopes up.

"I'm afraid I don't have the money to buy her another horse, even if I wanted to - but I do appreciate your offer. It's expensive enough just feeding and clothing these two kids and I just can't afford it. I will try not to be too tough on her for taking liberties with a horse that doesn't belong to her though," my father answered, leaving me relieved to know that at least I wasn't in too much trouble.

"I kind of figured that might be the case when I got here," he said as he looked around at our tiny one bedroom apartment, "but maybe she could work some of the price off doin' chores for me, and you could pay me the rest a little at a time… when you could afford it. I'm not hurtin' for money, and 'dI sure hate to see a natural horsewoman like your daughter goin' to waste."

"Well then, sir, I think maybe we **can** work something out. How much money are we talking about?" my father asked.

"The horse is worth double what I'll let your daughter have her for, and that's $500, tack included," he offered generously, which was a lot of money in 1962.

Now I was really jumping up and down, hand still held over my mouth… screaming inside, please, please, please, dad - say yes!!!

"OK," my dad agreed, still somewhat reluctant. "I guess you've got yourself a deal… and I guess my daughter has a fine horse now, thanks to you. She's been riding Prince, her horse over at the pasture, in all kinds of 4-H horse shows and can't seem to win a single ribbon, so maybe this will help. Thank you for your kindness, and if you'll leave your phone number and address, I'll be in touch so we can work out the details."

"Excuse me," the older cowboy asked, "but are you saying that young lady has been riding that old bay in 4-H horse shows?"

"Yes," my dad answered. "She did it for almost a year before I even found out about it. She's loved horses all her life, but me… I don't know a horse from a cow."

"Well then, it's no wonder she never won no ribbons. That horse a' hers, Prince you say his name is? Why he's a **pacer**. I know you're not much on horses, so you probably don't know what I'm talkin' about… but *pacers* don't trot, they 'pace', which would explain why a girl of her talent never won any of those horse shows. My three kids were in 4-H, and we used to hold trail rides and play days out at my ranch, but when the ringmaster says 'trot your horses' and all the other horses trot, her horse can't… it just paces instead. That poor girl was riding in those shows with no hope a' winnin', cuz she was ridin' a gaited horse."

Oh my gosh, I thought to myself. That explains every thing! I was so relieved to find out it wasn't my lack of riding ability that had kept me from winning show after show, no matter how hard I tried. Why didn't anyone ever tell me, I wondered? Now that I knew what was wrong, and I'd have a horse like Dusty to ride, I just knew that I'd become a champion, and I was so excited that I could barely squelch my screams of joy, so I ran in place - and tightened the grip of my hand over my mouth.

"I think she'll be very glad to hear that, and I'd like to thank you, sir," my father added. "You're a fine man for taking the time to come over — and for caring about my daughter. I'll make sure you get your money."

"I got no doubt about that. My kids are grown and they don't care much about horses anymore. Cars are more their style... and it's nice to see a real cowgirl in the making. So just give me a call," he said as he headed for the door, still shaking his head and grinning. "If I was you, I'd do everything I could to encourage her riding. She's got what it takes - and there's a lot worse things a young girl could be doin' out there these days than riding and caring for horses."

"I agree," my father nodded. "So thank you; thank you again. But I **am** going to have a long talk with her about rustling other people's horses," he said with a laugh, which made my heart soar, knowing that if he was really mad, he wouldn't be laughing.

And that's how I got Dusty, the most beautiful Appaloosa I'd ever seen. I won so many ribbons that eventually they didn't even fit on my walls, and I won the Jackson County Fair Horsemanship class, Trail horse class and Western Pleasure class. I even earned the right to go to Salem and placed in the Oregon State Fair, representing Jackson County. I didn't get rid of Prince because he'd been a loyal friend and I loved him; plus he made a fine horse for my friends to ride – at least until I was a Senior in high school when I finally gave him to my best friend's little brothers and sisters because he was completely kid proof and wouldn't do anything but WALK by that time. But Dusty and I were soul mates - and no one but me could ever ride that horse. Just ask my step-mother Roma who, (at my assurance that Dusty was tame as a kitten), tried... and broke her ankle getting bucked off.

I don't know why I went on and on over such a silly story, but from the life I'm living now on the road in Lucky, you'd never know that I have such a deep and abiding love for animals, and an almost magical connection with horses. Since my 8th birthday when I got Prince, I've never been without at least two horses, sometimes as many as a dozen, until the day I left Gold Beach after the flood. Suddenly, on this New Year's Eve, I find myself horseless... and remembering the smell of leather and alfalfa hay - and the way the horses greeted me when I came to feed them and clean their stalls. I'll never forget feeling the ripple of muscles under me as I galloped them bareback, nor the way it felt like the reins weren't even necessary, as it was my will communicated directly to the horse through my weight, legs and voice that told the horse what I wanted. What wonderful memories these are... and how blessed I am to have them!

But that's enough reminiscing; time to get back to "today". I've been doing a lot of thinking about it, and I've come up with a plan for how to set up my poetry readings as I travel.

It's a lot easier now that I've seen the positive reaction I get from the audiences at my shows, because I'm no longer embarrassed to advertise and promote them. So in each town I go to, my first stop will be the Chamber of Commerce, where I'll get a list of local churches, schools, clubs, nursing and retirement homes, etc. I'll also get a list of available meeting rooms and the names of contact people at the local radio stations and newspapers.

That's where a bicycle would come in really handy because after I find a place to park Lucky, I'll go to each one of those places, recite a sample of my work so they can decide whether they'd be interested in hearing more... and then, assuming they ARE interested, I'll schedule a performance. The only show where I'll put out my contribution basket and hope to make enough money to get me to the next town, will be the one "open" show I'll put on in each town - and for that one, I'll use a rented meeting room.. I still feel kind of bad about putting a monetary value on my art because the words are "free" to me, a gift from God...

and I'd rather pass them on the same way. But the reality is that I'll need money for food and gas, as well as for flyers and copies to hand out. Oh well, maybe someday it will be different - and I'll be able to share my art freely with everyone who cares to listen.

So looking at it that way, I figure I'll need to stay in each town for about three weeks to a month, because I'll schedule the "open show" during the last week and use the three weeks preceding it to put on shorter programs at all the places I mentioned, (and even more if I can think of any). That'll also give me enough time to post flyers, do radio interviews, put ads in the local newspaper and visit the local businesses - where I'll issue personal invitations, as well as a sample of my work, like at the auto shop. I figure that if the people I entertain at the schools, clubs, churches, and other places like what they hear… they'll come to my **open** show, and maybe even bring their family and friends with them.

At least now I have a plan, and although at this point, it's only an idea and open to change, I really think it might just work… as long as I can find a place to park Lucky close enough to walk (or ride a bike) everywhere I need to go. I just hope that my newspaper ad here in Sun City brings in enough jobs to earn the money I'll need to get started. I can still hear the "voice" after the flood that said so clearly, ***"I will do my part – but YOU must do yours."*** That's why I said in the ad, "no job too small or too dirty"… because I'm ready and willing to *do my part*. I have absolutely no doubt that if this is the path the Lord wants me to take, *"everything will be fine"*.

And tomorrow is the beginning of a new year… 1999. I can't believe how quickly the time has passed, which only makes me want to grasp onto each and every moment and treasure it for the amazing gift it is.

OK, that's enough rambling. It's time to get my tape recorder out and start a new tape for my mother. By the way – I bought one of those long distance cards at the convenience store so I could call her and see how she's doing, and she says she LOVED the tape I sent her for Christmas!

Happy New Year!

THERE'S A REASON...

There's a reason for every yesterday...
every feeling that ever came your way.
All the heartache – you thought would never end...
and every moment you'd like to live again.

Life's a puzzle - each day another piece...
so don't regret things you know were meant to be.
In the morning – the day is new again.
and you can make it... the best there's ever been!

Don't look back with a heart that's full of tears.
You ARE who you ARE – because of all those years.
So even when you're tired; when you have no more to give...
remember Jesus loves you – and he died so you could live.

— Poem by Abigayle

chapter 35

January 5, 1999

10:00 P.M.

W hew… am I ever beat!

The newspaper ad worked like a charm - and I've got the blisters to prove it! I've been working non-stop for the past three days now, and since I'm only charging $8.00 an hour, I've still got a long way to go. Let's see… in order to make $400 at $8.00 an hour, I'll have to work 50 hours. Thank goodness for Elaine's Christmas gift because I'm using that money for food, gas and propane, so I figure I should be ready to go back to Blythe, (and see John and Mary), in a little over a week.

I truly must have been out of my mind when I said "no job too dirty" in my ad, because that turned out to be an open invitation for all the work that no one else would do. And these past few days have been an important learning experience for me too, because since leaving Gold Beach, I've been working with my *mind* rather than my *body*… so not only is this heavy manual labor getting me back in shape, but it's giving me a chance to see first-hand what it's like to clean up other people's messes for a change, which is one small step toward understanding what so many of my brothers and sisters have to go through every single day of their lives just to feed their families. That was, after all, one of the main purposes of this trip; to learn, to understand, to encourage, and to help wherever possible.

But as it turns out, there's an even **greater** benefit that dong the work the ad is bringing me… and it's not getting in shape, or the money I'm earning. As I discovered rather quickly, the **true** joy is in helping people who are too old, too crippled, or for some reason unable to do the work themselves. That's the one "plus" I hadn't expected… and here's a perfect example.

Yesterday and today I worked for an 88 year-old woman named Norma who lives alone. She's been a doll-maker and craft enthusiast all her life and for the past 20 years I don't think she's thrown a single thing away. Her back yard was literally filled with stack after stack of boxes and containers of every size and shape… piled higher than even my tall frame and long arms could reach without a ladder. According to Norma, they've been sitting there for years… some under the patio roof, some in the carport, and others just stacked against the house in the back yard. When she saw my ad, she decided it was time to sort them all out, throw away what she didn't need, and organize the rest… and believe me – it's a big job!

Most of the boxes weren't just filthy; they were literally rotting away from years of exposure to the hot Arizona sun, so every time I tried to pick one up - it just fell apart and all the contents spilled out onto the ground. And Norma didn't merely want to get *rid* of the boxes; she wanted me to empty them, item by item, and then divide the contents into several piles, one pile to keep, one for charity, one for the dump, etc. But there were two rather large problems; *one*; I didn't recognize what most of the craft items were, which meant I was constantly running into the house to ask Norma if the item I was holding was something was worth keeping or whether I should throw it away or give it to charity… and *two*; **the boxes were full of bugs**!

One time when I went to pick up a box, a big brown spider almost the size of my palm, scurried back underneath it. I immediately let go of the box and let out a squeal of panic, which brought Norma hobbling outside to see what had happened. I told her about the big brown, hairy spider and she said, "Oh yaa, we get those all the time around here. I don't know what you call them, but you better watch out because they can jump three or four feet – faster than you can blink an eye."

Great! That was just what I wanted to hear. Although I've been an avid camper and wilderness hiker/horseback rider all my life, even when everything I brought on a trip had to be contained in a single backpack and carried for many miles, I ALWAYS managed to find room for a can of "Yard Guard" – Raids super bug killer. It's kind of like the story of the elephant and the mouse; I'm not afraid to break wild horses or milk kicking cows or even of worry about sharks when I swim in the ocean. I would never consider taking a weapon camping because I'm not afraid of bears or cougar, or even evil people. But I WOULD do everything within my power to keep a tiny bee or a tick from landing on me; especially *bees,* my biggest fear of all. Well, it looks like this very large and hairy spider has just made *second place* on my *fear* list.

"Do you have any bug killer?" I asked Norma hopefully, preferring not to touch another box until I had sprayed the entire stack and there was no possibility of giant spiders leaping out at me.

"Nope," she answered. "But you just come with me dear, and I'll find something that'll do the trick," she said calmly as she turned and walked slowly back into the house.

After a few minutes of searching, she retrieved a spray can from one of her many cabinets and proudly handed it to me. And no … it wasn't bug spray; it was a can of *spray paint,* and I actually had to turn my head to keep Norma from seeing the look of disappointment (and disbelief) on my face.

"This'll do the trick," she announced with great satisfaction. "You just let me know if it doesn't, and we'll try something else."

Easy for her to say, I thought to myself as I looked at the can of spray paint and actually laughed at the idea of "painting it to death". But since Norma seemed absolutely positive that it would work, I decided to give it a try, and believe it or not, she was right. The problem was that I couldn't spray the whole stack of boxes to get rid of the bugs BEFORE I ran into them. Nope, I had to wait until I actually saw one - and THEN *paint him to death*; (a brilliant green, I might add).

It wasn't long before I saw my palm-sized spider friend again, so I stood back as far as I could, (having been duly warned about his leaping abilities), and gave him a dazzling green coat. And surprise, surprise... that big brown furry spider rolled right over onto his back, apparently stunned by the paint just long enough for me to smash him. And even though I was relieved to know that I would no longer have to worry about him leaping out at me, I couldn't help but feel sorry for him. That poor spider had been living in those boxes for who knows how many years, bothering no one – and then I come along and kill him. I even wondered if he (or she) had a family. But then... it WAS a matter of self-defense.

Anyway, I worked on those boxes for 8 full hours yesterday and another 8 hours today, and the entire time I felt like I had bugs in my hair and crawling in my clothes. But sweet elderly Norma was counting on me... so I put my silly fears aside and tried to do the best job I could. And actually, it made me feel really good, because if I didn't do it, who would? And that was the unexpected bonus I was talking about.

The people who are hiring me need help... and apparently they can't find anyone else to do the job. I thought I was doing these dirty chores for the money, but as it turns out... the *biggest* benefit of all is that I'm getting a chance to help people who really need it. That means I get DOUBLE the joy; the *joy* of earning the money I'll need on the road and the *joy* I'm bringing these people who no longer have to worry about whatever it is they've hired me do. There's always a silver lining...

Opps... back to my story: After I finished getting rid of all the boxes and cleaning up the yard, Norma asked me if I would please stay and visit with her for awhile and although I wanted nothing more than to go back to Lucky and get cleaned up, it was obvious that she was lonely... and that giving her some of my time meant more to her than my rest meant to me; which is why I agreed to stay, and why I listened to story after story about her life – and boy has she seen a lot in her 88 years. I shared a few of my own stories and poems with her and she was so enthused that she insisted on writing down the name and address of her son, who lives in Texas, and putting it in my pocket; assuring me that she would call him and tell him all about me… so if I ever got to Texas, I could park my RV at his house.

It was such a small price to pay … and the pleasure that my time and attention brought Norma was worth every minute of it. She asked me if I would please come and visit with her again, but I explained that I was completely booked up with cleaning jobs and would be leaving town as soon as I was finished. But my heart ached for her when I saw how disappointed she was, so I drove back to Elaine's house feeling like I had somehow let Norma down. I can't help but wonder if I should have done more; at least tried to find some way to keep in touch with her… but there are so many lonely people out there – and no possible way to befriend them all!

Elaine's phone is still ringing off the hook about my ad; some of the calls even more surprising than the jobs, such as the paraplegic who wants to travel with me – and the retired gentleman who needs a personal assistant. (So many people… and so little time.) I can't believe I was actually worried about finding enough work – and now I not only have more work than I can handle, but I'm getting a chance to make a small difference in the lives of those I'm working for. It's a "win-win" situation… and I'm so thankful for this amazing opportunity, (even if I am dead tired)!

Speaking of tired, I have to get up at 6:00 tomorrow morning for an early job, so it's "lights out" for this manual laborer!

COLOSSIANS 3:23, 24
23) And whatsoever ye do, do it heartily,
as to the Lord, and not unto men;
24) Knowing that of the Lord ye shall receive the reward
of the inheritance for ye serve the Lord Christ.

chapter 36

January 11, 2009

I'm not parked at Elaine's house anymore because my last two jobs before I leave for Blythe are pretty far away - and since I'll be working all day anyway, I figured it was best to say our goodbyes and then I can concentrate on working. It will be almost the middle of January by the time I leave, so I wonder if John and Mary will still be waiting for me... but only time will tell, and for some strange reason I find myself thinking of that RV Park in Blythe, California as "home"... and I can't wait to get back to my baby palm tree (as well as some much needed REST)!

Guess what? Elaine insisted on taking me shopping before I left her house and bought me an amplifier and a microphone for my shows. Now all I need is lighting and I'll be ready to go! Thank you, Elaine!!!

Right now I'm parked in front of the big and beautiful house I'm cleaning today in Sun City West, which is the "high dollar" district of Sun City. (And I mean mansions!) I don't think Eda, (the lady I'm working for), was too happy when I pulled up in my big old RV (which took up her entire driveway), especially in this classy neighborhood, but it didn't take long before her attitude did a complete 180 and she stopped treating me like second-class "hired help". It was an interesting experience though... because for the first time in my life, I got a chance to see what it was like to be treated like a lesser person just because of the work you do. I had no idea how sheltered my life has been until I began getting so many chances to walk in other people's shoes. I still don't know what the Lord has in mind for me, or how He wants me to best use my gift to do His work, but I DO think that every bit of this, every single experience and every single hardship I endure… is all training.

But even as a "maid" or "dirty work laborer", I still have an unfair advantage over those who have no choice but to do this kind of labor all of their lives. The fact that I'm obviously well-spoken and well-educated is quickly noticed by those who employ me, and it doesn't take long before they come right out and ask, "What are you really doing here?" And that's when I get to tell them the story, bear witness to the glory of my Lord and share some of my art. I still can't believe how quickly their attitude towards me changes. One minute I'm face-less, (just the hired help), and the next I'm someone they want to know – and often they'd rather talk to me than let me work. Even though their perception and treatment of me changes, I'm actually glad that it's only AFTER I've had the opportunity to see what I **would** have been treated like if things had been different.

How many times have I seen that in my life? So many that it makes me feel repelled by the respect of people who shouldn't be giving it to me. Take playing foosball for example.

My two boys were born only 18 months apart, and my youngest, (Jeremy), was only 6 weeks old when I discovered that I had no choice but to have a hysterectomy. For a woman whose marriage to her high school sweetheart had just ended, but who still wanted at least 6 more children, it was devastating, to say the least. At the time, I was a legal secretary, making $400 a month in 1973, but during my recovery period from the major surgery and the pneumonia which followed, I was unable to work, and going crazy being cooped up in my house… even with two babies to care for. That's why a friend brought me a foosball table to keep me entertained, which was a very popular game during the 70's.

He set the table up right in the middle of my living room so I could play and watch my boys at the same time; although I'm sure the doctor wouldn't have approved because I still had staples from my belly-button clear down to my… well, let's just say, all the way down.

But I loved the game! It was fast and intense, (just like me), and as it turned out, I was pretty darn good at it. The early 70's were "party time" and as soon as the word got out that I had a "free" foosball table at my house, there were ALWAYS people coming over who wanted to play. Even when I went to bed at night, it was often to the sound of slap, slap, bang, bang… and to the cheers of someone scoring a goal or winning a game.

I guess I was so unusually good at foosball that one day the same friend who had brought the table over to my house, (who also happened to be a foosball table and pinball game distributor), showed me a flyer about a foosball tournament in San Francisco, California. First prize in the women's division was $500; more than I made in a whole month working as a legal secretary.

So, to make a long (and very interesting) story short, I had no money, which is why I hitchhiked to that first tournament in San Francisco, where I won first prize… a whole months wages! Because I'd gone to the tournament without so much as a dollar in my pocket, I slept on the floor of some other player's room and didn't eat anything but the sandwiches and fruit I had carried along with me, but I won… and it was the beginning of a new way to make a living. There was a quarter-million dollar tour that year, which meant I could be with my children all day - every day, (rather than taking them to daycare while I worked at the law firm), and then leave them only on the weekend - which to me seemed like a much better arrangement.

I can't count the number of lawn chairs I slept in, or hotel lobbies where I stayed awake all night during that first year because I couldn't afford a room. I hitchhiked or begged rides from other players as I traveled all over the country, sometimes alone and sometimes with my mixed-doubles partner, Danny… often going days without food or sleep and yet *almost* always winning my event. At the end of that first year came the Nationals, with Wild World of Sports and Sports Illustrated present, as well as many other sports reporters, and suddenly I became noticed. Suddenly, people were offering me rides and wanted to pay for my room. Suddenly people who hadn't given me the time of day before… wanted just to be able to say that they knew me - and treated me like someone special; someone they were honored to help.

And it literally made me sick to my stomach! I was the exact same person I had been before I became a National Champion… and yet now they treated me completely different. It was all so fake; like rhinestones that meant absolutely nothing. That's why I quickly became publicity shy and stayed out of the limelight as much as possible, even going so far as to enter some tournaments under a false name. And that's also why I retired from playing foosball on tour when I was 26; the year that I began rooting for my opponents rather than myself. You can't play a competitive game and want the opposition to win, but that's exactly how I felt. For me, it was all about the "joy factor". See, I was a world champion… so the people who walked up to the table hoping to beat me, were excited and eager to show their family and friends in the crowd how good they were - and that they could beat one of the best players in the world. Yet to me, it was just another game, in another tournament, in another city, and I'd never even remember their faces soon after the match was over. So if winning that game could bring a HUGE amount of joy to my opponents if **they** won - and just a LITTLE bit of joy to me if **I** did, I felt like I was robbing the "joy pool". And since I felt their joy every bit as much as if it were my own, how could I possibly root for myself? I couldn't, which is why I retired from the sport. I played an occasional tournament for several years after that, but not for a living, and usually just to see everyone and have some fun.

But I still don't understand how (or why) people can treat you so differently just because of something you've accomplished – or something you're good at? It's not right… and here I am, seeing the same thing in action once again, but this time it isn't foosball.

After we talked, Eda not only stopped treating me like a servant, she even invited me to have dinner with her and her husband, something I highly doubt she would have offered to any other maid or housekeeper. But then, I can't blame her for that, because that's just the way society has taught us; from looking up to actors and athletes to treating the rich and/or beautiful people differently. She's a product of her circumstance and environment… so maybe instead of begrudging the respect she has for me, (unearned or not), I should **use** it to make some very important points.

And what points could I make with Eda? That's an easy question to answer. Eda is a very proper elderly Jewish lady who was interned at Auschwitz, a World War II concentration camp. She was only 19 years old when she was forced to watch helplessly as both of her parents, as well as her younger brother, were marched into the gas chamber. She told me, with tears of agony in her eyes, "You just can't imagine the things I was forced to do to stay alive," she sobbed, and although she wasn't specific, I think I **can** imagine what a pretty young girl of 19 might have suffered at the hands of evil men. That poor young woman had experienced such horrible and unspeakable trauma that (according to her), she's never been able to speak of it since… not to anyone.

And then I came into her home… and it wasn't long before she felt the urge to share her entire story. While I scrubbed the floors and washed the windows, she literally followed me from room to room, telling me things that according to her - she's never even told her husband. What an honor it was to be able to give this lady some small amount of comfort and relief, as she allowed her pain to be released and spoken of for the first time. And it also served as a big reminder to me that I should be very grateful for the life **I've** been blessed with… and for the fact that I was never forced to suffer like she and so many others were. I can't help but wonder what kind of person I'd be today if I had walked in her shoes.

And why was she able to open up to me? I think it must have been easier for her to talk about something so personal to someone she'll never have to face again… and someone who has no pre-conceived notions about her life, and someone who will just hug her and listen, without making judgments, and then leave. It's my honor to be that person and there's no doubt in my mind that the Lord is the one responsible for the way she opened up today. It was step one in her healing process and long overdue. That's why I decided to accept her dinner invitation, and use the respect she obviously has for my opinion, to talk to her about Jesus.

She kept asking me one question over and over again as she sobbed, "How could God let such horrible things happen?" That was a difficult question for me to answer, so I just said, as I put my arm around her, "We can't possibly hope to understand His reasons, Ada, but we **can** overcome the pain and look forward to a joy-filled eternity in His presence. All you have to do is accept Jesus as your Savior.

I know that you, as a Jewish woman, believe in the Old Testament, right? So what if, just for the sake of discussion… what if the Jewish leaders of those times were wrong – and what if Jesus really **was** the messiah they were waiting for? Look at how many years have gone by since then and no other messiah has come. Can't you at least consider the possibility that THEY were wrong… but that YOU don't have to make the same mistake? Look into my eyes, Ada, and believe me… Jesus WAS and IS the messiah, our Savior, the son of God, and He loves you. So turn to Him, and HE will heal your pain."

It was obvious that a lifetime of religious teachings weren't going to be wiped away in a single day, so I added, "Just please, do me one favor - and pray about it. That's not asking too much, is it? You don't really think that my coming here today to clean your house was merely a coincidence do you?" I asked as I looked deeply into her tear filled eyes. "No, I didn't think so - and now I'm asking… no I'm begging you to pray, and ask God to let you know if Jesus is truly the Savior. And a smart woman like you certainly realizes that no major decision should be made without considering ALL of the evidence, so I'm going to leave you a copy of the New Testament, and I BEG you to read it before you decide. Jesus can heal your heart, Ada, and I'm here to tell you that!

After our discussion was over, she told me that I'd done more than enough work to earn my salary today, so perhaps I should go out to my RV and get ready for dinner because her husband would be home soon. (I really think she wanted some time alone, so I agreed.)

An hour later, her husband came home - and he was a nice elderly Jewish man, but not very talkative, so we never again broached the subject as I helped her finish preparing dinner and the three of us enjoyed a meal together before I bid them a final farewell and gave her one last loving and encouraging hug.

I wish I could do more... because it feels like I just drop into people's lives for a few moments, plant a few seeds, and then off I go... wondering - but never knowing whether those seeds took root.

But for now, that's the way it is... and if the Lord is leading me somewhere else, or has something different He wants me to do, perhaps that will change. But for now, at least, I'm just like Johnny Appleseed; wandering and planting... and maybe someday, when I get to the Celestial Kingdom, I'll see these same brothers and sisters again, and find out whether the seeds I was so blessed to have sown actually flourished.

chapter 37

January 11, 1999

7:30 A.M.

Good morning – and what a beautiful morning it is!

I can't wait to get back on the road again, and I keep hearing Willie Nelson's song playing over and over in my head; "On the Road Again". It's not that I mind the hard labor, since most of the blisters have turned into calluses and my muscles are getting stronger than they've been since I was cleaning stalls every day in Gold Beach… but I miss the freedom, and I NEED SOME REST!.

By the way, Lucky's new battery was just what I needed and the engine starts right up every single morning. (What a treat!) Yesterday I bought a used ten-speed bicycle for only $15.00. Wow… what a bargain. At least that's what I thought until I took my first fall last night. Ouch! I'm afraid I've never ridden the kind of bike where you lean over the handle bars and your rear end is sticking up higher than your head… and I'm not sure I like it. The tires are so skinny that I feel like I'm always on the verge of falling over. Oh well, it still beats walking, and I'm sure I'll get used to it eventually. I do wish it had a basket, though!

Right now I'm parked on the street in front of a new home construction site in a nice neighborhood in Sun City where I'm doing what they call, "new construction clean-up". The contractor, Scott, is teaching me a lot of things I never expected to learn. For example, this morning he just casually asked me to remove all the door hardware, (as if he expected me to know what that meant) and although I had absolutely no idea how to do it, I eventually figured it out… and when I was finished, I was pretty darn proud of myself. My boys would be shocked, (and I hope proud), because they always took care of everything to do with automobiles or home repairs, so here is yet another wonderful opportunity for me to broaden my horizons.

I do have to admit that I'm getting mighty tired of washing windows though, especially the really big ones. Just when I think I'm finished, the bright Arizona sun shines through and I see another spot I missed. Scott says they're fine, and that they don't have to be perfect…but it still bothers me, (always the perfectionist).

And guess what? They have lemon trees right here in the yard, so I filled several big bags of lemons, (with Scott's permission), so I'll have more than enough to make fresh lemonade and still have plenty to give away when I get back to Blythe.

I started working here yesterday, and it's a two day job, which is why Scott let me park Lucky on the street right in front of the house, which is where I'm sitting right now… waiting for the rest of the crew to arrive at 8:00. (Who'd have ever dreamed that I'd be part of a construction crew? (I still find it hard to believe.)

Opps… here comes Scott and it looks like he's carrying a whole box of doughnuts!

chapter 38

January 12, 1999

9:00 A.M.

"On the Road Again".... and it feels wonderful!

I'm parked at a rest area on Interstate 10 just east of Blythe where I spent the night last night and it seems that no matter where I go, I am presented with opportunities to share my testimony.

A nice middle-aged couple who clean the rest area bathrooms asked me what brought me here all the way from Oregon so, of course, I told them. It's funny how the doors keep opening, and no matter how far-fetched I think my story might sound to people, I've never once seen even so much as a drop of doubt in their eyes... and they always listen intently - asking questions and wanting to hear more. That's definitely the Holy Spirit at work... and all I am merely the conduit.

What a wonderful way to start the day! And now it's time to finish my drive to Blythe where John and Mary will be waiting, (I think).

Before I left Scott's construction site in Sun City last night, he and the other workers used scrap metal to build a bicycle carrier on the back of Lucky, so I have my new (used) bicycle with me; now I just have to learn to ride it! Who designed those things, anyway - and what happened to the ones like I had when I was young; the kind where you sit upright and have a headlight and a basket? Oh well, it's still better than walking!

And guess what? I have $500 in my pocket! Do you believe it? Since the owner of Blythe RV and Mobile Home Park said he would only charge me $50 a week, I figure I can stay for two weeks, spend $50 on groceries and still have $350 when I leave town. I'm rich... not merely in money, but in the ways that **really** counts!

So, John and Mary, here I come!

chapter 39

January 21, 1999

8:00 P.M.

Where does the time go? Once again I'm parked next to my little baby palm tree watching gorgeous sunsets, enjoying the warm winter sunshine and spending time with John and Mary. I've put on a few short readings here in town, but I've learned so much during the past few months that I've decided to wait to put on a full program until I do some more writing. My poetry over the years, (actually since childhood), has been almost like a journey… with the early ones full of questions and prayers, asking for guidance and a release from my pain and confusion, and now that my Lord has led me to THIS point in my life, I need to show where all those questions and tribulations led me; to complete peace and trust in God.

So much has happened since the flood that it's changed my outlook on life, and I want to capture it in words and then use my poetry to share it with others. Life is such an amazing journey… and it's important that this newest and greatest chapter is included. That's why I've decided to head for the desert when I leave here; somewhere between Yuma and Quartzsite, where I can be completely alone… and write.

Hey, guess what? I got a **new** bicycle. When John saw me riding that tall skinny 10-speed he had a fit. He said that I was just asking to get injured… and you know what? He was right. I rode that bike all over town; in fact one day I rode it for 4 ½ hours, and I still don't feel like I'm in control. John and Mary drove me to a flea market in Quartzsite, Arizona where I could shop for a better used bicycle, and I actually found one!

And this bike is different, (like the one I had when I was a little girl), and I knew it was meant to be mine from the first moment I saw it. In fact, the place where I found it wasn't even at a vendor's booth at the flea market; it was just sitting next to a tiny travel trailer parked a couple of blocks away. I spotted it as we walked from where John parked his car to the flea market and I was so taken by that bicycle that I decided to knock on the door and see if it was for sale. It wasn't… but after the man who owned it and I talked for awhile, he decided he would sell it to me. I paid him $100, and a fax machine I brought all the way from my business in Gold Beach, but it was well worth it.

The bike is a bright red Western Flyer with tassels on the handlebars, a big basket and a shiny chrome headlight, (complete with a secret storage compartment). It's perfect, because I can use the basket to carry my papers and groceries and on this bike I actually get to ride sitting up. I've already discovered a surprise benefit too, because everywhere I go people stop me to ask about the bike, telling me stories about the "Western Flyer they rode when they were young." It's a real conversation starter and you know where those conversations always lead. It must be the kind of bicycle that people remember because it's only been a week and already the folks here in Blythe refer to me as "the lady on the bright red bike". Cute!

John and Mary and I have spent so many hours reading the bible and discussing our feelings about what we've read that it's almost like going to church every day and I've learned many things. John has had some amazing experiences; ones that if I didn't know him as well as I do, I'm not sure I'd believe. But I do, without doubt – and I know that the Lord brought us together for some special reason. And we've also done some exploring. Together we drove all the way to Yuma, taking the back roads through the desert, and I saw some beautiful places where I could be completely alone. I'd have never ventured that far off the freeway by my-self, especially onto dirt roads heading out into the desert, if it hadn't been for John and Mary showing me the way, so they really are helping me in more ways than they realize.

Just think; a week from today, that's where I'll be; parked in the des-ert… hopefully where I can't see a single man-made light or hear the sound of an engine. I'm really looking forward to getting back to basics so I can hear what I need to hear – and write what I need to write.

Isn't life grand!

chapter 40

January 26, 1999

I'm still at the RV Park in Blythe, still filled with joy and humbled by the presence of too many miracles to count, and still on my way to "I know not where" but anxious to get there. Once again, the sun is shining brightly with 80+ degree weather in January. I'm healthier than I've ever been, and by the grace of God, I'm thrilled to accept the gift of yet another day on this amazing planet.

I've been riding my new bicycle (named "Candy" because of her bright red paint), everywhere I go, including the Laundromat and grocery store. As my teenage sons used to say, I'm really stylin' now and I'm so thankful that John and Mary insisted I get rid of that old one. I gave it to a young boy here in the trailer park whose family is so poor they couldn't afford to buy him a bicycle, so that way, at least someone is getting joy from it, and that makes me happy, too.

I had a rather serious meeting with John and Mary last night and it actually gave me a touch of the blues. I prayed about what they said to me before I went to bed and I woke up this morning feeling absolutely wonderful… so the blues are gone, and I'm taking what they had to say to heart.

Here's the gist of the conversation that left me feeling both wiser and sadder.

Let me preface the story by saying I had a dream the night before last… one of those dreams that are so vivid and so realistic that you don't forget a single detail - and it sticks with you for days. Here's what happened:

I was sitting in a church pew, surrounded by family and friends, when a sudden gust of wind blew right into the church. The wind was so strong that it literally blew my shirt off… and I hurriedly crossed my arms in order to hide my breasts. As I turned around to see if anyone else had lost their clothing, I saw that everyone else was fully dressed, and that they were staring at me… as though they were blaming ME for the fact that the wind had taken away my shirt. I couldn't believe it… because I was just sitting there worshipping God, and even though my nudity was no fault of my own, (and I was doing my best to cover myself), I couldn't figure out why they were blaming me for something that I couldn't control.

I think the thing that bothered me the most was the fact that I was in a church, a place where I felt safe and protected, and yet I wasn't. It just didn't seem right - and I felt both vulnerable and disappointed. And that's when I woke up.

So yesterday morning when I joined John and Mary for bible study and prayer, I told them about the dream and they looked at each in amazement. Apparently, they'd had a rather long and serious discussion about me the night before, (the same night I had my dream), and had been wondering how to broach the subject without offending me. They prayed about it before they went to bed that night and then this morning… I showed up with the story of my dream; a dream which just happened to open the door for the subject they had wanted to discuss.

First, here's John's interpretation of my dream:.

Because my faith in God and my love for Him is extremely strong, I feel safe and protected as I venture out into the world alone. And yet, that's NOT the case, which my dream was showing me by my being in a church, the place I feel closest to God and safe in his arms, when I was disrobed by the wind. His point was that as a woman alone on the road I'm not safe. I am vulnerable and must be more aware of that fact…even when I'm not doing anything intentional to cause it.

John's recommendations: Don't twinkle and sparkle with enthusiasm, like I always do when I meet people, (especially referring to men), without being aware of the possible dangers. Don't always look directly into people's eyes with a warm and welcoming smile like I always do; but instead...maintain some distance and perhaps even foster a perception of aloofness, (again, especially with men), knowing that my directness could possibly be misinterpreted.

He suggested tat I tie up and play down my shiny, long, blonde hair because it attracts attention. Cover my legs and arms - not just when I'm driving (like the lesson I learned from the tow-truck driver) but when I'm riding my bike, or shopping... or whenever I'm among strangers, because, and I'm quoting John here, "my muscle tone, long legs and smooth skin texture is noticeably attractive and showing too much skin can incite lust in some men.

So, the bottom line is... I need to present myself in the light of how "other" people *might* perceive me, rather than as what I really am. Not good news – and a lot to think (and pray) about.

After that conversation, I went back to my RV last night feeling sad and a bit out of sorts because I've NEVER been one to advertise any feminine charms I might have. I don't wear low cut blouses or adorn myself with eye-catching jewelry. My shorts are just above the knee most of the time and I wear very little make-up. I thought that was enough... but could I have been wrong?

And if I decide that John and Mary are simply being protective and over-reacting because they've seen the appreciative stares I get from some men when we go places together – why did I happen to have that vivid and disturbing dream just the night before they brought up the subject. I remember feeling so confused in my dream because I was sure I hadn't done anything wrong... and that it was the wind that was to blame - and yet the other people thought I was somehow responsible. Could they have been right? Does a woman have to be even more careful than I already am to avoid inciting lust in godless men?

And why did I end up in this particular RV Park, parked next to John and Mary in the first place? And why did they come out that first morning, feeling strongly that the Lord wanted them to protect me somehow? I was confused – so I did what I always do and asked my Lord for guidance and studied my miracle Bible.

By the time I went to bed last night, I decided that perhaps John and Mary's concerns were well-founded and I should pay attention. My friends and co-workers have always called me names like "Pollyanna" and "Susie Sunshine" because I always see the best in everyone and think the world is full of joy and good intentions. Of course I've never traveled the back roads of America by myself before, all too often finding myself in situations where I have to depend on the kindness of complete strangers. I don't know if I can change the way I smile at people or the way I look directly into their eyes because that's WHO I am. The fact is, I can honestly say that I've never met a stranger because I truly do feel a familial bond with every single person I meet, and I refuse to give that up. But maybe I could at least play down the long hair and cover my bare arms and legs when I'm in public… so that's what I decided to do.

When I woke up this morning, I was feeling absolutely wonderful… on top of the world, you might say. I have a little extra money right now, so I'll ride my bike to the second hand store and buy some loose fitting pants and long sleeved blouses, which should still be cool enough in this heat. If that's what my Lord wants me to do in order to keep me safe while I carry out His work, then I'll happily comply.

Gee, another day… and another lesson! I have so much yet to learn that I'd better keep my eyes and ears open at all times.

Two more days and I won't have to worry about what anyone else thinks, because I'll be parked somewhere out in the desert where I can be completely alone – with God.

I can't wait!!!!

chapter 41

January 31, 1999

You're not going to believe this, but instead of being alone in the desert, I'm sitting right smack in the middle of a bee-hive of activity... a bee-hive consisting of a half-million RVs gathered in a town of only 500 people; Quartzsite, Arizona.

When John and Mary told me that every year they spend a couple of weeks parked in the desert about 10 miles south of Quartzsite, and asked me if I'd like to come along, I accepted their invitation thinking that this would give me a chance to get familiar with the area, guided by someone who's been there many times before. According to the map I had with me, Quartzsite was just a tiny little town in the middle of nowhere... so I was sure that 10 miles away from it would be the perfect place to find the retreat I was so looking forward to.

I think I first knew that something was amiss when we stopped for gas 25 miles from Quartzsite and had to wait in line for over an HOUR. By the time I made it to the pumps, I had less than one gallon left in my tank, (a fact I know - because it took 29.5 gallons to fill my 30-gallon tank). And to make matters worse, Lucky's engine was red hot from the hour spent waiting in line. I guess what my sons warned me about my recharging system must be true because Lucky starts fine - as long as I drive for awhile between starts, but if I turn the engine off then start it up... turn it off again and then start it up, even my new battery goes dead. That's why I had no choice but to idle the engine the entire time I spent waiting in line... and why I barely made it to the pumps before I ran out of gas. (Thank goodness for my little spray bottle of water that keeps my right leg from burning from the heat of Lucky's HOT engine!)

And where did all these people come from? The line to the gas station pumps was backed up all the way to the freeway exit – and then down onto the freeway. John doesn't have to worry about his big coach overheating, but the minute I saw him pull over into that line, I knew I was in trouble.

But eventually, I made it to the pumps and got the gas I needed, so we headed back onto the freeway toward Quartzsite. It's a one-stoplight town and believe it or not, it took us another hour just to get through that one stop light. I guess Quartzsite becomes a mecca for RV travelers every February, when the little town suddenly grows to over a million people. Gee... just what I was looking for!

But that's ok, I thought. I'll park near John and Mary for a few days and share some of the activities they seem to enjoy so much, after all, it's the least I can do for them, after all they've done for me. And THEN, as soon as I possibly can, I'll leave the RV madhouse and find a place where I can truly be alone. We actually drove 10 miles **past** the little town of Quartzsite in order to find a place in the desert to park, and in every direction, as far as the eye could see, the cactus and rock covered ground was littered with motor homes and trailers. I've never seen such a thing ... and I hope I never get to see it again. It's crazy!

I was following John in his coach, and I was so relieved when he finally pulled off onto a little dirt road and drove out into the desert where we found room for both of us to park, maybe 50 feet away from each other. I'm pretty good at making the best of unpleasant situations, and believe me – this is one of those times. So, on the positive side... I'm sure I'll meet lots of nice people and, who knows, maybe I'm supposed to be here for some reason; maybe there's someone the Lord wants me to talk to.

I spent last night sleeping to the steady hum of RV generators and late arrivals. The dust is two inches thick on the desert floor and it's so light that it's almost like talcum powder that floats in the wind. We just got here today and I can already write my name on almost every surface inside Lucky.

Soon after we arrived, I went to gather firewood from a little ravine that runs through the desert near where we're parked, (probably a place where the rain water runs off during flood times – because there were "flash flood warning" signs all along the bank). It was filled with little bushes and gnarly twisted mesquite trees, and they make great firewood, so we had a lovely campfire tonight, and spent hours greeting dozens of strangers who stopped by to visit.

John is insisting on helping me fix a few things on Lucky before I take off because I've made it clear that I need to get away from civilization for awhile and he wants to make sure that at least some of the vital things are tended to before I go; like my auxiliary battery which is now dead, so I can't use my water pump or my 12-volt lights.

And yes, I enjoyed all the company around the campfire… but I'm still searching for the silence – and I'm determined to find it… soon!

John and Mary are taking me to town tomorrow so we can do some grocery shopping and I can fill my propane cans, which means I should be ready to take off on my own as soon as I can possibly can, without hurting their feelings. They've been so good to me, but "I really need to be alone for awhile!"

chapter 42

February 4, 1999

I thought I'd spend one last night in an RV Park before I headed out into the desert… so right now I'm in Yuma, Arizona. It sure makes me appreciate all the nights I spent parked in rest areas, truck stops, in the desert with John and Mary, or even on a quiet side street in Sun City – because it takes a whole lot of time and effort to get everything all hooked up in an RV Park, (especially for a "green pea" like me). But since I've only done it a few times since I left Gold Beach almost seven months ago, I have no doubt that it will get easier with practice – and today was just one more opportunity to learn.

The RV Park I'm staying at is filled to capacity with "snowbirds", (who are people from other states…and even from Canada, who leave the snow behind and spend winter in the South; a place where the sun shines almost every day, and the temperatures are warm – even in January and February). Because this park is so crowded, there were only a couple of spaces left, and they weren't exactly the cream of the crop. In fact, the spot I pulled into was so far from level that I had no idea how I was going to get my refrigerator to work, but then a kindly neighbor must have seen my predicament, because he walked over and asked me if I had any leveler boards. (So that's what those big pieces of wood in my outside compartment are for; to place beneath my tires and level me out on un-even ground.) I sure wish I'd known that sooner... and sometimes I just can't believe how ignorant I can be.

Hooking up to the sewer seems to be a new adventure at every single RV Park. I don't know why they can't all have the same fittings, but the first time I went to hook up and the end of my sewer hose didn't fit the hole where you're supposed to put it, I was completely stumped. I searched my storage compartment and found all sorts of different ends for my big grey sewer hose, from plain black rubber - to screw-in ones -and even a few that I still haven't figured out how to use...but eventually, (and almost always with the help of a kindly stranger), I figured it out.

And then there's the water... for some reason I can't seem to get the hose on tight enough to keep it from leaking. I'm afraid that if I use pliers or a wrench to tighten it, I might bend the metal end, and then it would be ruined for good. Oh well... what's a little drip, drip, drip.

But frustrating or not, I guess hooking up once in a while is a neces-sary evil - since I **do** have to empty my black and grey water tanks and refill my fresh water tank, which is why I decided to spend the night here in Yuma. I'm trying to be as prepared as I possibly can before I head out into the desert alone... and I also figured it would be a good chance to recharge my batteries, as well as my jump-start battery pac. The drive to Yuma from where I left John and Mary in the desert was long and hot, so on the "pure pleasure" side of things, I was really looking forward to a night with air conditioning and television before I left both the good and the bad of civilization behind me.

I spent three more days in the "over-crowded" desert outside Quartzsite with John and Mary, before I said goodbye and headed for Yuma. Of course I thanked them profusely, hugged them repeatedly, and assured them, (al-though I don't think John was completely convinced), that I would be just fine on my own. As I bid them farewell... by then almost desperate to spend time alone, John insisted that I accept a personal alarm; a gift from him and Mary, which he instructed me to place somewhere near my door.

That way, in case of emergency, all I have to do is pull a little plug and an ear-splitting, high-pitched alarm will sound, which was very thoughtful of them - and I have to admit that since I don't carry a weapon, (unless you count a kitchen knife), it does make me feel a littler safer, although if I find a place to be completely alone, who would hear the alarm?

Of course, we're never *really* alone... as the Lord is always with us - but I'm looking so forward to removing myself from the mayhem of everyday activity and finding a place where I can hear nothing but silence; a place where I can quit worrying about dead batteries, gasoline and propane tanks, where I can park - or whether Lucky will start in the morning.

I literally yearn for unlimited time in which to pray, study my Bible, write new poetry and songs, practice my guitar (at least enough to firm up the calluses on my fingers), and write in my daily journal. With no phone, no television, no neighbors, and no chance of anyone knocking on my door, I can have that time; time alone with God. (Gee, I sound a bit anti-social, don't I?) And yet for some reason; one which I can't possibly hope to understand, the Lord give me the gift of being able to touch people - to get them excited about life and to encourage them to face difficulty and confusion and to make the most of whatever their situation might be. It doesn't matter whether it's one person or a thousand, nor whether it's through the written word or by story telling and entertaining... but the light of the Lord's love for them, (and my own), seems to shine through me - and they feel it! And yes, although it might not sound like it right now, I do enjoy my calling. It's just that I need time to re-charge my "spiritual batteries" - and time to think.

After I checked in and got everything hooked up, it was so warm outside today that I spent a couple of hours at the swimming pool, (hoping to add a little color to my very white skin), and even though I was wearing a conservative one-piece swimming suit - I still felt like a piece of meat at the butcher shop, being eyed and appraised by men I thought were too old to even notice, let alone care. So I guess John and Mary, (whom I love dearly and am SO grateful for everything they've taught me), were right. I need to be a lot more discrete, (which I will), and I need to do everything I can to make sure that any men I meet on the road know that just because I'm alone, it doesn't mean I'm looking for "company"… if you know what I mean.

That's why tomorrow morning when I leave Yuma; I'm planning to stop at the local Wal-Mart - not only for groceries, but to buy some big, bright reflective mailbox letters, which I'll then use to place an easy-to-read message on Lucky's back bumper. It will say "WALK WITH JESUS."

Isn't that a great idea? From now on, when I'm driving down the road, every car that passes me will be reminded to think of Jesus - even if only for that one brief moment. And when I stop, whether it be at an RV Park, rest area, truck stop, Wal-Mart parking lot or neighborhood side street, any "hopeful" males will know exactly what kind of woman is inside this RV; a Christian lady. Those three words will serve as my shield; protecting me as I travel - and reminding others to "walk with Jesus".

When I was staying at the RV Park in Blythe with John and Mary, they took me on a four- hour day-trip through the dessert on unpaved back roads - all the way from Blythe to Yuma. As we drove the dusty dirt road, we ran alongside a water-filled canal and John told me that the canal eventually led to a big lake, which was created by a dam called "Imperial Dam". He also said it's where the flash-flood run-off water is stored, (like a big reservoir), and a great place to fish for bass. I thought… hmmm; now if I could just start out at Yuma, (which is where we ended up on our day trip), I could find the same canal from the opposite end… and then follow it back to the lake. There must be places to camp along the shore, and I miss the water so much! It may not be the ocean, with crashing waves and salt-water in the air, but at least it will be water - and I love it.

Tomorrow morning on my way out of town, I'll fill both gas tanks, and add the bottle of gasoline additive John gave me that he said would get rid of any water in my tank. That way I'll have all 60 gallons of gas available for use again, because 30 gallons at 5 mpg doesn't get me very far;

especially with a broken gas gauge and me nervously trying to calculate how much fuel I have left based on the mileage I THINK I'm getting at the time. Then I'll fill my two propane tanks, buy groceries, and find the biggest reflective mailbox letters I can find for my bumper message. And then… it's goodbye Yuma, and cars, and noise, and people - and off on a whole new adventure… as I search for the dirt road that will lead me to the canal - and eventually to the lake. I just wish I'd been paying more attention to the route John took, but when you're sitting in the back seat (and visiting most of the way), it's easy to miss what could turn out to be a very important turn… and who knows where I could end up if I do.

But then, who CARES where I end up? I'll have gas, food, propane and shelter… so even if I get lost, everything will be fine. I know, because my Lord told me it would, and I trust Him completely. I still can't figure out how I could possibly be worthy of such favor, but I also know that "to whom much is given – much is expected". That's why I'm going to spend the rest of my life making sure that someday… when I stand before my Heavenly Father in judgment, I'll hear the words that will be pure music to my ears; when He says, "Well done, my daughter. Well done!" Those are the words I live for… and I would do, say, sacrifice or suffer absolutely anything just to hear those wonderful words of approval from my Father God.

Well, I guess I'd better hit the sack - because I need to get an early start in the morning. And since it takes me almost as much time to unhook everything as it does to hook it all up, I mean a REALLY early start. Lucky's engine is still overheating… so I try to do as much driving as I can in the cool morning hours - but with stops at both the gas station and Wal-Mart before I leave town, who knows what time it will be when I find *whatever* (or should I say "**where**-ever") it is I am searching for. I have a feeling tomorrow could be a very long day… but I'm not worried. *"Everything will be fine!"*

chapter 43

February 5, 1999

As I drove east out of Yuma this morning, the land was flat, brown and covered with nothing but cactus and prickly brown bushes... when suddenly, much to my surprise, it suddenly turned into acre upon acre of beautiful, lush green farm land, as far as the eye could see. There were dozens of workmen in the fields and the smell of both manure and mud was filling my nostrils. Ah ha, I thought; this must be where the canal runs, because they probably use it for irrigation. How else could they maintain so much beautiful farmland in such a dry desert?

That's why at the first well-used dirt road I saw, I headed north, (in the direction of Blythe), hoping that I was on my way to Imperial Dam. But it wasn't long before I began to worry - when the lush, green fields disappeared, and the canal I had been following dried up and became nothing but a big, empty ditch; ready and waiting for the next flash flood. By then, I had no idea how many miles I'd driven, but at least I was pretty sure I was headed in the right direction, (north) or I **was...** until the dirt road suddenly came to a T, and I had no choice but to go left or right, east or west. Unfortunately, there were no signs to guide me - just brown, dry desert, so I decided to turn right, (although I have absolutely no idea why).

A few miles later, the once dry, dusty (but fairly smooth) dirt road turned into a wicked washboard; with unevenly spaced bumps - so large they reminded me of the dreaded speed bumps in my mother's trailer park. But these were never-ending... mile after mile of bump after bump. Being an avid downhill snow skier, I'm pretty familiar with "washboard" roads, but I've never encountered them anywhere but in the snow before, and these bumps were much worse than those I was used to. No matter how slow I went, Lucky lurched back and forth and the cupboard doors began to fly open with the contents falling out onto the floor. Even at 5 miles an hour, the bumps were spaced so unevenly that the front tires and the rear tires hit them at different times, which meant I wasn't just going up and down, but rolling to the right and left as well.

This can't go on forever, I thought... just be patient and eventually it will smooth out – and so I pressed on, and on, and on. By the time I'd finished my shopping and filled my gas tanks in Yuma this morning, the day was already well on its way to becoming a hot one, and as the heat from Lucky's engine began to burn my leg, I reached for my little spray bottle and used it to keep my right leg wet. I was still optimistic... sure that just around the next corner I'd find the lake I was searching for - but to tell the truth, by then I'd have settled for a flat, safe place to park... water or no water.

But there was no such place... because the deep, empty canal was on one side and a steep incline, leading down into a dry, rocky ravine was on the other, which meant that the road itself, (with absolutely no shoulder) was the only place I could possibly stop. Nothing changed for several hours, as I guessed my way through too many unmarked turns to keep track of, and I just hoped that I'd be able to remember which way to go if I had to give up and try to find my way back to Yuma.

I hate to admit it, but I seriously doubted that I'd be able to remember all the turns I had taken, because they all looked the same... and there were so many of them. Eventually I had no choice but to admit to myself that I was lost – lost in the desert... and not only was Lucky's engine beginning to glow red from the heat, but now the air inside the RV was filed with the overpowering smell of gasoline. Great – just what I needed. I'd been driving for at least five or six hours, (which isn't far when you're only going 5 to 10 miles an hour), and I still hadn't found a single place to pull over – or anything even closely resembling a dam or a lake.

Luckily, I had filled both gas tanks when I left Yuma that morning, so I decided to switch over to the other tank, just in case I'd used more gas than I thought, and it seemed to be working fine. Now I needed to find a place to stop before the engine got so hot it ignited the fumes that were so thick in the air that it was giving me a headache. That's when I began to feel the first sharp pangs of *fear*... as I slowly made my way further and further out into the dry, inhospitable desert, with no place to turn around, an overheated engine and gasoline fumes getting stronger by the minute. I knew I was in trouble... but I had no idea what to do about it. "Well, Abigayle, you wanted to be alone..." I laughed at myself, more in nervousness than in humor. "So how do you like it so far?"

And to make matters even worse, now it was beginning to get dark... and although had everything I needed to survive, what I DIDN'T have was a safe place to stop, except the middle of the road. There MUST be something coming up soon, I told myself again and again. Every road leads somewhere... right? But still, there was nothing but dry brown desert, an empty canal and a steep rock and brush filled ravine. That's when I decided I had no choice but to risk letting the engine idle for a few minutes, (which always makes it get even hotter); while I did something I **knew** was my only hope. I put Lucky into "park", got out of the driver's seat... and kneeled in prayer.

"Dear Lord... I'm afraid I've really gotten myself into a pickle this time, and I need your help! I know you're always in control - but you gave me free-agency... and I really blew it! I made some very bad decisions today... and now I'm lost and afraid - and I don't know what to do? Should I turn around and try to find my way back to Yuma - or should I keep going? And that's when I began to cry, something I seldom do - unless it's tears of joy or empathy. *"I'm sorry*

I was so stupid. I never should have come out here alone without more informa-tion, and I probably should have turned around a long time ago. It's my own fault, so I hate to even ask you to get me out of a mess I got myself into because of my own stupidity... but please, Lord - help your ignorant daughter find a safe place to spend the night. I don't even care about the lake anymore... I'm just afraid - and I don't know what to do. I need a place to stop before Lucky bursts into flames, which I have a feeling could happen any minute - and I need your guidance. Please, Lord, take control of this vehicle. Please lead me to a place of safety. I'm on my knees Lord, humbly... begging you for your help and your protection - which I do in the name of your beloved Son - our Savior, Jesus Christ."

As I stood up and got back into the driver's seat, I suddenly felt better... as though I'd called for reinforcements and I just knew that they were on the way. I quickly made the decision to drive for five more minutes, (since the sky was already turning red and orange as the day was quickly fading into night), and if by that time, I hadn't found a place to pull over, I'd somehow figure out a way to turn around, (if I could find a spot in the road wide enough) and then do my best to retrace my steps back to Yuma. I was SO HOPING it wouldn't come to that... not only because I wanted to spend time alone in the wilderness, (hopefully by the lake), but because I was almost SURE that I'd never remember how to get back to Yuma; not with all those forks in the road, and especially not in the dark. Just five more minutes; five minutes in which to hope, and pray....

And **praise God**... because it couldn't have been more than three minutes later when I rounded a corner and there was the most gorgeous sight I've ever seen! IT WAS the LAKE I'd been looking for - and it was bathed in the red and orange glow of a perfect sunset, surrounded by trees and breathtakingly beautiful! The lake was off to my right, and the incline to get down to the water was steep and rocky, but there - right next to the shore was a huge flat gravel area that would be perfect for parking, and there wasn't another vehicle or camper in sight. I can't honestly re-member EVER being more relieved, (or praising God more loudly), as I yelled, "Hallelujah! I made it! Thank you, God! Thank you, Jesus!" I shouted again and again. I still couldn't believe my eyes... not only had I found the lake I'd been searching for, (as well as the perfect parking area), but the sunset was absolutely magnificent as I pulled onto a flat little rise in the open gravel covered area so I could have the best possible view of the lake; and then gratefully... and tearfully... still praising God - I turned off that red hot, stinking engine and jumped out of the acrid smell of gasoline and into the fresh desert air.

Those first few moments of surprise, relief and gratitude will be imprinted on my heart forever... and the first thing I noticed was that it was almost eerily silent; which was just what I was looking for! And yes, I was crying again, but this time it was tears of pure joy! I could have praised God all night long and it wouldn't have been enough! After all those hours of bouncing, smelling gasoline, keeping my leg wet so it didn't burn from the heat of the engine and gripping the steering wheel like it was my lifeline -I was actually here... and it was as though the brilliant colors of the sky were welcoming me to my new home. Naturally I grabbed my camera and hurried to take pictures as the fiery red globe slowly disappeared behind the hills that surrounded the lake; the lake I now called **home**.

Whew! That was a close call, I thought - as I hurried to use what little light there was left to gather enough big rocks to build a campfire circle, and then hurried even faster to gather brush and mesquite branches so I could build and maintain the fire on my first night in *paradise*. And then, just to show you that I DID take John's advice seriously, I then put out **two** lawn chairs next to my RV, (one that I already had - and one that John and Mary insisted I take with me). "That way," as John explained, "it will look like there are two people in the RV, rather than just one." See... I'm learning.

What a day! What an adventure - and what a wonderful answer to my prayer. I believe I have truly found the Garden of Eden in the desert! Thank you, Jesus! Thank you so much!

chapter 44

February 8, 1999

At least I had an amazing two full days of solitude… with nothing but the sound of the ducks and the wind rustling the branches of the trees that line the lake shore before two other RV's discovered my beautiful spot. And even though I was a little disappointed at first, (shame on me), I thought about it and realized that I was being selfish. After all, there's plenty of room for everyone, and the Lord certainly didn't make this beautiful place just for me. But I'm so grateful that I had those two days alone; so alone that I could pretend I was the only person on Earth.

Of course I've already met my two new neighbors, one of which is an elderly retired couple while the other is the complete opposite… an older trailer filled to capacity with children and dogs. (So much for the silence!)

But surprisingly enough, I'm actually enjoying the sound of the children laughing and playing in the water, and I'm happily reminded of my pre-flood life as they throw sticks into the water for the dogs to fetch, who bark happily as they proudly drop their stick at the feet of whoever threw it - and then shake the water from their fur, as the people squeal in protest as they get doggie-water wet. They're all having such a great time that I can't help but get caught up in their joy just as much as if it were my own… because it is.

The night before my new neighbors arrived, I decided **not** to make a fire so I could have a perfect view of the stars… and it was amazing! I'm quite a ways from Yuma, so there were no city lights to block their brightness, and there were so many stars in the clear black sky that you couldn't separate one from another; all different shades of white and blue – some twinkling and blinking while others were bright and stationary. .It reminded me of how little we humans are… and how our earthly minds can't even begin to comprehend the vastness of "infinity".

And here I am; just one little grain of sand on all the beaches and deserts of the entire planet, and still my Father in Heaven always has time to listen to me, and guide me, and love me. And like those grains of sand, no one single grain is any more important than any other, and no two of them are alike. It gives me a chill just to think how magnificent Father God must be – and that He loves and watches over every single one of us.

Tonight I think I'll build a nice campfire and just stare into the flames as I let my fingers play whatever they want to on my guitar. Who knows, maybe I'll compose a new song. Although I do enjoy playing my guitar, my true instrument of choice is the piano… and what I wouldn't give to have one sitting right here next to the lake. Second to the piano, would be the violin… and then the guitar. I've always loved music, but the only music lesson I've ever had was for three months while I attended the third grade in West Linn, Oregon. I loved it… and I practiced until my father and brother begged for me to stop.

But it's always been the piano that was my true passion. None of the homes I lived in during my childhood had a piano, (except for my grand-parents… which is where my passion first took bloom). I only spent a few months living with them before I had to move again, (where unfor-tunately there was no piano), so I cut out little pieces of black and white paper and taped them to the kitchen table… just like piano keys. Then I'd scrounge for returnable pop bottles or do any odd jobs I could find and spend the money on music books. I can remember sitting at that (and other) kitchen tables for hours on end, studying my lesson books

and playing soundless notes on the pieces of black and white paper...
which was good enough for me. Believe it or not, I actually got through
lesson book four using a table rather than a piano, but then it became too
difficult - and I put my learning aside until I finally got my own piano
when I was 26 years old.

That was in 1977 and I lived in a little cabin on the top of Parrot
Mountain with my two little boys, ages 4 and 5. I had just retired from
playing foosball, so I went back to work as a legal secretary at the Legal
Aid Clinic for Clackamas County, a place where the poor could find legal
representation. I was making $700 a month, but with two small children,
day care and rent to pay, it took me awhile to save money for a piano, but
eventually, I had $300. I knew that wasn't enough for a decent piano, but
I also knew that there were many people out there like me; people who
thought of instruments as more than just objects - and wanted theirs to
be loved and appreciated... so much so that they would be willing to sell
it for less than it was worth to the right "home".

So I put an ad in the local newspaper that said, *"At last – I have $300
for a piano. If you have a piano in need of loving care and attention, please call
me at #......."* And boy-oh-boy did that ad ever work. A lady called me
whose husband had taught music at one of the local colleges before he
died and they had a beautiful upright grand she had vowed never to sell.
But now she was getting too old to take care of such a big house and was
moving to a condo at the beach and had no choice but to find a home for
her husband's beloved piano. She asked if I would like to come over and
talk to her about it... but I think she really wanted to size me up... you
know; see if I was the "right person" for such a precious possession.

"Oh yes," I answered eagerly. "I'll be right over, if that's ok?" And it
was... and I went...and an hour later, she said the piano was mine – for
FREE. She wouldn't even accept my $300 once she saw how lovingly
my fingers caressed the keys and the pure admiration and passion in my
eyes. What a blessing that lady was – and what a beautiful piano! Within
a week, I'd written my first classical song and it never stopped from that

moment forward. I liked to wear a blindfold when I played - so my eyes wouldn't get in the way of the music pouring forth from my soul - and I loved it!

I had that piano right up until the flood, and even though with the help of neighbors, we got the piano out before it was ruined - it, (like my horses) was something I had to sell to avoid bankruptcy. But this isn't a sad story... because I can still play the piano just like I did when I was a little girl... at my kitchen table. And until I can afford a keyboard, or maybe even someday have a house again - with a real piano, I still have my guitar... and for now, that is enough.

These past three days have given me a lot of time to write, so I've been taking full advantage of it. Although I've written a couple of new poems, most of my time has been spent writing in the journal I keep everyday and studying my Bible. It was so silent last night when I went inside after gazing at the stars and playing my guitar... that as I wrote in my journal I could only hear two things; one, the beating of my own heart... and two, the sound of my pen as it raced across the paper - trying to keep up with my rapid-fire thoughts. Now that's what I call quiet... and I'm so grateful that I had at least two days to enjoy it.

And you're not going to believe this. My new neighbor, the elderly gentleman and his wife, told me that if I had come to this parking area from the *opposite* direction, I was only a few miles from a cement road and then another 10 miles to the main highway into Yuma, (which is only 35 miles away). What a laugh – and the joke's on me! I took the back roads, winding through turn after turn on a washboard dirt road through the desert for almost 70 miles, and ended up somewhere I could have gotten to easily, (and only 15 miles off the highway). Oh well, at least I know which way to go when I get ready to leave, which I'm assuming will be sometime next week. They tell me the Ranger comes around once a week to collect $20 from each camper, so depending upon when he comes, I can only stay one week from that day. It's still a bargain, and I'm being very careful not to fill up my holding tanks and to conserve my fresh water.

And one more thing… when I was looking at the stars last night, I stood on a little knoll gazing off into the distance across the lake, and on the far side I saw an area that was nothing but twinkling lights. I pulled out my binoculars and there must have been hundreds of them, but they were too far away for me to tell what they were, and (fortunately) too far away for me to hear any sound coming from them.

So this morning I asked my neighbors what they were, and they said that it's a BLM campground, complete with dump station and fresh water. He and his wife don't like to camp there because the way he described it, it sounds much like the crowed desert outside Quartzsite, with RV's parked anywhere they can possibly fit, generators running constantly and never a quiet moment. I'm so glad that I ended up here – on the far side of the lake… even if it was a nightmare getting here. I guess this planet is getting more and more crowded all the time, and it's getting harder and harder to get away from civilization.

Well, time to build that campfire now, and maybe I'll even search my cupboards for some marshmallows to roast. What a wonderful day this has been!

chapter 45

February 9, 1999

THE NEXT DAY

It looks like I'm going to have a **lot** more time parked here by the lake than I had expected; in fact, I'm lucky I'm not lying in a hospital bed right now in Yuma - or in some Burn-Center in Phoenix because last night, tragedy struck! Well, I guess it wasn't really a tragedy because I'm alive to tell the story - and I still believe there's always a silver lining in every cloud, but I'm just not sure what it is yet. I trust God completely though, and I know that He always has my best interests at heart, so I'll figure it out!

Here's what happened:

Last night I was standing next to my campfire visiting with the elderly couple who had become my neighbors, when I decided to burn my little plastic grocery bag of garbage. I have two separate garbage containers in my RV; one for non-burnable items, like cans, and used-up batteries, and the other for paper plates, paper towels and paper cups. I've been using paper as much as possible so waste my limited fresh water by washing dishes, so I'm absolutely positive there was nothing in that little sack but paper.

The bag wasn't quite full, so I used the two handles to tie a knot, which left two little rabbit-ears of plastic on top as I tossed the bag onto the campfire. From that moment on, everything seemed to happen in slow motion, and I can remember every sight, sound, smell and feeling – just as clear as though it were happening right now.

The three of us stood there staring into the fire and watching with amusement as the little plastic sack seemed to grow in size as the heated air filled the sealed bag like a balloon. Then the fire grew brighter and brighter, especially inside the bag and it began to glow intensely just before it started to melt. Suddenly, there was this LOUD explosion, even louder than the sound Lucky made when the fan blade had struck the loosened bolt on my way to Portland. I've never heard a propane tank explode, but if I were to guess what it sounds like, THAT was how loud the explosion was, and I watched… again in slow motion… as the bag literally blew out of the fire and headed directly for me – as if it were a flaming bullet and I were the target. Then bulls-eye; it landed on my face! I could see it coming, but even in slow motion, I didn't have time to move… just enough to think, "This can't really be happening!"

But it did… and once again, in slow motion, I thought, "Oh my gosh, I'm on fire!" The bag had landed directly on my face and the front part of my head – and I could see the burning plastic as it melted and then suddenly my bangs were on fire and I could see the flames, bright yellow, just above my eyes. The funny thing was, I didn't feel any pain, or panic… just slow rational thought, as I said to myself, "Gee, Abigayle, any child knows enough to stop, drop and roll when you catch on fire," which is exactly what I did. The problem was that the ground was made up of nothing but gravel and rock solid dirt, but I fell to it anyway and laid facedown in the dirt, clawing at the hard surface… trying to pile something – anything on my head to put out the flames.

The elderly couple who were standing on the opposite side of the fire, were in total shock, so by the time they made their way over to me, I pretty much had the fire out. When I realized that my hair was no longer blazing and that the remains of the melting/burning plastic bag was now lying on the desert floor next to me, I opened my eyes and saw the elderly couple standing over me – with sheer panic on their faces and I also noticed that I was at least 15 feet from the fire pit. "How did I get over here?" I wondered out loud - without realizing I was speaking.

"You just blew over here like you'd been shot out of a cannon!" the man answered as he reached down to help me to my feet. "I've never seen anything like it. You just flew backwards. I've got a cell phone in my rig so I'll go call an ambulance," he said when he saw my badly burned face and hair.

"No," I argued, "That won't be necessary. I'll be fine. I don't have any medical insurance, so let me just go inside and stick my head in the water. Don't worry, I'll be fine," I insisted as I ran up the steps and into Lucky before he could mount another protest.

When I got inside, I turned on the kitchen faucet and let the water pour over my face and head, and I can still remember the horrible stench of burning skin, hair and plastic as I realized how close I had just come to a life-changing disaster. "I wonder what happened," I asked myself as I continued to let the cool water run over my face. I could still see that white ball of fire coming directly toward me, like it was fired from a gun, and it just didn't seem possible.

That's when I decided to go to the bathroom sink and survey the damage in the mirror, and even though it was bad... it could have been much worse. My face was bright red and bleeding in a few places, (as well as my neck), but because my hair had been drawn back in a ponytail, only the front half had been burned off. I no longer had bangs or hair in front of my ears, or eyebrows or eyelashes. Instead I had a fiery (no pun intended) red and already swollen face; somewhat bloody - but scabbing up quickly, as though the blood had been cauterized by the heat of the fire, and now... instead of hair on the front half of my head, I had quarter-inch long frizzled curly-cues... like hair that had melted and rolled into little balls. "Oh my dear Lord," I thought. "No one is going to believe this!"

So I grabbed my camera before I went back outside to reassure my neighbors that I didn't need to go to a hospital, and I asked them to take some pictures of my face. I'm sure they must have thought that I was crazy to think about taking pictures at a time like this, but when I explained that someday I was going to write a book about my journey and would need pictures to go along with the story, they relented and snapped a few... continually insisting that I still should to go to a hospital.

And that's when we heard the sirens. Like I said earlier, by using the highway, Yuma is only 35 miles away, so apparently the LOUD explosion had been heard by the RV's on the other side of the lake and someone had called the fire department. "Great," I thought to myself. "Now they're going to try to talk me into going to the hospital, too."

When the firemen arrived, accompanied by a rescue/ambulance vehicle, I was holding an ice filled towel (courtesy of my neighbors) over my face and head, and the fully uniformed firemen ran from their truck toward me, asking, "What blew up? Where was the explosion?"

I didn't know how to answer that, because *nothing* blew up... and I had no idea what the huge blast was, and neither did my two witnesses. When I told the firemen about the garbage sack, they looked at each other like they didn't believe me. No paper bag could have done such a thing – so surely I must have mistakenly put something in that bag that was explosive. I couldn't blame them for doubting me – and even though I was absolutely positive that the bag had contained nothing but paper, I watched as they spent almost an hour sifting through the remains of the campfire, as well as the surrounding area, looking for evidence of some kind of accelerant or explosive.

Eventually, they gave up and admitted that everything they found in the residue indicated that there hadn't been anything but paper and wood in the fire. Even the professionals shook their heads in disbelief... because it as much of a mystery to them as it was to me. By that time, my face was really beginning to swell up and the pain became intense as the initial shock wore off, and I must have let it show because one of the EMT's asked, "Are you sure you don't want us to take you to the hospital? You really should have a doctor take a look at your face because infection could be a problem, and it looks like you've got some third-degree burns."

They were so kind, but there was no way I could afford to be treated at a hospital and my first aid kit had some burn cream in it, so I figured I'd just tough out the pain, keep the burned area clean, and see how it went over the next few days. If it got infected, I'd have no choice but to go to a hospital… but if not, well, I guess I wouldn't be putting on any shows until my face healed. The EMT's gave me a big white container of burn cream and told me to keep it on my face until the redness and swelling went away, which I gratefully accepted and then thanked them for their help.

So, how's that for an adventure? There's just never a dull moment is there! As silly as it sounds, I almost feel like that bag was *aiming* for me… like it was **trying** to hurt me. I know that it doesn't make any sense, but I couldn't shake the feeling that I'd been the target… and it was a direct hit.

Well, my face may be down, but I'M NOT OUT! I'll just use the extra time I need to heal to study my Bible, (praising God for saving me from what could have been much worse), writing more songs and poetry for my shows, practicing my guitar, and enjoying my time at the lake.

This morning when I got up, I looked in the mirror, and it looks much worse than it did last night; because now my face is all swollen out of shape. It was so bad that I could barely recognize myself in the mirror, as I shaved the fuzzy burned hair off and applied more burn ointment. I also noticed for the first time that both my hands had been burned, probably from when I was trying to put the fire out with rocks and dirt clods. Well Lord, if this was a lesson in vanity… point well taken. I don't think I'll have to worry about any men hustling me for awhile! (See? A silver lining…)

The one thing I didn't expect is how shiny my face is, except the part that has scabs. I know our skin is covered with peach fuzz, some people more than others, but until it gets burned off, you don't realize how shiny you would be without it. And my eyes!!! With no eyelashes or eyebrows, they look like round circles in the middle of a very misshapen face, kind of like ET in the movie. (In other words, I look just LOVELY!)

Oh well… I know that no matter what happens, there's always some good that can come out of it. I just hope I heal fast! And maybe the Ranger will take pity on me when he comes by and sees what happened, and he won't charge me $20 a week since I obviously can't see well enough to drive right now and have no choice but to stay here until I get better. (Now see - there's another silver lining!)

But OUCH!!! My face hurts! It's a good thing I was sick for 20 years, because that's how I was forced to learn to separate my body from my spirit; the only way I could possibly have endured 20 years of intense pain. The first 10 years I had Lyme Disease, (an especially virulent and rare strain I picked up on one of my wilderness camping trips), but since it was in the early 1970's, the doctors had never heard of Lyme Disease - so it not only went undiagnosed, but MIS-diagnosed. For many years, I was in the hospital several times a year, (sometimes for two or three weeks at a time), and dozens of doctors thought it was everything from Rocky Mountain Spotted Fever to San Joaquin Valley Virus, (among other things). All I know is that it was like having a bad case of the flu for 10 years, and that every joint in my body was in constant pain, not to mention the rash, sores and boils that eventually covered my entire body.

But no matter how sick I was, there was no way I could raise two small children alone, train and show horses, ski or play foosball for a living if I didn't learn to control the pain… so out of complete necessity, I learned to separate my body from my spirit. Other than a few times when the fever got so high I became delirious and wandered out into the street in my pajamas (once in the middle of the night) and was rushed to the hospital by ambulance, almost no one knew I was even sick, because with the help of God, I learned to find joy amidst the pain, and the worst part of the whole ordeal was NOT KNOWING what was wrong… as doctor after doctor poked, prodded and tested until he gave up and sent me to someone else.

If it hadn't been for the fever and swelling of my joints, I think they would have thought it was psychosomatic, because all the other symptoms **could** have been caused by extreme stress. And yes, even though I was always happy, (little Miss Susie Sunshine), I did have two babies, (18 months apart), and had just ended my marriage to the only man I had ever kissed, when I was 21, (after being abducted and raped by a complete stranger who grabbed me in the parking lot after work). And then I went through two trials, (the first one being called a mis-trial).

And then, after being warned NOT to have another baby when I was only 20 years old and my first son Scott was born, because the doctors discovered two grapefruit sized tumors in my uterine wall during his cesarean birth. They told me that another pregnancy could kill me when the baby grew large enough to puncture the growths, (or whatever they were... since back then we didn't have ultra-sound or any of the modern diagnostic tools we have today). They wanted to do a hysterectomy right then, but I refused, insisting that I was going to have more children, danger or no danger.

And then, of course, there was the fact that my ex-husband convinced me to spend his birthday with him, even though we were separated and getting a divorce... and then slipped something I think they call a "mickey" into my drink, carrying me home unconscious and raping me, (if you can call it that – when the victim has no memory of the event whatsoever – and the rapist happens to be the only man you've ever even kissed, let alone slept with)... or the shock that followed two months later when the pain in my abdomen became so severe that my parents rushed me to the hospital and I discovered that I was pregnant – even though I hadn't had sex with ANYONE... which meant it had to be a virgin-birth, because there was no way I could possibly be pregnant, (or at least so I thought until I told my ex-husband – and he admitted what he had done... apologizing and saying that he was hoping a second child would convince me to give him another chance.

Of course the doctors wanted me to have an immediate abortion (and hysterectomy), which I still stubbornly refused... somehow knowing that I was meant to have this second child. And yes – it was stressful when

Jeremy, (my youngest and last son), was born almost two months early because the doctors were afraid he was already big enough to burst the tumors and I wouldn't have time to make it to the operating room before I bled to death.

And then there was the hysterectomy I finally let them perform - when Jeremy was only 6 weeks old because the pain had become intolerably severe, and even though I knew in my heart of hearts that my inability to have children would mean that I would NEVER find my soul-mate - and would most likely live the rest of my life without a husband; a fact which I mourned for several years, because I wanted at least 8 children, and the kind of man I wanted was one who loved kids and would coach their teams, be a scout leader and be active in every aspect of their lives. But I also know that **that** kind of man would also want children of his own… something that at age 22, I could no longer give him. Yes, it was devastating. And yes, I was under stress, to put it mildly! But the one thing the doctors ALL agreed on was that stress doesn't cause raging fevers… which was the only thing that convinced them that I was definitely in-fected with something… but they still had no idea what it was.

But even through all those tribulations, I lived my life to the fullest. That's when I got my first foosball table, and that's when my boys, (even as babies) and I spent as much time as we possibly could camping and hiking in the wilderness. That's when I learned to ski and got back to raising and training horses. We sole purebred puppies and even Siamese Cats. We raised our own chickens, and I put up jams and preserves and we always had a huge garden. Once both kids were in school, I even went back to work as a legal secretary… and at age 26, got my first piano. I taught Sunday School, and was room mother, PTA member, and what we now refer to as a true "soccer mom"… and no one knew how sick I was, except for my immediate family and a few close friends; at least not for the first ten years.

Because once again, (as always), there was strength and good that came out of the suffering. I even wrote a song about how "every teardrop is a blessing". I not only learned to separate myself from the pain, but I learned to think of my body as a vessel... a gift from my Lord in which to house my spirit, and mine just happened to have a few problems.

But during the 1980's, after ten years of undiagnosed pain, fever, vomiting and all the other flu-like symptoms, the medical community finally discovered Lyme disease... so of course I was rushed in for testing. All the symptoms I'd had for so long fit the disease perfectly - and the doctors were sure that they had finally found the culprit.

Imagine their surprise, (as well as my own), when all the tests came back negative, even though they repeated them several times because they were so sure that Lyme disease had to be the answer. But no... my blood had absolutely no Lyme disease in it, and now - my symptoms were beginning to change.

In the early 1980's, I was hospitalized with Spinal Meningitis for the first time. After a few weeks in the hospital, (and more antibiotics than I thought possible), they sent me home, but within a few weeks I was back again, and then again, and again. Now they were calling it "Chronic Meningitis", and – just like before, the doctors had no idea what was causing it... or how to stop it.

And another ten years went by... and even though I didn't let it stop me from making the most of my life, the headaches became so intense and so unbearable that it was like an ice cream brain-freeze that never went away. I actually thought I was going crazy and I couldn't sleep or even think clearly.

One time I was so out of my mind that I tried to kill myself, even though I knew the religious repercussions. I put a hose in the tailpipe of my car, duct taped all around it and then ran the hose into the window of the little Chevrolet Station wagon I had at the time. Why? Because I couldn't even imagine facing one more day with pain so severe that I'd have rather bashed my head in with a hammer than suffer one more minute.

At that point, separating my body from the pain was no longer possible - as my brain had become infected with the Lyme disease, (although the doctors didn't realize that until years later) and I could no longer control my actions... at least not for short periods of time. I can remember going weeks with no sleep - to the point of hallucinating and going to bed in my own cabin on Mt. Hood, and waking up out in the horse pasture or face down in my flower beds with the hose on, as though I'd been watering my flowers in the middle of the night - with absolutely no memory of how I got there.

Now I was becoming frightened... afraid to live another day and afraid of what I might do when I "wasn't myself". Thank goodness my children were grown by the time it got that bad, because I really **did** think I was losing my mind... especially since the doctors couldn't find anything wrong - even after a dozen spinal taps and testing for every infections disease they could think of. My father and step-mother, Roma, even talked me into going to see a psychiatrist, who pronounced me completely "sane", (in fact, he said "maybe I should be the one talking to you."), and he said my illness was physically – not psychological... so it was back to the doctors again.

That's why I decided to start the project in Gold Beach in 1990. I could no longer punch a time clock, because one day I could manage to fool everyone - and the next, I huddled in my bedroom, afraid to come out because I was sure that some evil spirit was trying to get me. The only thing I could do to earn a living was to start my own company; one that I could be in control of - and use every coherent hour, (which was **most** of them, by the way), to find the land, incorporate, sell shares, and build the project. My workers may have nicknamed me "big cheese" on the job, but I felt more like Swiss cheese, with holes in my head!

The only respite I found, now that my kids were grown and no longer living at home, was when I was planning to kill myself. I'd get up every morning, (if I went to bed at all that night), and sit down with a notebook and make lists of all the possible ways I could do it. I drew columns, one for the "method"; one for the "percentage of success", one for the "pain involved", and one for the "mark it would leave on whoever found my body".When I was making those plans, it was the only time I felt relief... and I still have those notebooks, just in case I ever take being healthy for granted and need to remember how much worse it could be. My grand-father, (who I worshiped before he died when I was a teenager), always used to say, "I cried because I had no shoes – until I met a man who had no FEET." I live by that saying, and I still had two arms, two legs, a family who loved me, and I had God... and a Savior who died so I could have eternal life. Pain or no pain... I was blessed.

I kept journals my entire life, but the ones from those most difficult of years were not written for my great-great grandchildren, (like the others); they were written to "let out the pain" and to make sure I never forget what it felt like to lose all hope.

And speaking of how I felt... the day I put that hose in my tailpipe and ran it through the window of my car, I had driven my little station wagon into the shop, (a large building with a loft and workshop - as well as parking spaces), and the door was one of those big, old heavy, sliding doors that roll on metal runners when you pull it open or closed. I'll never forget how relieved I was as I started the engine and climbed into the back of my station wagon to lie down, with my journal in one hand and a pen in the other. I wanted to let my family know that it wasn't their fault - and that "death" would truly be a blessing, so please... celebrate for me, and don't cry.

And so I wrote, and wrote... and gradually the words got bigger and bigger on the page. (I still have that book too, by the way.) At the very end, on the last few pages before I passed out, there were only three or four huge and sloppily scrawled words on each page of my spiral note-book... and I had stopped making any sense whatsoever.

The next thing I knew, after having written my goodbyes in my journal and trying to explain to God why I couldn't go on living another day in such pain... day after day - year after year - and begging Him to please forgive me, when suddenly I woke up. And I wasn't in the car any more. I could tell with-out even opening my eyes... because it was cold and hard, and the car had been warm and soft. And THAT was the first time I actually heard "words" from my Lord; not the Holy Spirit messages that come from deep within your heart, but actual verbal words, just like my visitation after the flood… and it was those six words that brought me back to reality.

It was those six words, (heard not with my ears but coming from everywhere, both inside and out), that literally saved my life and my soul. And those six words were spoken by the same wonderful voice I would hear again - seven years later - after the flood; the voice that was so familiar and so beloved that it made me desperately want to open my eyes and see who was speaking… and yet I couldn't. And it was those six words that changed my life forever… from that moment forward. That was in 1989, and it was those six words that got me through the pain and confusion of the next five years of pain and torment yet to come - before the doctors finally figured out what was wrong and cured me, in 1994. But I didn't hear my Lord speak aloud to me again until after the flood in the winter of 1996/1997, several years after I was healed. It was those six words that gave me the strength to form my own corporation, move to Gold Beach, start and complete (at least enough to be open for business) my childhood dream project, and stop me from ever trying to kill myself again, no matter HOW unbearable the pain became.

The six words were: "IT IS NOT YET YOUR TIME!" They were so simple – and spoken with such unquestionable authority, (and love), that I never even thought for a moment to question them. It simply wasn't my time yet; I had been told – and I believed it.. Then I opened my eyes to see where I was and found myself lying face down on the cold cement floor of the shop, with my nose stuck in the tiny space between the giant rollers that supported the big rolling double door to the shop and the, (I'm not sure the right word is here), heavy iron runners that the wheels fit into as you roll the door open and closed. There was about a half inch of space at the most, and somehow, **after** I had passed out, I got out of the car and was breathing through what little clean air was seeping in between the wheels (or rollers) and the runner.

I knew right then that it was my Lord who wouldn't **let** me die, and even though I believed Him when he said *"It is not yet your time"*, I began to sob hysterically because I was so sick and the pain was so indescribable, and yet He wouldn't even let me kill myself. In my infected brain... which I didn't know about at the time, I felt like even God didn't want me.

And so I continued to live, but this time with renewed strength and joy... because even though I had always known that my Lord loved me, (as he does ALL of us), I didn't know He cared enough to literally "save me from myself"... and that kept me going My Lord had told me that it wasn't my time yet... so I had no choice but to make the most of whatever time I DID have.

In looking back on that experience, (one anyone who knew me would never have believed possible), I realize that it, too, was simply training... training for whatever I can possibly do to encourage and inspire my brothers and sisters who are battling unbearable pain or depression, (or anything else that makes them feel like they can't go on another day). Because of that fateful (and wonderful) day, I can now look them in the eyes; see through their tears of despair and depression, and say, "I understand. I know how you feel." That was truly a *gift* from God that I will use for the rest of my life.

And if I hadn't been sexually abused as a child or raped as a young woman, how could I possibly offer comfort to others who have experienced those same things? If I hadn't been forced into a hysterectomy so young, raised two children as a single mother, and never been able to find the love of my life, how could I understand how so many women feel - knowing that she will grow old alone? I never could have... so it was all training - and that's why I am so thankful for everything, both bad and good, that has ever happened to me. Every moment I suffered became a tool; something to help me understand and encourage others - as well as opportunities to show my Heavenly Father that I'm not a "good-time Charlie"; one who is happy and thankful only when things are good, but that I will love, trust and praise him NO MATTER WHAT the circumstances!

I certainly wouldn't have been ready for the way the Lord called me into service after the flood; eager to drive away from everything and everyone I've ever loved - with nothing but joy in my heart and complete trust in God without those experiences. Yes..."I am WHO I am - BECAUSE of all those years." (A line from one of my poems.) There's not a single person out there who hasn't suffered - or who isn't hurting as we speak, so - as a "cheerleader for the people", as an "encourager", the Lord armed me with a limitless supply of compassion, because I HAVE walked in so many of their shoes.

Finally, four years later, after moving to Gold Beach and working on the project for three pain filled years, and running back and forth to doctors hundreds of times during those three years, (which is why I said when I left Gold Beach for Portland in Lucky that I knew that stretch of road like the back of my hand - but that I'd always been in a hurry before; always on my way to a doctor or lawyer appointment). In 1993, the best Infectious Disease specialist in the northwest, (Dr. Dwarkin at Providence Medical Center), set me up for yet another spinal tap, because he wanted to send a sample of my spinal fluid to the New England Center of Medicine. He explained that researchers there were discovering that when some strains of Lyme disease are allowed to run their full course untreated... the disease actually leaves the blood stream and goes into the meningococcal fluids, which would explain why they couldn't find it in my blood, as well as the "chronic meningitis.

It made sense... and this time I dared to hope. Yes, I hated spinal taps, (doesn't everyone?), but I'd already been poked and prodded for 20 long years so what was one more painful test? Nothing... and Dr. Dwarkin, even years later when I spoke to him, said that I was the ONLY patient he'd ever had who recited poetry during a spinal tap.

And it worked! They discovered that my especially virulent and rare strain of Lyme disease had invaded my meningococcal fluid... so my brain really WAS infected, which explained why I thought I was going crazy - and why the pain was so unbearable. They didn't waste a minute... and immediately put a shunt directly into my heart and zapped me with 30,000 milligrams a day of the strongest antibiotic known to man (in 1994, anyway). That went on for 21 straight days, and even though I somehow was under the mistaken impression that I would go home WELL after such radical treatment… it didn't work out that way. Instead, I went home crying - and pleading with Dr. Dwarkin. "Doc, why does my head still hurt? Shouldn't I be well? Didn't the antibiotics cure me?" I cried, almost in a panic because I had truly expected to be pain free for the first time in 20 years.

And that's when he sat me down and patiently explained that even though we had bombarded my body with the maximum amount of antibiotics that it could take, I had had the disease for so long that it could take months before all the diseased cells were purged; possibly even a year. Oh boy… was I ever disappointed, but at least I could see a light at the end of the tunnel, and I can honestly say that six months later, when I woke up for the first time without a wet pillowcase from tears of pain shed during the night while I slept, I felt like I'd been reborn! At age 42, I felt better than I had when I was 23, (when I contracted the Lyme disease! In fact, I had no idea it was possible to FEEL so good… and it was amazing!

At the time, I was busy building the equestrian center in Gold Beach, and the flood wouldn't be for another 2 ½ years yet, but at long last, **I was well**. And, as always… even those last six months I spent waiting for the symptoms to dissipate were part of my training. I'm afraid I've never been a patient person by nature… and suddenly I had six months in which to on my practice. Nope - I wouldn't change a thing, not even if I could… because I know now that it was all part of learning how to become a true servant of my Lord Jesus Christ, and how to put my complete faith and trust in Him; not to mention a way to help others who are suffering.

It may have been a long story, but my 20-year bout with Lyme disease explains why the pain of the burns on my face and hands don't seem nearly as bad as they might have to someone else. To me, pain is comparative - and unlike the Lyme disease and Lyme Meningitis I lived with for so many years… these wounds will heal.

And I know this is really silly, because my name doesn't deserve to be spoken in the same breath as Job's, but I sometimes like to picture God saying to Satan, *"See, I told you that my daughter Abigayle wouldn't blame me, or even ask me why. She trusts me - because she knows that I love her and her faith and obedience is unshakeable."* Wouldn't that be wonderful... and in your face, Satan!!!

So even though I'm not sure what I'll look like after the burns heal, (which doesn't really matter because "vanity" isn't one of my problem areas)... because of my injuries, I've been blessed with more time to spend parked next to this beautiful lake. I've been given extra time in which to pray, study my Bible, write, draw, (did I mention that I love to draw?), play music, and more... all while I'm recovering from my burns.

So this, too, was just one more "speed bump" in the road of life... AND THIS, TOO, SHALL PASS.

That's my story – and I'm sticking to it! (Ha! Ha!) Ouch! Don't make me laugh!

PROVERBS 24:10
If thou faint in the day of adversity, thy strength is small.

chapter 46

February 23, 1999

Two weeks of rest and healing and you wouldn't believe how much better my face is. Even my hair is growing back faster than I expected, (although I think I'll have a "mullet" for awhile), but even the scabs on my face are almost completely gone. But now comes the peeling, as layer after layer of skin comes off in huge pieces… and just think; most women have to "pay" for a "face peal", and I got mine for free!

I'm still bright pink, shiny and swollen, but my skin heals quickly, that those who don't know me will just think I have a pudgy face and a ruddy complexion. I've decided to stay here for one more week, and then I'll be ready to move on… and now I know exactly where I'm going.

I've had time to study my maps and talk to the other campers who have come and gone during my last two weeks here at the lake. They tell me that there's an Indian reservation, (CRIT, which stands for Colorado River Indian Tribes), which is just a few hours north of here, so I thought it would be interesting to go there. I'm almost out of money, but I still have enough left for gasoline, propane for my tanks and even a few groceries. I just wonder if there'll be anyone interested in hearing my poetry, (more like a quiet *revival* in disguise), on an Indian reservation? I don't know – but I guess there's only one way to find out, and that's to try it and see what happens.

When I spent time with my mother in Sacramento, I found out that her grandfather was half Cherokee, which was a complete surprise to me. Apparently, my great-grandfather was a fire and brimstone German preacher who went west to Arkansas and opened a mission. His goal was to save what he called the savage souls while his wife, my great-grand-mother, would teach the children to read and write.

The problem was that his daughter fell in love with one of the "breeds', a half-Indian boy... and at that time, it was strictly TABOO! They insisted on being together, no matter the consequences, so they were promptly disowned and left the reservation. My mother tells me that even though her father, (my grandfather), had a real problem with "firewater", he was also a kind, gentle man who loved music, children, animals and his family. She said he was a friendly drunk; the type everyone in town made fun of as they continued to buy him drinks just so they could watch him dance on the tables or play music on anything he could find. She said he was so talented that he could make music with almost anything and that she remembers many a night when the neighbors gathered on the front porch while everything from spoons to washboards were used to make music while they all sang and danced the night away.

So, I guess that explains where I got my love of music and my ability to play almost anything I can get my hands on, (at least well enough to enjoy around the campfire). I wondered about that, because my father's side of the family isn't exactly strong in that area. A couple of my aunts play the piano, but they took lessons, and it was never the "love of their life"... just something proper ladies did and an ability to be admired.

So how about that... I'm part Indian and part hillbilly!

The town on the reservation I'm going to is Parker, Arizona. I have no idea what I'll find when I get there but I'm really excited. If my face wasn't still swollen and red, I'd leave today, but I think another week ought to do it... and I'm more than ready to hit the road again. I've never been on an Indian reservation before and I can't wait to see what it's like. After all, no matter what a person's race, (or color), they are ALL my brothers and sisters, and other than reading every western I could get my hands on, I know almost nothing about their culture. It should be quite an adventure!

So - next stop; Parker, Arizona, (after one more week of healing).

THE GIFT OF LIFE
Enjoy the gift of Life, my friend...
Don't linger - there's too much to see.
Adventure lays waiting for those who jump in.
So hurry - admission is FREE.
When you look 'round the corner that looms up ahead,
be eager to see what it hides.
Tomorrow the road might be slippery and wet...
but challenges sweeten the ride.

— Poem by Abigayle

chapter 47

February 24, 1999
THE NEXT DAY

Another day – another adventure! I just hope the Lord isn't disappointed in me because I still have so much to learn, but at least I'm trying. And once again, today - just like everything that's ever happened to me, from the day I was born until this very moment, has all been part of my training; getting me ready for whatever it is I can do for the Lord and hopefully worthy of His presence and praise.

And this morning was a perfect example of how far I have yet to go. I was sound asleep in my comfortable little couch/bed, when suddenly I was startled right out of my dreams by the sound of a big diesel engine that was so close I thought it was about to hit my bedroom wall - right next to where I was sleeping. Of course I sat up like a shot, fully awake with my heart pounding, as I parted the curtains to see if I should run for cover. And there, right next to my window, was a huge 5th wheel trailer, being backed in as close as it could possibly get to Lucky, by a large (and loud), diesel truck.

I looked at the clock and it was only 8:00 in the morning, but the fact that I had just woken up and didn't have time to think about what was happening was no excuse, and I'm ashamed to admit that my first thought when I saw how close they were to me was, "Why – with all this room to park, is this person putting their trailer so close to Lucky? How rude can they be? Surely they could have found somewhere else, instead of practically on top of me."

But then I took a moment to think… constantly working on my patience and knowing that I shouldn't rush outside and take the chance of appearing angry or unfriendly, at least not until I had more information and had calmed down enough to wonder what Jesus would do if He were here.

That's why I made a cup of tea, took out my miracle Bible, kneeled in prayer, and then read a few chapters… just to get my attitude right before I let my selfish earthly emotions overcome what I KNEW Jesus would want me to do. And boy, am I ever glad that I did!

When I stepped outside my RV into the already 80+ degree morning sunshine, I was dressed in the lightest long pants and long sleeved shirt that I owned. (See, you **can** teach "an old dog new tricks.") But still I was hot, (and missing the shorts and sleeveless tops I used to wear), and beginning to regret the fact that I had decided to heed John's warnings. Of course, with my face so red and swollen, I'm not exactly "lust material"… but then, many a sexually obsessed man never makes it as far as the face when he appraises a woman. (See, I'm getting pretty good at arguing with myself!)

Much to my surprise, the huge (and brand new) 5th wheel trailer that was parked so close to Lucky that I could reach out and touch it out my bedroom window, wasn't alone. There were three other similar vehicles; all looking brand new and expensive - and all being drawn by big trucks.

As soon as the man and woman who owned the trailer parked closest to me saw me step outside, they left their job of guiding one of the other trailers into a different spot, and approached me with big, (and somewhat sheepish) grins on their faces.

"Hi there," the man greeted me as they approached. "We're the Miller's and we're so sorry we had to crowd you like that. See, we're farmers from Canada and the eight of us, (meaning four couples and four rigs) come down here every winter and park for a month. We always like to form a square, so we have a central courtyard with one campfire in the middle where we all gather. I'm afraid the only way we could fit everyone into position was for my wife and I to park right next to you," he explained politely while his wife smiled and nodded in agreement. "I'm so sorry," he apologized again. "I sure hope you don't mind."

Now I really felt like an idiot for letting it bother me - for even that first instant when I woke up, because these people were genuinely concerned about my feelings, and any angst I may have had quickly disappeared, and I immediately recognized my new neighbors as brothers-and-sisters in Christ. It's funny how you can just *tell* when you meet someone who loves the Lord. Jesus told us in the Bible that we would know each other - and here was a perfect example. In only three sentences, I already knew and loved my new neighbors and was looking forward to their company, (even if they were practically parked in my lap).

"No problem," I answered with a smile – hoping to reassure them that they were welcome and that I wasn't bothered in the least by their close proximity. "I can see what you mean by trying to park in a square so you have a central courtyard - and it sounds like a good idea. I'll be leaving soon anyway, and I've already had a chance to enjoy my privacy, so now it'll be fun to enjoy some company for a change."

"That's very hospitable of you," the husband responded appreciatively. "I'm not sure I'd be so gracious if I was in your place… and we really appreciate the warm welcome. My name is Ken and this is Paulette," he introduced both himself and his lovely wife as he reached his hand out to shake mine.

"Hi there; it's nice to meet you. I'm Abigayle, and I'm from Oregon and traveling alone, unless, of course, you count my new roommate - a mouse that seems to have taken up residence in my RV," I laughed as I shook both of their hands.

"Hey, Greg," Ken shouted to one of his friends who had just finished getting his 5th wheel into position. "Bring Beverly over here for a minute. I want you to meet someone."

And so... one couple at a time, that's how I met my eight new neighbors; all farmers from Canada who have nothing to do on the farm until it's time to plant. Their ages ranged from 35 to 50, the ladies well dressed and wearing make-up and nail polish - even out here in the middle of nowhere, and the men polite, friendly, and obviously capable, from the organized way they went about setting up their camp.

So... my lesson for the day; never jump to conclusions... and always be 'slow to speak', even if it means turning to the Lord for guidance before you open your mouth.

As soon as I'd met everyone, we all sat down in the lawn chairs they'd set out in the middle of their courtyard to visit. It wasn't long before they invited me to join them for a big first-night barbeque potluck. I tried to refuse, (because I was getting a little getting low on food for a potluck, not having expected to be out here this long), but rather than admit to a food shortage, I just suggested that perhaps I could come over **after** dinner and roast some marshmallows around the campfire. But they insisted - saying, "Please, don't bring any food! Our wives always make enough to feed an army so we could use our help eating it."

And so I relented - and then decided to make sure that I didn't wear out my welcome and headed for the lake... while they sat in their lawn chairs laughing and exchanging stories about their trip from Canada.

That's when I saw a silver-haired gentleman pull in with a pick-up camper that was towing the most beautiful bass boat I've ever seen. It was painted like a silver bullet, but obviously set up for fishing... and the gentleman was alone. As I watched him work, from far enough away that he wouldn't notice me watching, I saw how deftly and purposefully he went about the business of finding a way to turn around in such a now-crowded area so that he could back his boat into the water and unload it from the trailer. He was so capable, and so focused on what he was doing that I found myself enjoying sitting there watching him, and couldn't help but wonder where he was from and what his life was like.

I wondered if he was a Christian and I wondered whether he was retired, or did the silver hair just make him look like he might be. Boy, I
guess this time alone has done more than allow me to heal. I'm actually
looking forward to being with people again.

So… since my face is healing unbelievably fast, I'll spend this next week
getting to know my new neighbors and who knows – maybe there's a
reason the Lord brought them into my life, (and lap!).

And then, before I know it… this poet will be "on the road again"; next
stop – Parker, Arizona and my first Indian Reservation. I can't wait!

Farewell to my front yard in Gold Beach, OR.

chapter 48

February 26, 1999

W hat a gorgeous Sabbath sunset! Thank you, my Lord... you are definitely the best artist there could ever be! It's absolutely awesome; so beautiful that I expect to see angels emerging from the big bright spot in the middle, where beams of bright light reach toward Earth - surrounded by rings of deep purple and lavender, before spreading out into shades gold and orange, and ten fading into pink and robin's egg blue. Wow! Happy Sabbath day to everyone!

This morning my new neighbors invited me to go to Church with them. I had no idea there was a church nearby, but I gladly accepted and we drove to the Yuma Army Proving Grounds, a military installation I didn't' even know existed. They have a chapel and a pastor who conducts a non-denominational service every Sunday for both soldiers and travelers, and it was a lovely service. Isn't that wonderful! Even out here, people seek out places to share their love of God and praise our Lord Jesus Christ.

After we returned from church, (at the request of my neighbors), I pulled out my guitar and we all sat in a circle of lawn chairs and I shared my poetry, songs and stories from the road with a very appreciative group of brothers and sisters. I also told them that I planned to leave in the morning, (a little earlier than I had expected), since my face is healed just enough to test my vanity, but not enough to repulse people I meet.

I've come to think of this place as a sort of second home... and I know that someday I'll return -once again seeking peace and quiet; but this time I think I'll take the shorter and more direct route!

And guess what? Yesterday, the silver-haired fisherman I told you about took me for a tour of the lake in his bass-fishing boat. I guess they're having a fishing tournament here next week and he arrived early to get the layout of the lake. It was great fun, and I'm really glad I got a chance to spend some time on the water before I say goodbye.

chapter 49

February 28, 1999

You know what they say about the "best laid plans of mice and men"? Well, I'm still at the lake, and yes... I have another story to tell.

I'm so glad I've been studying my Bible every day... because ever since the Lord saved it from the flood, I realized how important it is to make it a part of my everyday life. It's not only his "word", but it's really an instruction manual for living, and I've learned so much that I can't wait to finish it - just so I can start all over again. Every time I read a verse that strikes me as "especially meaningful", I underline it, and since I plan to read it over and over again, I'm hoping that each time I do, the Lord will open my eyes to the meaning of a new verse, (when He deems me ready to understand and accept it), and eventually, every word will be underlined.

Of course I **always** kneel in prayer before I read it, because I don't speak Greek or Hebrew, which means even the King James Version, which is the one the Lord saved from the flood, is subject to man's interpretation as it was rewritten in English... and only the Holy Spirit can make sure I understand what the Lord WANTS me to understand – in spite of the English words used to convey the message.

And the message I'm especially glad that I took to heart before my eight new friends parked practically on top of me, was a difficult one for me to learn - and that is to be "slow to speak". I've always been an "off the cuff" person, and usually the words come out before I even have a chance to edit them, let alone consider the effect they may have on those around me. I've been working very hard on that problem... and the day that my new neighbors woke me up by pulling in so close to Lucky, I used my newfound skill and **didn't** hurry outside to see why they were crowding me... but instead prayed about it first.

And thank goodness I did, because apparently these eight fine people were brought here to help me, even though I had no idea at the time that I would need their help.

Yesterday morning when I went to start Lucky so I could begin my drive to Parker, Arizona, the engine wouldn't start. It turned over, so I knew the battery wasn't dead, but it just wouldn't start... and before long – the battery WAS dead and Lucky still wasn't running. Great! Now what was I going to do?

That's when my new neighbors came over and offered their assistance. According to them, when you're a farmer, you have to work on your own equipment, so they consider themselves pretty handy with machinery, and all four men quickly went to work on Lucky. I was so grateful... and yet worried that whatever was wrong might be something they couldn't fix, and I would once again find myself broken down, and this time with-out enough money to make repairs.

After about an hour of tinkering, and using their vehicles to jump-start Lucky, to no avail, they told me what the problem was; I was out of gas. But how could that be, I argued. I filled both tanks in Yuma, and even taking the very **long** way I took to get here, (maybe 70 miles instead of 35), I couldn't have possibly used 60 gallons of gasoline.

That's when one of the men motioned for me to climb under Lucky so he could show me what the problem was. He pointed to a section of the fuel line that had broken, this time in several places - as years of non-use had dried out the plastic and then the heat had cracked it.. When I had the fuel line repaired at the base of the "Grapevine" in California, they had only replaced the part that was near the engine, which at the time was the only place that needed replacing, (assuming that they even bothered to check the rest). But now, the part that ran from the back of the RV, (where the gas tanks are), up to the front of the RV, (where the engine is) was crumbling and according to them, I must have been leaving a trail of gasoline behind me the whole time I drove over that washboard of a dirt road before I found the lake. No wonder I smelled gasoline fumes... and thank God I didn't burst into flames. (I think I've had enough FIRE to last me for a long time!)

So the four men put their heads together and decided what to do. Two of them would remove my old line, which was stapled to the frame and difficult to reach, while the other two took every gasoline container they had all the way to Yuma and fill them up for me. What kind and generous people – and how blessed I am that they parked next to me!

During their search for what the problem was, they opened my outside storage compartments and discovered that the wood flooring had gotten wet over the years, probably while parked outdoors in rain soaked Oregon, and the wood flooring had rotted until they were actually gone in some places and merely ready to collapse in others. They decided to take it upon themselves to put new boards on the bottom of several of my storage compartments so I wouldn't lose the things I kept in them as I drove down the highway.

After the two men returned with full gasoline cans, (20 gallons), and 25 feet of new plastic fuel line, they all went to work and spent the rest of the day getting me ship-shape and ready to go.

I can't tell you, nor could I tell them, how grateful I was... and how blessed I felt as I knew that the Lord was once again providing for my needs through my brothers and sisters in Christ. If it hadn't been for them, I'd have been stuck out here, perhaps finally figuring out that I was out of gas - and maybe even finding a kindly neighbor to lend me a gas can, but even then, it would have run out onto the ground as I drove and I've have found myself stuck again, (and who knows where).

No matter how many times I tell them, there's no way my new friends can possibly understand how much their help means to me. And even after fixing my fuel line, putting gas in my tank and replacing the floors in the storage compartments, they didn't stop. Nope… they're still helping me right now.

Unlike Lucky, they all have generators, so as we speak - they are running them, (taking turns so no one has to run theirs all night), and I have my battery charger hooked up, as well as my "battery pac" so by tomorrow morning, I'll be fully charged, gasoline in my tank, a new fuel line… and ready to hit the road.

My new friends have given me their addresses and telephone numbers and want me to come to Canada and do some shows while I park at their houses, but I highly doubt that I'll make it that far north. They also want to know how they can keep track of my travels, or contact me, so I gave them a card with my mother's address on it, but I wish there was some other way. Every time I say goodbye, it feels like the end… and if only there was some way to keep in touch with all the wonderful people who've made a difference in my life.

And something else they did for me that I forgot to mention. They had some mouse traps with them and put one in Lucky yesterday so I wouldn't be taking my little rodent friend with me when I left. When I got up this morning and found the dead mouse in the trap, I felt terrible… like I'd killed a friend – and I couldn't bring myself to touch it.

But I guess farmers don't think much about killing mice, so one of the men took the trap and got rid of "whatever his name was", and although I'm happy that I won't have to listen to him chew whatever he finds in my drawers all night, or spend every morning cleaning up little round pieces of "mouse poop", I still feel sad that I had to end his life.

And now - this really **is** my last sunset at the lake, and I find myself with a small case of the blues; sad that I'll be leaving my new friends behind, sad that I had to kill my little mouse roommate, and sad that I'm leaving such a beautiful place behind… a place where I've become comfortable - and have found so much peace, love and healing.

But this is only one place, and there is beauty and love to be found around every single corner… so once again – off I go into the unknown, trusting God to lead me, and wondering what tomorrow will bring. If you listen to the media, you'd think the United States has become a selfish, Godless, greed-driven society… but I know better! Every where I go, people are kind and helpful, generous and loving. These people are the "silent majority", (the backbone of our society), but unfortunately the very loud "squeaky wheel" minority is making all the noise and getting all the attention. I'm so glad I was given this opportunity to be poor… because it forced me into having to rely on others to help me along. For most of my life, I've been the one doing the helping, and now, as difficult as it is, I'm finding great joy in letting my brothers and sisters open their hearts to me.

Nature may be a glorious example of God's handiwork – but SO IS MAN!

chapter 50

March 2, 1999

Parker, Arizona... I'm not sure what I expected, (since I've never been on an Indian Reservation before), but it's not much larger than my home town of Gold Beach, (which had 2,000 people -including the suburbs), so it's definitely a small town, but it seems that the desert towns are a lot more spread out than the ones in Oregon.

After I left Mittry Lake, (I discovered the name as I drove **out** the way I SHOULD have driven **in** - and saw the sign), I decided to spend one last night at an RV Park because my holding tanks were full and my cupboards were empty. It was only 150 miles from Yuma to Parker, (approximately), which meant 20 gallons of gas wasn't going to be nearly enough, so if it hadn't been for needing to empty my holding tanks and to refill my fresh water tank, I'd have just gotten gas and propane and then driven straight through. But I do have to admit, it was really nice to have air conditioning and cable television for a change. I really wanted to catch up on the national news, (as I've always been a political junkie – as conservative as they come and proud of it), and I enjoyed some old reruns of Candid Camera, (which left me laughing hysterically), and another of my favorite television shows, Walker Texas Ranger. What happened to all those good old shows; you know the ones... the ones that don't need nudity or sex to be entertaining, and where good always prevails over evil. It's a shame that the media doesn't use it's power to influence and teach in a more positive manner, but at least there are still a few shows that not only entertain but bear an important message - and I enjoy watching them.

Since I approached Parker from the south, I drove north - all the way through town, and just as I got to where it was apparent that I was leaving all signs of civilization behind, I came upon what looked like a big grocery store with a McDonald's right next to it. It had a huge parking lot, so I pulled in... and that's when I noticed that half of the grocery store building wasn't a grocery store after all... it was an Indian Casino. Hmmm, I thought to myself. Casinos are open 24 hours a day, and they almost always allow RVs to spend the night in their parking lots, (hoping the owners will gamble, of course), so maybe I could park here for a little while, at least until I figure out what I'm doing in Parker.

And that's where I am right now – in the Casino/grocery store parking lot. It's a good thing too, because after I spent one night in an RV Park in Yuma, bought food, gas and propane, I have exactly $5.00 left. But I'm not complaining, because like I said... I have food, gas, and propane; not to mention a soft bed, a shower and even a toilet - so I am truly blessed. But now I just need to figure out where I can put on one open show - so I can hopefully make enough money to move on to the next town, which would be Lake Havasu, Arizona. Naturally, I'll put on some free ones while I'm here, (where I **don't** put out my little contribution picnic-basket), but unfortunately, money is a necessity and I can't afford to do the "free" ones if I don't at least do one where I accept contributions.

So tomorrow morning I'll go to the Chamber of Commerce, since I checked in the telephone book and they DO have one. (I didn't if they did on Indian Reservations), and I'll find out where the local nursing home/assisted living care facilities are, the Senior Center, if they have a Woman's Shelter, and any other possible places where the people might enjoy some encouragement in the form of entertainment. I wonder if Indians like poetry? Since discovering that I'm part Indian myself, I certainly don't mean that in a derogatory way... I'm just truly wondering – because if they don't, I might be in the wrong town with no money to go anywhere else.

But as always, I trust the Lord completely, so I must be here for a reason... and I have no doubt that somehow – everything will be fine.

I think I'll walk over to the Casino and see if I need permission to park here before some security guard come knocking at my door in the middle of the night. I hate to admit how tempting it is to see those golden arches and remember how good a hamburger and french fries taste... but there's no way I'm going to spend my last five dollars on fast food; not when it could buy me a whole loaf of bread, a jar of peanut butter and maybe even a dozen eggs. But it sure does smell good!

chapter 51

March 5, 1999

I'm afraid things didn't go too well when I asked if I could spend the night in the Casino parking lot because they only give you a 24 hour permit - and you have to gamble in order to get it extended. Obviously, I'm not gambling... so that meant I only had one night before having to find someplace else to park; someplace free.

But fortunately, that turned out to be easier than I thought, because on the main highway, not far from the casino, was a whole line of vendors... most of them Indian – but some who weren't. They had tents set up all along both sides of the road and were selling everything from Jewelry and Dream Catchers to 2nd hand household goods. Most of them had RV's or campers parked near their tents, and immediately behind them was a large, (probably two or three acres) dirt field that was completely empty, unless you count the three inches of talcum powder-like desert dust. When my 24 hours was up at the Casino, I decided to pull into that dirt field and kill two birds with one stone. First; I'd have a free place to park - and second; I could walk up and down the row of vendors and get acquainted with some of the local people.

What better way could there be to find out what life is like here on the reservation than to talk to the people themselves? I can share some of my poetry and stories from the road, and, of course, whenever the opportunity presents itself, I can bear witness and encourage those who are receptive (or in need)… to turn to Jesus for help and comfort.

The Chamber of Commerce turned out to be a bust, too – because their **aren't** any rest homes/retirement centers or women's shelters here in Parker, so other than the Senior Center and private clubs, (like Rotary, Soroptimist, Lions, etc.), I still need to find a place to put on my one **open** show so I can earn enough money to move on to the next town. I rode my bike to the Senior Center today and talked to the lady in charge, and after sharing a poem or two with her, (right there in her office), she asked if I'd put on a show for them next week. And who knows; perhaps that will lead to something else. The lady at the Chamber of Commerce kindly suggested that I talk to the Mayor, (who, according to her, is a very nice woman), and tell her what I do – and that I need a place to put on a show. Because I don't charge admission, she might be able to help me find a good location at no cost – as well as give me the names and numbers of some contact people for the local clubs. I wrote down her name, address and telephone number, so calling her is definitely something I plan to do this afternoon, and maybe even make an appointment to meet with her tomorrow. .

It's so HOT here, though, I can't believe it! I've been using my little spray bottle, (the one I use to keep my leg wet when I drive so the heat from the engine doesn't burn my leg), and I'm using it to spray myself constantly, letting the water cool me down as it evaporates. Luckily, Mc-Donalds has an outdoor faucet, so I can refill my little spray bottle whenever I need to without using up the water in my freshwater tank, and believe me… I'm filling it every couple of hours!

I also found out from the nice lady at the Chamber of Commerce that there are two radio stations in Parker, so I I'll ride my bike (Candy) over to their offices as soon as I figure out the actual date and location of my open performance and see if they'll announce it for free, (since I'm not charging admission which makes it a public service). Then I'll put notices up everywhere I can think of; like the Laundromat and the grocery store bulletin board. But right now, it's too hot to do any more bicycle riding today, so I think I'll just wander over to the vendor booths and introduce myself. Tomorrow I'll go see the mayor and get the telephone numbers of at least the President of the Soroptimist Club and the Lions Club and then use one of my five dollars to make a few phone calls. The first one will be to the President of the local Soroptimist Club, (since I'm a Soroptimist Sister and I'm sure I can count on them for some advice regarding a location for my open show, and then I'll ask her who else I should call… and go from there.

So, wish me luck… because this isn't as easy as I thought it would be. I guess I should just be thankful that I have a bicycle — because there's no way I could possibly walk to all those places in this heat! (Thank goodness for my spray bottle!)

chapter 52

March 9, 1999

Things are going absolutely great! I've picked March 24th as the date of my open show, and after sharing a poem or two with the mayor, right there in her office, at first, she was understandably skeptical – but after listening to a couple of my poems she became extremely enthusiastic and helpful. She immediately stopped everything she was doing, and not only offered me the free use of the public library to put on my show, but took the time – right then and there – to take me to the Head Librarian and tell her who I was, what I was doing, and that she wanted them to let me use one of their meeting rooms. That was so far beyond the call of duty, I still can't believe it. The library closes at 7:00 in the evening, so that's when my show will begin, which means I have a little over two weeks to do whatever advertising I can manage, and put on a short program at the Senior Center and Lion's Club.

I posted all the flyers I already had made, and since they're in color, (and not cheap to copy), I don't dare use my last $5.00 to have more printed up. But I'm hoping that by word of mouth, (through the local clubs and the vendors I've met), it will at least bring a small audience. I did a short reading at the Soroptimist Club luncheon yesterday, which should help with publicity via word of mouth, and in fact, it was one of my Soroptimist Sisters who called her husband (who just happens to be the President of the local Lions Club) and he arranged for me to speak at their luncheon tomorrow. I can't believe I still haven't learned not to worry yet... because somehow, no matter how bleak things seem at the time - everything always has a way of working out. It's just hard not to wonder if I'm on the right track; especially when it's so foreign for an A-type personality like me to be completely without resources or at least working toward a definitive goal.

And speaking of definitive goals... I'm STILL not sure **how** the Lord wants me to use my gift of inspirational writing and speaking for His work. I guess that's why I'm still wandering the country; hoping that when the time is right, the Lord let me know... and whatever doors He wants opened **will** be opened. And in the meantime, I'll just keep trying to learn everything I can about the people and what they need most... and praying and studying my Bible.

I rode Candy to both local radio stations but only one of them was interested in doing an announcement about my show, but at the other one, I did an early morning talk show and shared a couple of poems, so maybe that, too, will bring in a few more people. I'm starting to worry though, (oh boy – here I go again)... because the Indians I've met so far not only don't seem interested - they actually HATE me!

And I'm not kidding. I've NEVER felt hatred like this before, but I can see it in their eyes when they look at me. I'm here in Parker as an inspirational poet because I **love** them and want to bring them some joy and encouragement - but they take one look at my blonde hair, slim figure and blue eyes, (the exact opposite of them) and I can literally feel the hatred, (mostly from the women). It's so strong it's almost palpable. More than once I've had an Indian woman stand by the door, like they were kindly holding it open for me, and then let it slam in my face just as I got there... and they laughed – not even bothering to hide the pleasure they got from insulting me. They really DO hate me... and yet they don't even know who I am!

I actually think that experiencing such unrestrained racial hatred is a wonderful learning experience; once again, a part of my training for whatever it is the Lord has planned for me. I know that times have changed... but being Caucasian and having grown up in an almost completely Caucasian state, and attending completely Caucasian schools, I've never really known anyone who was the victim of racism. We had one black boy in our high school – and we all loved him dearly. In fact, we bent over backwards to make sure he never felt excluded or left out.

When I was in the sixth grade, I wrote a poem about a little black boy and how terribly he was mistreated - and my message was how horrible racism is, and I can honestly say that I've NEVER judged anyone by the color of their skin... but I am aware that it happens, and probably quite often. Mexicans complain about it, as do African Americans and Asians, but I never thought of racism in connection with American Indians because everyone I know, (including me) is PROUD of our Indian blood. But apparently, at least here in Parker, it IS a problem. It's not that I blame them, (in fact, I understand why they feel the way they do), but on this reservation... the racism is reversed – and it's ME feeling **their** hatred.

That's why I look at this experience as a wonderful opportunity for me to show the local Indians that I love them, even though they hate me... and that Jesus loves us all - white, black, yellow or green. I'm actually kind of excited about it... since this is the first time I've been a victim of racism, so I find it enlightening... and now, because of my stay here in Parker, I'm aware of a problem that I didn't even know existed. While I'm here, I'm going to do my very best to stand as an example of what Jesus would do - and return their hatred with nothing but kindness and love, and I mean "sincere" love. Just maybe I can get through to at least a few of them – and even that would be a start!

And as far as the vendors go, at least half of them are Indians and the rest are just poor white people; some even disabled veterans who are trying to eke out a living in a most inhospitable climate. One of the tents along the road is a really big one, almost like a circus tent, and they sell sandals and thongs, and the man who runs it says I can cover for him once in a while when he goes to lunch and I get to keep 10 percent of anything I sell. What a blessing that is! Even if I only make two dollars, I could get some of those wonderful smelling french fries at McDonald's. My mouth has been watering ever since I saw those golden arches and caught a whiff of that delicious aroma.

But at least I'm gradually getting to know a few of the Indian vendors, and after the first hour of instant mistrust and hatred, I've actually managed to make friends with several of them; one lady in particular. She makes and sells dream catchers and beaded necklaces, and lives alone in a beat up old RV; one that makes Lucky look luxurious. I can't help but notice that she spends everything she makes at the casino every night, and that she's not a happy person, so maybe I can encourage her a little bit; at least plant a few seeds. Since they call her "Sister Sarah", I have to believe that there must be a reason… so I've invited her over for some tea and conversation tonight. She didn't exactly say yes… but instead tried to get me to go to the casino with her - so I ended up compromising and offering to watch her gamble at the casino for a little while if she'll then come and visit with me at my RV; and so that's what we're dong tonight.

I don't mean to be repetitive, but I still can't believe how **HOT** it is here, and it's still March. I can't even imagine what the summer will be like - or how people survived before they had air-conditioning. They must have been really tough because I can barely stand it already. Of course, I'm not hooked up to electricity, and therefore have no air conditioning, and I'm living in what amounts to nothing more than a tin-can that holds the heat like an oven, without a drop of shade to block the sun. But that's only because I'm still parked in my three-inch deep dirt-filled field behind the vendors, and hot or not, the desert is still beautiful… and every day is clear and sunny; and I have so much to be thankful for that I wouldn't DARE complain. There are places in this world with 20 people living in mud-floored huts with no bathroom facilities or even fresh water… so I'm the one who is truly blessed. I not only still have food and shelter, clothing and facilities, but I get to spend hours every day studying my miracle Bible and praying for guidance and wisdom, forgiveness and understanding.

But is this really what the Lord wants me to do? Or is this preparation and training for something else? I know I have so MUCH to learn… and I have a feeling that as the Lord leads me… sojourning among the people, doing what little I can to inspire and encourage those I meet, it's all leading me to something else. Maybe – maybe not… only God knows for sure… but sometimes I can't help wondering. So, in the meantime, I'll just keep doing what little bit I can – one person at a time - one town at a time.

chapter 53

March 14, 1999

I just finished reading my bible and singing and playing my guitar for Jesus - and I'm so filled with emotion right now, that I can't stop the tears; tears of gratitude and joy.

I'm feeling so many things that I can barely separate one emotion from another. First and foremost, it's **gratitude**. Thank you, Jesus, for taking our sins on your back… for suffering and being tortured and humiliated so that **we** could have eternal life. I'm thankful for your Word (the Bible), my health, my food, the roof over my head, my family, my country, my clothes, even my bicycle…. and the list goes on, and on, and on… never ending.

And at the same time, I feel **ashamed**… ashamed that it took me so long to understand what life on Earth is really about. I spent too many years enjoying blessing after blessing, from nature to children, from accomplishments to the gift of many talents… and though I was always grateful - I never realized that the gifts the Lord gave me weren't meant just for me; they were tools… tools with which to glorify God and tools with which to spread his Word and encourage others.

And then I feel **fear**… fear that I might somehow disappoint my Father in Heaven; fear that I might not be righteous enough, or that I might take the wrong path - driven by my own earthly desires rather than by

the Holy Spirit. That's why I pray every day for the gift of discernment…
but I still FEAR that I'm not doing everything He wants me to do - or
that I'm not being all that he expects me to be.

And then there's the **joy**! Boy did those french fries taste good, and the sun
is so bright and warm - and I'm so comfortable here in my little home on
wheels. I can't seem to wipe the smile off my face as I'm finally making head-
way in getting to know some of the local citizens, both Indian and white, and
people are actually beginning to stop by my RV, (still parked in the dirt field),
just to talk; sometimes because they've seen the "walk with Jesus" sign on my
bumper and sometimes because of something I said at a vendors booth that
brought them here for more conversation or clarification.

Here's a perfect example:

Don, one of the gentlemen who was at the Lions club meeting where I
shared a few poems and told an abbreviated version of my story, showed up
at my RV yesterday. He's an older man; (in fact a WWII veteran), and as he
sat at my kitchen table - telling me how much he enjoyed what I had to say
at the Lions Club meeting, it took only a few minutes of general discussion
about life here on earth before he literally began pouring out his heart. He
was a strong man… a soldier from the greatest generation – and yet his
spirit had been broken. He went on for several hours… recounting horror
story after horror story from the war; things he had never been able to put
into words before. He sobbed… and I sobbed with him, as I held his hands
across the table. His were tears that spoke of suffering and soul-wrenching
pain… and together we cried over the inhumanity of the horrible things
he had been forced to endure. But after awhile, (and words that I have no
doubt that the Holy Spirit put into my mouth), Don began to feel better.
He wiped his tears away and smiled in relief… saying "I guess the Lord
wouldn't have let me go through all those things if He didn't think I could
put the experience to good use somehow."

And believe me, I KNOW that none of the credit is mine. I'm just a
poet, a sinner - and a servant of Jesus Christ, but I think that Don opened
up to me because, (like the Jewish lady in Sun City West who watched

her family led into the gas chambers in Auschwitz), it's sometimes easier to share your innermost pain (and shame), with someone who is not only a stranger – but someone you'll never have to face again, (at least if you don't want to). And to me, crying with Don was a great privilege, and it's because of men like him that I'm free to sit here in this dirt field today. I reminded him of that fact, and hugged him, and thanked him profusely for his service to our great nation. And then he thanked me as well - telling me that the pain he had just shared with me were emotions that had remained unspoken; trapped inside his heart, for more than 50 years... and I was so honored to be there when the dam finally broke that my eyes may have been filled with tears – but my heart was filled with joy!

Don may have opened up his heart – but he also opened my eyes. Since I'm only putting on one open show in this little Indian reservation town, I had been beginning to wonder if I was sitting here in this dirt field wasting precious time; time the Lord would rather see me spending in some other way... but now I know better. Where ever I am... **HE** will bring them to me. Once again, the amazing voice, (who ever it was), that spoke to me after the flood - and said, *"I will do my part – but you must do yours,"* comes back to me every single day... especially as I wonder if I truly AM following right path - or doing and saying the right things. What is **my** part? I know one thing for sure; and that is I must continue to study the Bible and pray unceasingly. I must continue to listen and learn – and continue to plant seeds every where I go. And just maybe, with the help of my Lord and Savior, I can make a small difference in this very big world. Don just reaffirmed that – and now I'm feeling a lot more confident that this dirt field is where I belong right now.

Because Parker isn't exactly what you'd call a rich town, (nor am I sure that anyone will even attend my show at the library), I've been hanging on to my last $5.00. (I even earned the money I spent on french fries and phone calls by working at the vendor booth selling thongs.)

But last night, I attended my very first tent revival meeting, (now there was a new and different experience), and on the way home, (riding my bicycle, of course), as I rode toward the dirt field where Lucky is parked, I saw a local newspaper, (or at least a page or two of it), blowing in the wind in front of me. As I rode, it continued to almost lead my way as I pedaled down the street. Then, as I turned onto the dirt field I now call home, the wrinkled pages turned as well, still blowing right along with me, just a few feet ahead - but never quite close enough for me to run them over. It was almost surreal, the way the newspaper never once veered in its course, so when I reached Lucky and parked my bike… I was stunned to see that it too, had stopped and was now lying on the ground next to me. This **had** to be more than mere coincidence, so I decided to pick up those crumpled pages and take them inside. I don't know why I felt the urge to do that – because I would never normally pick up a dirty, piece of newspaper, (not knowing where it had been or what germs it might hold), but there was something strange about the way it almost led me home… so I decided to see what sort of news those wrinkled and dirty pages contained - and there's when I saw this ad:

"Help wanted. We're just about ready to open our new multi-million dollar casino resort in Parker, complete with 300 rooms, 200 boat slips, 5 restaurants, and a 4 story pool and atrium overlooking the Colorado River. We are looking for help in all areas, from food service to cleaning staff. Call ###### or stop by the Human Resources Department located next door to our current casino."

And that's when it struck me like a bolt of lightening! I'd been fasting and praying about what I should do next, asking the Lord to guide me. And now an idea I hadn't even considered suddenly popped into my mind. Every time I give a reading, or even meet someone on the road, they ask how they can keep in touch with me, or how they can invite me back again next year. They love the stories of how my Lord has guided and protected me along the way, and always want to know how they can find out what happens next. I usually give them a business card - but the address on it is my mother's house in Sacramento, (because I call and check in with her every now and then(, so really, for all practical intents and purposes, there's no way for people to reach me - or to follow my journey. And then it dawned on me as I sat there reading that ad.

I need to apply for one of those jobs, like maybe serving food in one of the casino restaurants. Even though I've never been a waitress before, it's one of the few jobs that you can do for a little while and then move on - unlike being a paralegal or business executive. If I got a job at the new casino, I could work long enough to buy a computer. I've never used one before, but how hard can it be? Then I'll create a website, call it "poetry on the road", and that way, everyone who wants to - can keep track of my travels as I keep an "on-line journal". That would give people a way to reach me via email - for everything from encouragement and advice to invitations to speak to their clubs or churches... or perhaps just to talk if there's something they want to get off their chest.

The minute I thought of it - I was absolutely positive that the Holy Spirit was leading me (as well as the newspaper)... and that my prayers for guidance had been answered. I already keep a written journal as I travel, (and the cassette tapes I send regularly to my mother), so I'll just put an occasional entry on-line so people can feel like they're riding along with me, sharing the pain and the joy, the wonder and my trust in God. I'll post copies of my poems, (at least some of them - since there are way too many), so anyone who wants to can download them... and of course, I won't charge anything. It will be a gift for them - from me, (and from God). Wow! That's perfect... Thank you Jesus! Now I just have to get a job at the new casino, earn enough money for a computer, learn how to use it, and figure out how to design a web-site. (I have a feeling that my plan sounds a whole lot easier than it actually is... but oh well – I think I've finally learned my lesson about worrying.) *"Everything will be fine!"*

I'm the first to admit that I'm not exactly technically savvy... but my son Jeremy is, and I'm hoping he can walk me through the basics over the telephone. And with the Lord's help, through my website, I'll be able to reach people from all over the world.

I'm so excited... and now – first things first; I have to put on my show at the Parker Public Library. Then I have to get the job. But now that I think about it – why wait until after my show to apply for the job? I should put in my application right away… just in case all the best positions go first. So that's what I'll do first thing tomorrow morning.

Right or wrong, I have a sort of "litmus test" for whether it's MY will or the Lord's will when I feel like I'm being called somewhere. If it's a place I really WANT to be, like a beautiful beach town or a mountain cabin with an unending view… then it's probably ME who's influencing the decision.

But when the Lord makes me feel like He's calling me somewhere I would NEVER choose on my own; (like a dusty, flat, HOT, HOT, HOT small town that's rife with racial hatred, anger and resentment toward me), it's probably God who wants me here – because it certainly wouldn't be my first choice!

And that's how I feel right now. Parker wouldn't exactly be where I'd choose to live… with no forests or waterfalls, no ocean or salt-air breeze, and right in the middle of a group of people who **hate** me for the horrible things my ancestors did, and for the color of my skin. So the fact that I'm so unbelievably excited right now… so SURE that this is where my Lord wants me to be, (at least for a while), means I have no absolutely no doubt whatsoever that it's not my carnal desires leading me astray.

So… it looks like I'm starting a whole **new** adventure! And what better place could there be to stop and work than on an Indian Reservation… where I can work side by side with my Indian brothers and sisters, gradually learning about them - while they learn about me. And what better place to work than at a restaurant in a casino, where I'm sure there are bound to be lost and miserable people; people who, (like Jon and Sister Sarah), are held captive by an addiction to gambling… and are using their food and rent money to make that big score they all dream of making. I'm sure there will be people who need help; people I can love and encourage… and many, many seeds to be planted.

I'm so excited! I can't wait to apply for that job tomorrow! And I can't wait for my show at the library, (assuming that anyone shows up). Wow! You just never know what's around the next corner…

chapter 54

March 16, 1999

I'm not sure whether this is good news or bad ... but at least it's news, and very interesting news at that.

Yesterday morning, (Monday), I went to the Human Resources Department dressed in a businesslike suit with my resume' in hand, but when I walked in, I felt as out of place as a piece of licorice in a fine dining restaurant. Everyone else in the room was Indian, rather large, (especially compared to me), and dark complexioned, (again compared to my almost snow-white skin). Most of them were dressed in t-shirts and blue jeans; completely the opposite of my businesslike attire, and every head turned my way the moment I walked in the door... because I stuck out like a sore thumb – and they weren't smiling!

The application packet that the lady at the counter handed me was huge; at least two inches thick – because you have to apply for a gambling permit in order to work at a casino. Apparently, they investigate not only your credit – but your entire background, a precaution taken to make sure you won't be tempted to steal. The packet was so big that I decided to take it back to my RV so I could spend the day filling it out and then return it in the morning – which the lady at the desk said would be just fine.

I spent all day yesterday filling out the myriad of forms, and then... first thing this morning, I rode Candy back to the Human Resources office, papers in hand, where I was told by the lady at the counter that the Director of Food and Beverage, (who was the one who would be interviewing me), was over at the old casino, but should be back soon; so I waited... and waited... and waited... (Thank goodness I thought to bring a good book.)

Finally, two long hours later, I approached the woman at the counter and asked if I could schedule an appointment with the Director - when he wasn't so busy... and she laughed as she said, "Oh, I doubt that he's busy. Why don't you just go over to the casino and find him," she suggested. That seemed like an odd thing to say, but since I didn't know the man, (and she did), I just took the piece of paper on which she had written down his name and description, and headed down the block to the old casino, hoping to find him.

When I walked in, even though it wasn't even lunchtime yet, the place was already crowded, and filled with the sound of jackpot bells and whistles, people cheering, and the din of constant conversation. I looked around until I was pretty sure I had spotted the man I was looking for, but decided to ask one of the cocktail waitresses first, just to make sure I had the right person.

When I asked her, she, too, laughed rather disrespectfully, as she said, "Yup, that's him. But good luck... he's a hard man to corner."

"Thanks," I replied, wondering what she could have possibly meant. That's why before I approached him, I decided to watch for a few minutes and see why both the lady at Human Resources and the waitress seemed so disrespectful... and it didn't take me two minutes to figure it out.

He was a fairly young man, maybe 35-ish, and dressed more like a gambler than a businessman, with a flashy shirt and tie, (loosened at the collar), hair shiny and slicked back, and a small, neatly trimmed mustache. He was laughing in a very loud and flamboyant way - more like a winning customer than any boss I'd ever worked for, and he was standing next to one of the waitresses at the bar - who was obviously waiting for her drink order to be filled by the busy bartender. One of his arms was around the attractive waitress's back... a bit too low and lightly grazing the top of her well-formed bottom; a fact made even more apparent by the short, tight mini-skirt/uniform she was wearing.

And I noticed that as he was speaking to her, he held his face so close to hers that if it had been me in her place, I would have firmly objected, (and most likely lost my job). He then began whispering something in her ear... once again laughing as though they were co-conspirators in some secret joke - but her return laughter was more like that of one who is subservient and has no choice but to respond in-kind... even though she was obviously uncomfortable. It just didn't feel right... and it seemed to me, (in the few minutes I watched him), that he was using his position of authority over her in more ways than any employer should. I felt the hairs on my neck begin to tingle because something wasn't right here – and I not only felt like I was walking into a situation I didn't approve of... but now I understood why both women had spoken of him with such obvious disrespect.

But if I wanted to submit my application, I guess I'd have to face both the evil and the good ... and I had a feeling that I knew exactly which one I was dealing with here.

But at least I was dressed like a lady... and I've discovered throughout my life that *almost* always when you look like a lady - and act like a lady, you're treated like one. So now it was time to find out.

"Excuse me, Sir," I said as I intentionally kept a distance of at least 4 feet between us. "Are you Mr. XXX, the Director of Food and Beverage?"

As he turned to face me, and before he responded to my question, I could feel his eyes looking me over as if he were removing my clothes - and he made no attempt whatsoever to hide his appraising look... which started at my face and ended at my feet. "Why yes, I am," he answered with a grin bordering on lewd. "And what can I do for you?" he asked as he took a step closer to me. How could this man could make such a normally respectful question, (what can I do for you?), sound like a dirty proposition? Oh boy – I had a feeling that this was going to be quite a challenge.

"I was given some application papers to fill out yesterday at the Human Resources Office because I'm looking for a job at the new Casino," I explained, "and the lady at the front desk said I might find you here so I could schedule an interview."

"I see," he answered, with what looked more like a leer than a smile, as he once again made an innocent response sound like a proposition. "So you're looking for work," he announced rather than asked. "Well then, I guess I'm the one man that can make that happen," he informed me, obviously enjoying his power as he continued to close the distance between us - and I quickly reacted by backing up another step. "We could meet later tonight, after I'm done here at the casino if you'd like, and talk about it then," he suggested - but then quickly thought better when he saw the look of disbelief on my face. "Or if you'd rather, you could meet me in my office in the morning; let's say about 10:00."

"Thank you. That would be great," I answered with relief. "I can see you're busy right now, and I was hoping we'd have some time to talk because my application might need some explaining." What I was referring to was the fact that I had no address, no telephone number, and was living in a dirt field. Also, it was obvious by my resume' that I was over-qualified for a food server position, and had absolutely no food serving experience - and I wanted to explain why... and tell him how to get in touch with me.

"Ok," he nodded, "I'll see you at 10:00 tomorrow morning over at the Human Resources Department. But don't worry about your application. I base my hiring on more than just those papers," he said, obviously making sure I knew how much power he had. "And I have a feeling we can working something out," he said in a disgusting tone that once again left me feeling like a piece of meat at a cattle auction.

And why did those words sound so evil? If you took them at face value, they should have been hopeful... and I should be celebrating the fact that even though I had no address or telephone number, and no previous experience as a waitress, he had just said "he was pretty sure we could work something out". Under any other circumstances, that would have been good news... and yet, I felt like they were more like a warning... a message from him to me that he had OTHER ways of deciding who did and did not work for him.

"Thank you, sir," I responded, sticking to my polite and businesslike tone. "I'll be there at 10:00 sharp. I appreciate your time, and I'll see you in the morning," I said as I smiled, (not TOO friendly...), shook his hand, and walked away - feeling like I needed to find the restroom and wash my hand as soon as possible.

As in many casinos, I noticed that this one didn't have a single window, (or even a clock for that matter), on its walls. Sister Sarah told me that they do it on purpose, so that the gamblers can't keep track of time... and are therefore likely to spend more hours at the gaming tables and slot machines. So instead of windows, these casino walls were lined with mirrors... obviously intended to make the surprisingly small room, (which was extremely overcrowded with people, noisy slot machines, gaming tables and even a buffet restaurant), look larger and more inviting. But for me, they served a completely different purpose, and because of them, I was able to watch Mr. XXX's reflection as I turned and walked away. I wasn't even slightly surprised when I saw that his eyes never once left my hips; and being aware of that fact, I made a concerted effort NOT to let them swing, but instead to walk purposefully and self-confidently all the way to the exit.

They say that men who prey on women can actually make a fairly accurate judgment about who are the weakest targets just by the way they walk, so I made sure that Mr. XXX didn't think I was trying to entice him, or that I was even slightly intimidated by his position of authority, as I headed straight for the nearest door.

So - tomorrow morning it is... and since the newspaper ad said that the big, beautiful, new Blue Water Resort and Casino is due to open in two weeks, it would sure be nice to know if I get the job as soon as possible.

(And you can be sure of one thing; I'll definitely be wearing a long skirt or a loose-fitting pair of slacks for my interview with Mr. XXX tomorrow!)

One of my new Indian friends, Sister Sarah, told me about a beautiful place about 15 miles from here that the Indians consider *sacred ground*, and she offered to take me there. She loves my poetry, and has even introduced me to some of her Indian friends, gradually making my circle of acceptances on the reservation grow, which is just what I was hoping for. She introduces me as, "*Abigayle – Spirit Woman*," which is quite a compliment… so when she offered to lead the way to the sacred grounds in her RV - with me following in Lucky, I didn't hesitate to take her up on her offer.

But first - I need to see if I have a job… and then if I do, I'll have two whole weeks before the casino opens and nine days before my show at the Parker Public Library, on Wednesday, March 24th, so right now would be the perfect time to get away for awhile. I could use the peace and solitude of the desert to decide which poems I should do, study my Bible and ask the Lord for help with my new boss, (assuming I get the job). I'll write in my journal, make a new tape for my mother, and even practice a couple of new songs I've written on my guitar. Plus, I don't think I'm supposed to park (legally anyway), in this dirt field, so it might be a good idea if I'm gone for a week, so the local police don't think I've moved in permanently.

If tomorrow morning goes as I hope it will… Sister Sarah and I plan to leave town tomorrow afternoon, on Thursday the 17th, which will give me plenty of time to enjoy my adventure in the desert before I have to return to Parker and do my show at the Library. According to her, (my trusted Indian guide), the sacred ground isn't flat, brown and treeless like it is here in Parker, but instead it's more like a hidden oasis; a deep gorge carved out of the desert floor by thousands (or millions) of years of raging flashfloods. She says there are amazing trees, (indeed - a rare desert site), as well as bright and beautiful red and gold colored cliffs, and - (best of all)… complete privacy. She says we'll be driving for about six miles out into the desert AFTER we leave the last paved road, so even though it didn't work out too well when I had my first skinny-dipping adventure on Mt. Hood, maybe the desert will be different and this time we really WILL have complete privacy, (even though I don't plan on doing any skinny-dipping!)

I'm really looking forward to seeing such a special place, (although I'm not sure I'd consider it *sacred* – I'll have to wait and see how it feels)... but right now I can't concentrate on anything but my job interview tomorrow morning. I can only pray that the Lord puts every word in my mouth – and that he opens the heart of Mr. XXX, I'm not using his name in case he eventually repents for his evil ways and, (Praise God), if he does, I wouldn't want to embarrass him by using publicizing his behavior. So now, once again, my future is in hands much larger than my own. If Parker is where God wants me, then He'll open the door. But if not – I Have no doubt that Mr. XXX will happily slam it right in my face, no matter what I say or do.

It's so comforting to be able to lay all your burdens at the feet of our Lord. Not a day goes by that I don't repeat the words said to me after the flood; ***"Do not worry; everything will be fine."*** But JUST as often - I find myself repeating one of the other things He said... and those words were, ***"You must do YOUR part – and I will do MINE."*** I just hope I'm doing my part!

I wonder if filling out two inches of paperwork and dealing with Mr.XXX counts?

chapter 55

March 18, 1999

Why is it I can find no peace; no place to rest my soul…

That's a line from a poem I wrote many years ago, and it came to me now because here, at Sister Sarah's sacred place, I seem to have found a place to "rest my soul".

Whether it's sacred or not isn't the point, because out here… in the midst of never ending sameness, I can see why the Indians would consider this place special. It was like driving into another world. One minute the land was brown, flat and void of life for as far as the eye can see, and then we were going steeply downhill, on an unmarked road (if you can even call it that) that twisted and turned around boulders and over dried brush and gravel. Then suddenly, we were at the base of a sheer cliff, layered by millions of years of both life and death, and the effects of weather, erosion and time. Its beauty is magnified by the blandness of its surroundings - as well as by the surprise of finding something so unique and colorful in a landscape that seldom changes.

The highest layer is a combination of numerous hues of grey, black and brown that gradually formed into a cement-like stripe, appearing nearly petrified by the years and the elements. The second and wider stripe is streaked with shades of red and orange, light peach and even pink. The last level, (the one closest to the desert floor), is colored with every shade of brown imaginable, interspersed with greens and yellows, as it seems that some sort of plant has found a way to survive by living in those rocks. It's amazing… and best of all, there are trees!

I didn't realize how much I missed trees, having lived most of my life in Oregon where I took them for granted, but this afternoon when we pulled into this place of such unique beauty, I reveled in the trees most of all. Of course these aren't like the trees I'm used to, but here, each tree is different. One was a huge gnarled giant; twisted and bent, with short, sharp branches protruding leafless from a stout grey trunk which was at least three feet in diameter - and looking more like giant thorns than branches. Then there was the one that resembled a giant bouquet of flowers, with bloom covered branches that bent down and reached all the way to the ground, like the willow trees I'm so familiar with, but these branches are stiff and unyielding… as though they are protecting whatever it is that resides beneath their shade. And the flowers are brilliantly colored; from yellow to orange, and even red and purple.. But the thing that impressed me most was that no two trees were alike… and yet they all seemed to give off an aura of power and individual character. It's as though their very existence was a testimony of hope and perseverance; an acknowledgment that the will to survive will triumph… no matter the circumstances.

As we parked our RVs, the first thing I noticed when I got out, (after the cliff and the trees, of course), was the almost perfect silence… not even the sound of a fly or a squirrel; just the wind as it whistled through the trees, bouncing off the cliff and then returning once again to rustle the branches. It was like desert music – but it didn't come from one direction or another; it came from everywhere … and I watched, entranced - as it blew a single leaf in a never-ending circle.

Now if only it wasn't so HOT! In my town of Gold Beach, the average winter temperature is 60 and the average summer temperature is 70, so I guess I'm not what you'd call acclimated to this kind of heat - no matter how "dry" they say it is. Including my time at Mittry Lake, Yuma,

Sun City, Blythe and now Parker, it hasn't dipped below 80 degrees for a single day, (and it's usually even higher), and this is still early Spring!

Naturally, I parked as close as I could to one of the bigger trees, hoping to find shade and relief from the hot, desert sun, but even that doesn't help… so I'm back to using my spray bottle and keeping myself wet all the time - and I may even have to pull out the summer clothes I so carefully tucked away after my lecture from John and Mary about modesty if this heat doesn't let up.

Sister Sarah parked her RV about 30 yards from mine so we could be alone… and yet still be together, which is nice because I'll have both company AND solitude. When we first got here, I pulled out my miracle Bible to read while Sister Sarah gathered her beads and set up a table outside her RV, where she is busily making necklaces and bracelets to sell alongside the road in Parker. I'm so glad she brought me here – and so glad to have uninterrupted time to study, pray and think about everything that's happened so far – and everything that might lie ahead.

I really **need** that right now - especially after my meeting with the Food and Beverage Director this morning. I was there at 10:00 sharp, but of course he was late… which I had expected, (and why I brought a book to read), so I didn't mind the one-hour wait. When he finally did arrive, looking disheveled and half-asleep, without so much as a hello, he motioned me into his office and ordered one of the women to get him a cup of coffee.

I don't think he was actually reading my two inch-thick application, because he didn't ask me a single question and leafed through it in a matter of minutes. When he finished, he looked up at me and said, "I see you're applying for a job as a food server. You **DO** realize that we'll have 5 restaurants at the new resort - and that it will be completely up to **me** whether you work in fine dining or at the hamburger stand, don't you," to which I nodded yes, and he continued on. "Assuming you don't have a criminal record or anything in your past that would prevent you from getting your gaming license, I think I can find a place for you."

"Thank you, so much," I said as I smiled with relief. "Of course, I'd rather work the fine-dining restaurant, and I think I'd be a good addition to your team - but where ever you can find room for me, I'm willing to work my way up,." I added enthusiastically.

"Well, there's no 'working your way up' around here," he stated without hesitation. "It's simple; I decide where to put you – and that's all she wrote. I see you don't have a telephone number or address – so why not?"

I quickly told him that I'd been traveling in my RV, (deciding that this probably wasn't the best time to tell the whole story), but I told him I was a poet who put on shows in places where people didn't have money to pay, so I needed to find a regular job so I could buy a computer and set up a web-site, as well as live and eat. I also told him that since the resort wouldn't be opening for two weeks yet, I'd already scheduled a show at the Parker Public Library on the March 24th, and would be leaving town in my RV until then. After the show, I would be parked in that big dirt field just past the grocery store and McDonalds, and that I'd really appreciate it if since I didn't have a telephone, I could just stop in at Human Resources every few days and check on the status of the opening date. He had no way of knowing that I was down to my last five dollars, (nor did I want him to), but he answered my question in a way that completely caught me by surprise… especially after my reaction to his previous advances. He looked up at me, grinned in an almost evil way – shook his head and said, "Well, I think maybe it would be better if I stopped by your RV and let you know when we're opening. That way we could get better acquainted and I could decide exactly which restaurant to put you in."

Oh great… just what I needed, I thought. A power-hungry skirt chaser who thought he could have anyone he wanted - for a price. Instead of my earlier reaction discouraging him, I got the feeling that he considered me a challenge, and just couldn't help giving it one more try. Well, I thought to myself, I hope he DOES stop by, because maybe I can plant a few seeds in that dry, desert heart of his! I'll just make sure we stand outside and talk – right next to my "walk with Jesus" sign!

"Yes, sir," I answered. "That would be fine. I'll let you know as soon as I get back. In fact, maybe you'd like to come to my show at the public library on the 24th - because that would be the best way to get to know me."

"We'll see," he said… with obvious disinterest as he lightly brushed off my invitation without even considering it. "Right now, I've got work to do, so let me know when you're back in town and we'll figure something out."

And that was how it ended… and that's why I'm so glad to be out here… away from all the glitz and glitter, greed and lust. I know Jesus used to preach in such places… because that was where he was really needed – and so I wasn't about to let this one evil, lecherous man discourage me!

So here I am - alone at last; well, almost alone, anyway, since Sister Sarah seems to be as much of a loner as I am, so we haven't talked all day. Now everything would be just perfect if it wasn't so darn HOT outside! I've got screens on my windows, so they're all open… and I'm very thankful for the wind, even if it is so hot it's like standing in front of a blast furnace. But at least it's moving air… so if I stay wet, it helps. I think it's time to put on my shorts and a sleeveless top and thongs. In fact, I'm even considering donning my swimsuit, (which is what Sister Sarah is already wearing). I mean really… what are the odds that some strange man will show up way out here?

Yup – time to change clothes!

chapter 56

March 21, 1999

My worst nightmare caught up with me today, and in a supposedly "sacred" place, (which, by the way, I'm now absolutely SURE isn't sacred). In fact, I tremble every time I even think about it. I'm glad I took pictures, because I'll NEVER see that beautiful place in person again!

It was a typical blue-sky morning, too early to be unbearably hot - but clear, sunny and quiet, as even the wind hadn't yet begun to blow. I was sitting at my dining table reading my Bible, (with all the windows open to take advantage of the early morning coolness), when suddenly I heard a loud buzzing sound. I probably wouldn't have noticed it had it only been the sound of a few flies (or even bees), because I was inside with screened windows, but this was no normal buzzing. It sounded like nothing I've ever heard before... like a million bees - angry and coming directly toward me... and the HMMMM was getting louder by the minute!

Then I heard the sound of hail, which wasn't possible because it was at least 80 degrees outside, but the occasional loud ping, ping, ping quickly became so rapid-fire you couldn't tell one ping from another, and I suddenly realized that the RV (with me inside) was being attacked! I think I mentioned before that I have only one real phobia, and that's bees... and here they were, attacking me - and ping, ping, pinging against the walls and roof of my RV.

As I ran around from window to window, closing each one in case the screens had little holes in them, perhaps large enough for a bee to squeeze through, I looked outside and saw literally thousands of what looked like either very large, oddly shaped and angry honey bees or hornets of some kind... and they weren't just going about their normal business; no... they were interested in only one thing – getting inside Lucky.

I hate to admit it, but I was in a state of panic as I ran around like a crazy woman stuffing socks and washcloths into any possible openings where I thought the bees might squeeze in. I also took the time to turn on my tape recorder so I could share the experience with my mother as I was doing my best to bee-proof my little home on wheels. That way she, (and I... when I wrote a book about my adventures someday) could hear the humming and pinging as I told her what was going on exactly *as it happened*.

But there were so many places for the bees to get in... such as the vent for the furnace and the vent for the water pipes, and the vent for the refrigerator, and even the little space between the "dog house" and the driver's seat, where the heat from the engine kept burning my leg because the wood had rotted and was falling apart.

As I ran around the RV, looking for any places I might have missed, I carried a big book with me so in case a bee found its way in, I could smash it. I certainly wasn't going to rely on a rolled up newspaper, and other than my Bible, I'd gladly sacrifice any book I had to keep from getting stung. According to my mother, I was deathly allergic to bees when I was a young child, and once when a hornet's nest fell from a tree in the local park where we were having a family picnic, I was stung and they had to rush me to the hospital. She said that we barely made it in time as my throat was beginning to swell shut and I was unable to breathe.

I personally don't remember that particular event because I was too young, but it does explain why I was always so unreasonably afraid of bees. I've never been stung, as far as I can remember, because I can outrun just about any bee in the country, which is what I've done all my life. As soon as my mother told me the story, it all began to make sense. I know

I should be carrying one of those shots people who are allergic to bees keep on hand, but I haven't been to a doctor since they cured me from Lyme Meningitis in 1994, which has been five years now, so I was completely unprepared - and too far from a hospital to get help in time if I was stung and had an allergic reaction.

At last… I found myself able to relax for a moment… fairly sure that I'd covered every possible entry point. So I sat down at my table - where I could look out the window, talk to my mother on the tape recorder, and hopefully wait until bees eventually gave up and went away. With the windows closed, it was quickly turning into an oven inside Lucky and I was dripping with sweat, (although I'm not sure if it was from the heat or the fear; most likely both. I had a feeling that they were after the water in my tanks, which I could understand in this hot, dry desert… but surely when they realized there was no way they could get to it, they would move on.

And that's when it happened. All of a sudden one of the buzzzzz-ing sounds came from inside, rather than outside… and my heart sank as I realized that they had found a way in.

I was more frightened than I can ever remember being, (including having a knife held to my throat as I was being raped), and I looked over at Sister Sarah's RV, only 150 feet away, and I could see that she had deserted her tables of beads and feathers and was sitting inside looking over at me, probably wondering what I wanted to do. Because I love to draw, I just happened to have some sheets of poster board on hand, so I grabbed the biggest piece I could find and a big, black marker pen and wrote in large bold letters, *"I'm allergic to bees. Let's go!!! Now!!"*

She waved emphatically to let me know that she had read the message I was holding in my big front windshield, and immediately climbed into her driver's seat and started her engine. I was also in my driver's seat, but I was busy trying to kill the few bees that had found their way inside before starting the engine, and praying that I had enough battery power (after being parked for three days) to get just one good start out of Lucky without having to go outside and use my battery pac. (No way was I going outside!!)

And that's when I looked over and saw that Sister Sarah was stuck in the sand. She tried and tried, but the hole her back tires were digging just kept getting deeper and deeper, until finally she threw up her hands and yelled as loud as she could through her open window, "HELP ME! I'm stuck! Come push me!"

Sister Sarah's beat-up RV didn't have screens on the windows, so when she shouted at me through one that was open, I thought, "How could she leave her window open?" I knew this tough old Indian woman wasn't afraid of bees, but having an open window at a time like this was beyond my comprehension. Then I looked closer... which wasn't easy with her RV parked so far away, and I noticed that there weren't very many bees around HER vehicle, so they must have picked mine to swarm. I really wanted to get out and help her push, and I felt terrible that I was too much of a coward to do it, but there was no way I was leaving the comparative safety of Lucky... and even as I sat there in the driver's seat trying to figure out what to do next, I was constantly using my book to hit (and hopefully kill) the few bees that had found their way inside and were now buzzing angrily around me.

I finally decided to turn my big sheet of poster board over and quickly wrote another message on the other side, **"I can't! You come here!"** And again she yelled louder than I thought humanly possible, "NO WAY! I'M STAYING HERE! At the time I didn't understand why - but it wasn't long before I did. But for the time being, I was out of options. I couldn't possibly just drive away and leave her there... even if Lucky DID start, because she refused to come over. So what could I possibly do?

I've been through a lot of things in my life, some of them very frightening, but NEVER, not until that very moment, had I literally SMELLED fear. I've heard the "saying" "don't run or the animal will smell your fear," but now I realized first-hand that it wasn't merely a saying... it was a fact! Suddenly the air around me was literally filled with the acrid stink of ammonia, like one of those capsules you break open and put up to the nose of someone who has fainted. The smell literally burned my eyes, as well as my nose, and was like sniffing a bottle of ammonia. And the worst part of all was that the smell was coming from **ME!**

That's when I decided it was time to 'call for reinforcements', as I was sitting in the driver's seat with no idea what to do - and still batting at bee after bee with my book. But every time I killed one, another one took its place, so I was completely helpless against a swarm of what I was beginning to think must be the dreaded *killer bees*. So I climbed out of the driver's seat, put my "bee killing" book down and kneeled in front of my couch/bed. And for the first time in my life, I didn't pray in quiet humility... no, I actually shouted as I called upon the power of my Lord and Savior, Jesus Christ, to **banish** these deadly creatures. I completely shocked myself as I literally commanded them to **be gone**, and continued to call upon the Holy Spirit to surround and protect me. I've never even considered doing such a thing before... but as I stood there, now more angry than fearful, I yelled at the top of my lungs and demanded, in the name of my Lord, Jesus Christ... that these creatures leave me alone. I didn't even stop praying long enough to use my book to kill the ones that were already inside the RV and buzzing around my face as I prayed - because I was long past that point. Then, as I finished my prayer, I got up from my knees... and it was as though my whole countenance had changed.

Suddenly I was no longer afraid; instead I was angry - like I was a soldier in a raging battle between good and evil and I stood up without fear - and held my Bible in the air, as I pleaded with God, "My Lord... if it is truly my time, then **take me**, and I shall revel in the glory of being with thee again, and I ask forgiveness for my sins. But if it **isn't** my time, then I command these deadly creatures to leave. I command them in your holy name - and I stand in the circle of your protection. Get thee behind me, Satan... you and your evil minions have no power over me - because I belong to Jesus, and in **His** name I command you, **BE GONE!**"

And that when it happened... not slowly or a little bit at a time, but in a matter of less than a minute, the constant sound of hail hitting my RV and the hmmmm that was so loud I could barely hear myself think just moments before was now quiet. I couldn't believe it! The bees were gone! I had called upon the power of the Lord in perfect faith – and they had vanished! I shouted with joy and praised God over and over again, tears rolling down my cheeks... no longer worrying about the few that were left inside because they had no power over me anymore. This feeling was completely new to me - something I'd never experienced before... and for that moment, I felt completely bathed in the light of both His power and His protection.

But that's when I heard a horn honking, and I turned my attention to Sister Sarah in her RV. Oh no! I couldn't believe my eyes! I hadn't thought of that! The possibility had never even crossed my mind that when I, (through the power of the my Lord and master), commanded the bees to be gone, that they would move over to Sister Sarah's motor home. Now I understood why **she** refused to come over to Lucky when she was stuck in the sand. Until that moment, I had no idea just how many bees there actually were! Sister Sarah had a white RV and now the entire side of it was black; solid black and moving, like a coat of living paint... as the swarm had left Lucky and gone over to her.

Oh no, I cried! I would never want my own safety to come at the cost of someone else's! Why didn't I think of that? I'd gladly give my own life to save another – and yet that's what had just happened. I was fine – and now Sister Sarah was the one in danger! I was heartsick... and even more upset than I was when they were attacking me.

But apparently, the Lord wasn't going to let that happen, and (as always... so you'd think I'd learn eventually), there was a really BIG silver lining to this particular cloud. As I watched Sister Sarah's RV, trying to figure out how I could help her, I let out a cry of relief and joy when I saw her suddenly come flying out of her door, (with her cat in her arms), and running straight for Lucky. Now if we could get out of this dreadful place! No wonder she had refused to come over when I asked her with my big poster board sign; it was because she could see the solid wall of bees on my RV that weren't visible as I looked out my window. But now that they were swarming **her** RV, she was more than willing to make a run for mine and together we could escape. "Thank you, Jesus! Thank you," I said tearfully as I hurried to open the door and let her in.

"Let's get the heck out of here," she said, as she sat down in the passenger seat, still holding her cat.

"Sounds great to me… but let's just hope Lucky starts," I answered as I prayed out loud, "Please Lord, just one start… just one start – that's all we need." The problem was that I was parked with my front end as close to a tree as possible, (hoping for some shade), which meant that now I had to back out… and the desert floor behind me wasn't flat, but full of dips and ridges, not to mention boulders and cactus. Usually, even if Lucky **does** start, I have to let it idle for a few minutes, allowing the engine to warm up before I put it into gear, or it dies. I knew that if that happened, there wouldn't be enough battery power left for a second start… and since there were still quite a few bees inside, there was no way we could take the time to let it warm up - which left us only one choice; I needed to start the engine and then immediately throw it into "drive" and gun it… hoping that enough gas would make it all the way up the long fuel line, from the gas tank in the far back of the rig, to keep it running. Lucky doesn't have an electric fuel pump, (those came on later models), which is why it always takes a few minutes to warm up… but hopefully, if I gave it enough gas, there was a chance that we could lurch backward fast enough to keep going. It was a gamble… but it was our only option at the time, unless, of course, I wanted to sit there for a few minutes while the engine warmed up and possibly get stung, and maybe even die before we could make it to the hospital in Parker.

"Please Lord," I begged. "Please help us," I said again and again as I turned the key; and halleluiah… the engine started! I immediately pushed down on the gas pedal as hard as I could, not caring if we flew over the first couple of bumps and not caring about and damage to Lucky… but I'm afraid our joy was short lived as the minute I put it in gear and pressed on the gas, the engine sputtered and died.

We looked at each other in disbelief; stunned even though we had known it was a possibility. We both knew that the chances of a second start on what battery power I had left were slim to none, but we HAD to try. Again I begged, "Please Lord, just one more time! Please!" And again, I turned the key... but this time I got an 'almost dead battery' groan, groan, groan... each one getting weaker and not knowing whether to pump the gas pedal and take the chance of flooding the engine - or whether I should just hold it all the way to the floor... the usual thing ones does when an engine floods.

But the Lord must have been with us still, because on the fourth groan... just as it sounded so weak I was sure all hope was lost - the engine started - and I slammed it into gear and OFF WE WENT, so fast that the cupboards flew open and the floor was littered with everything that had been on the countertops. When we arrived, we drove over this stretch of desert doing 5 miles an hour because it was so wild and strew with obstacles - and now, here we were doing at least 30, and literally flying through the air.

I smashed the oil pan in my 1957 Chevy back in the late 1960's by going so fast over a rise in the road that when I landed, the weight of the car brought the middle right down to the pavement, and I began to wonder where the oil pan was in Lucky, because we were flying over those bumps and landing so hard that both of us were actually hitting our heads on the ceiling as we bounced in the air - and I was and holding onto the steering wheel like it was a life-line, flinching every time we bottomed out.

But we made it... and after half a mile or so, I slowed down and we were both too stunned to even speak. It was like we were in a traumatic trance... both of us speechless and probably both wondering what had just happened back there. Sister Sarah had left every thing she owned in the world inside her motor home, and yet we couldn't go back and get it. In fact, I was afraid that the bees were still following us, and a half mile didn't seem nearly far enough away to satisfy me.

That's when Sister Sarah suggested that we drive to the Police Station in Parker and tell them what had happened, which is exactly what we did. They, in turn, called "Fish and Game", and the Reservation Police, asking them to join us as we drove back out to the site. I parked Lucky and then Sister Sarah and I climbed into one of the police cars so we could show them exactly where the bees had attacked.

When we arrived at the fateful spot, the Fish and Game Wardens used high pitched whistles, (like dog whistles - unable to be heard by the human ear) to drive the bees away and while we waited, the policemen told us a horrible story. They said that 4 people, (two adults and two children), had been killed by a swarm of Africanized Bees not far from here during the past two days, and that Fish and Game was going to take a sample of one of these bees to the lab so they could study it and see if these, too, had been those dreaded "killer bees".

Oh my gosh... what a day! So much for peace and quiet! And talk about spring cleaning... I couldn't shake the feeling that there were still bees hiding everywhere inside Lucky, from closets to bedding, so I removed practically everything - shaking each item out and searching every cupboard, nook and cranny for any of those little devils that might be still lurking inside... waiting to get me while I was sleeping. I doubted if I'd get much sleep for the next few days, but at least I was alive... and I couldn't hear the hmmmm of bees anymore. Whew! What a nightmare – but what a miracle!!!

When we returned to the police station, I drove back to my dirt field, and the Fish and Game Rangers promised that they would let me know when they found out whether our attackers had been the Africanized Bees.

So how's that for an adventure? I think I've had more than my share of excitement for today, so now that everything has been searched, shaken and declared "bee-free", and I've bathed, washed my hair and ALMOST feel like I don't have bugs crawling all over me, I think it's time for me to TRY and get some much needed sleep.

But wasn't it AWESOME the way the Lord came through when I needed Him most? Seeing and feeling the power of His protection was well worth the fear and danger. Perhaps this was just another lesson in my preparation for whatever it is He wants me to do.

chapter 57

March 24, 1999

Tonight is the night I put on my show at the Parker Public Library...
and I have no idea why I'm so nervous. I've had three days to calm down
since my "adventure" with the bees... and guess what? That particular
cloud had more than **one** *silver lining*.

First, there was the fact that when the bees moved from Lucky to Sister Sarah's RV, it scared even that tough, bee-friendly Indian woman into
leaving her place and running for Lucky... silver lining number ONE.

Then, when Sister Sarah and I got back from our killer bee encounter in
the desert, I parked Lucky in the same dirt field behind the vendor booths,
and suddenly every single vendor, along with many of their customers,
crowded around me, wanting to hear every single detail about what had
happened to us. (And talk about a chance to bear witness! How much
more profound can you get?) People, who wouldn't even give me the time
of day before – were now clamoring for every excruciating detail. Some
of them seemed to enjoy hearing about how terrified I was, (you know –
white woman, big chicken...), while others showed genuine concern and
expressed happiness at the fact that neither of us had been hurt.

But either way, it didn't matter. Sister Sarah, who they'd all known for
many years, was there... when for some unexplained reason, (her version,

since she hadn't been with me in Lucky as I prayed), the bees suddenly made a mass exodus from my RV and went over to hers. That's where I was given the perfect opportunity to bear witness to the power of our Lord, when I told them about the prayer, (my story), and not a single listener questioned it; at least not after I turned on my tape recorder and played the tape I had left recording throughout the entire episode. So there it was; the perfect example of how faith can move mountains, (and killer bees); silver lining number TWO.

And by the way, this morning a representative from Fish and Game dropped by and told me that yes... they WERE Africanized Bees. That's why they were so aggressive and yes... they were probably after the water in my holding tanks. Whew! Talk about facing your biggest fear and living to tell about it. Once again... for the thousandth time... Thank you, Jesus!

Ever since I drove into Parker for the first time, I sensed a big, brick wall of hatred and mistrust standing between the Indian residents and the white residents, (especially this skinny white girl), so it doesn't matter if they found joy or humor, (or even satisfaction), in my tribulation because it gave me a chance to talk about Jesus – and the power of prayer. At least the bee story opened the door... which then allowed me to show them not only humility, (as I told the story and gave ALL the credit to whom it belongs... God), but to treat my Indian listeners with both respect and courtesy... something they didn't seem to expect from whites, (and who can blame them).

So, why am I so nervous today? After everything that's happened, putting on a show should be a walk in the park... and yet I can't get rid of the butterflies in my stomach. (Oh well – at least they aren't bees!) Ha! Ha!

The fact is, I don't expect many people to show up tonight because I didn't have very many color flyers to put up, nor am I sure that Parker is the kind of town where people would come to hear an inspirational poet anyway; especially one they've never even heard of. The radio show I appeared on to advertise the location, date and time of my reading, (something I really hate to call it because I don't use a single piece of paper), aired at 7:30 in the morning, and from what I've seen so far, the local Indians live pretty hard-drinking, late night partying lives… so I doubt that many (if any) of them heard the sample poems I did on the radio show – nor heard my personal invitation for them to come and hear more at the library tonight at 7:00.

That's why I decided at the last minute, (yesterday morning), to spend the five dollars I'd been hanging on to for food, and had the print shop make some more photocopies of the poetry I hand out at each show, and to have a three more color flyers printed, which I immediately posted on telephone poles in likely spots around town. I emptied my purse a few minutes ago and I have exactly 75 cents left; not even enough to even wash a load of clothes at the local laundromat.

Since the flood, the miracle of the Bible, and the visitation, I no longer think of money as being important anymore. But under my current financial circumstances, I have no choice but to move it up on the list. I need gasoline… because every time I drive to the public sewer dump to empty my tanks, I have to drive around town long enough for the alternator to do its job and recharge my battery – or Lucky won't start the next time I need to empty my tanks or get fresh water. I used quite a few gallons wandering (and speeding), through the desert with Sister Sarah, so gasoline has become a must. I also need money to buy drinking water, because the water here in Parker isn't even close to potable. Then there's my propane tanks, which are nearly empty, (another thing I MUST have in order to keep my refrigerator running), and it would be nice, (after almost a month since I last went grocery shopping in Yuma) to have some money for food. I know the true riches are in Heaven, and I also know that God will provide, but I'd sure be thrilled if there was enough money in my little yellow picnic basket after the show to pay for these items; but do I dare to hope? (There go the butterflies again…).

I need to calm down… so I keep reminding myself that I'm doing MY part, and now the rest is up to God. *His will be done; on Earth as it is in Heaven,* so it's time for me to quit worrying about money, and propane and food… and start looking at tonight as just another opportunity to gather among friends and share my art and my testimony… like I've done so many times before. If it weren't for my critical financial situation, I'd be happy if only **two** people showed up tonight… but since I have no idea how long it will be until the casino opens, (nor how long it will be until I get my first pay check after that), I'm having trouble controlling my nerves. (You'd think I'd have learned not to worry and that *everything will be fine* – like it always is. But that's much easier said than done!

I don't remember having a single birthday party when I was growing up, but I did have a Halloween party, and it was the same year that my father, my step-mother Roma, my brother and I first moved to Oregon City. It was only one month after I had made such a fool of myself by putting on a big campaign for cheerleader in the 9th grade, something never done at that school, and Roma, (bless her heart), offered to throw me a big Halloween party - hoping to help me get acquainted with my new classmates and to put my rather shaky introduction behind me. I can remember sitting in my room after all the preparations were finished… and being scared to death that no one would show up.

Together, Roma, my brother and I had turned the horse barn into a huge party room, complete with colored lights, music and bales of hay every-where. We also turned the garage into a "haunted house", complete with long cooked spaghetti noodles that hung down in front of the face of each blindfolded person who dared to walk through the "haunted garage" and we even had bowls of peeled grapes, which were offered up as "eye balls".

The reason I'm bringing up those memories from so long ago again, is because that's exactly how I feel tonight; like I'm throwing a party – and no one will come. But they DID come to my Halloween party… almost every single person I invited - and they WILL come to the library tonight. So I guess it's time to put those butterflies away and concentrate on putting on an entertaining (and enlightening) show.

Wow - what a week this has been – and now tonight will be the frost-ing on the cake; my first show on an Indian Reservation.

chapter 58

March 26, 1999

1:00 A.M.

I knew everything would turn out fine – and it did!

I just got back from my show at the library, and it went even better than I had hoped. All the credit, of course, goes to my Lord, because for some reason, not only did I play the guitar with skill beyond my ability, but I don't think my singing voice has EVER sounded so good, (and believe me - I'm no singer!). Isn't that wonderful… and even better yet is the way the audience reacted.

Sister Sarah came along with me to help turn the library reading room into a staging area, gathering all the chairs we could find for people to sit in and finding a table big enough to hold the copies of my poetry and my little yellow picnic basket. We had just finished getting everything ready as the people started to arrive and even though the crowd was small, it was bigger than I had expected; at least 25 to 30 people, and at least two-thirds of them were Indians.

But here's the real shocker… and it was so amazing that I still can't go to sleep, which is why I'm wide awake at 1:00 in the morning.

The show was scheduled from 7:00 p.m. to 8:00 p.m., because one hour was as long as I thought I could hold the audience's attention. But hot-diggity-dog… was I ever wrong!

At 8:00, when I thanked the folks for coming and began to say good-bye, someone in the crowd raised their hand and said, "I don't know about anyone else, but I'd sure like to hear some more."

And then other people started nodding and agreeing, and pretty soon someone stood up and said, "Everyone who wants Abigayle to keep going, raise your hand," and almost every hand in the room went up, some waving emphatically like children begging to be called on by the teacher.

I was both shocked – and honored… but I still didn't want to make anyone who wanted to leave feel uncomfortable, nor did I want to appear rude by not going along with the rest of the crowd. That's why I responded to their request by saying, "OK, folks; I've got an idea. Let's take a little break. That way those of you who need to leave can do so, and the rest of you can use the bathroom, get a drink of water or just stretch your legs. Then, in about 10 minutes, I'll continue for as long as you want me to. How's that for a deal?" I asked. I got my answer in the form of enthusiastic applause, so I thanked them profusely and promised to start again in 10 minutes.

That was at 8:00 – and it was at 11:00, (three hours later), when the police showed up at the door. It just happens that the Police Department is located right across the street from the library, and when they saw all the cars parked in the lot and the lights still on, they were concerned and wanted to see what was going on. And who could blame them… but their appearance gave me the excuse I needed to stop, because by that time, my voice was just about gone and my throat was getting sore from so many hours of talking and singing. (I knew I should have listened to the doctors in High School when they told me I was damaging my vocal chords by cheerleading every year!)

I promised the Police that as soon as we put all the chairs back and cleaned up the room, we would vacate the premises, but they didn't seem too worried about it - and told me to take my time. That might as well have been an open invitation for the two dozen people who wanted me to stay and sign copies of the poems they had collected from the table behind me. Some just wanted to talk, and others to share stories of their own, which was great. And even better, one lady asked me to speak to her garden club and another at her church group next week. I met some wonderful people tonight; and just like at all the other shows I've put on, these people are the reason I've decided to get a job and earn the money to buy a computer; so I can have a website… which will be my way of keeping in touch with them as I travel. .

Once everyone but Sister Sarah and I had left, I opened my picnic basket, and even though this is a poor town, I was amazed to find almost $100 in it. Much of it was in one dollar bills and even some change, so I knew that it wasn't *extra* money. No, it was more like the widow's mite, and it brought tears to my eyes to think of how generous and appreciative these people had been.

So, now I have enough money for gasoline, propane, more flyers and copies of my poems for the next show, and even a much needed night at an RV park, (so I can recharge my batteries; both in Lucky and in me). All in all, I'd say it was a wonderful night, and, as usual, my worrying was for nothing. And guess what… I might just have enough money left for some groceries.

chapter 59

April 1, 1999

It's almost midnight, and the end of yet another magnificent day! All I did today was talk… and talk… and talk – and although my voice is just about gone… is was a wonderful day!

It appears that I've been accepted - at least by SOME of my Indian friends - because they are now bringing their own friends over to meet me almost every day… and we sit inside Lucky and talk by the hour.

At noon today, I did three poems at the Ladies Garden Club luncheon, and afterwards we talked and then talked some more; the ladies asking questions, and me answering them and telling stories both from the road and from before I left Gold Beach.

And then, early this evening, my WWII Veteran friend, Don, came over and shared even more of the pain of his war experiences with me, and we talked, and talked and talked.

The only person I DIDN'T talk to was the Director of Food and Beverage at the Indian Casino, because when HE appeared at the door of my RV, it was already getting dark outside and I couldn't shake the feeling that he had more on his mind than just talking… which is why I greeted him at the door and then stepped **outside**, walking to the back of Lucky so "we could talk where it was cooler", I suggested. I was hoping he was there to give me a starting date for my job at the casino - as well as hoping he'd see the sign on my bumper that said "walk with Jesus"; which he did.

In fact, he didn't make any bones about hiding his intentions once he noticed the big reflective lettering, because he stared at it for longer than was necessary and then said, "Well, I came by to let you know that we're still behind schedule and that I'm not sure when the new casino will be open... and I also thought we might get a little better acquainted so I could see which restaurant to put you in - but then I saw your sign," he said as he pointed to my bumper.

"So I guess whatever I might have been thinking about you and I getting to know each other better went right out the window when I read it, because I'm already in enough trouble with the Big Guy and I certainly don't need to make him any madder at me!"

Wow... I didn't expect THAT reaction – and I was truly shocked that he had the nerve to think... let alone "say" what he said next.

"So it looks like you'll be selling hamburgers," he announced, "but I still don't have any idea when... so just stop by the office every few days and see where things stand," he said without even looking at me as he rudely turned and stalked away. I've never met a prospective employer like him before... and I thought it was unspeakably rude that he didn't even bother to offer a handshake or a polite goodbye.

"Ok," I answered to his backside as he almost hurried to his car, as if he was trying to escape whatever it was he was afraid of. "Do I need to talk to you directly - or can the lady at the front desk tell me?" I asked, almost yelling since by then he was already in his car with the engine running.

"She can help you," was the last thing he said as he left in a cloud of dust. Hmmmm... I guess my sign is working, I thought as I actually laughed out loud. And yet I'm really disappointed that I'll be stuck selling hamburgers for minimum wage - rather than making good tips in the fine dining restaurant? But at last, I've learned my lesson and this time I'm not worried. I trust my Lord completely, so if He wants me to sell hamburgers – that's what I'll do... and if not, then I'm sure everything will be fine.

But even after Mr. XXX, the Food and Beverage Director left, I still felt grimy and soiled. This man wasn't going to be an easy boss to work for, and yet - I always did love a challenge. The fact is, he just acknowledged his belief in God... or my sign wouldn't have bothered him so much. That means there's always the possibility that somehow, with the Lord's help, I could possibly influence him. Now I just need to make the little bit of money I have left last until the new resort/casino opens... and he gave me absolutely no idea when that will be.

And talk about coincidences; after I filled my gas and propane tanks, added two quarts of oil, restocked the photocopies of both my poetry and the color flyers for my next show, (when ever and where ever that might be), and did my laundry, I have exactly $5.00 left over, which puts me right back where I started before my night at the library - except now I have my tanks emptied, batteries charged, clothes cleaned and all the propane and gas I need, at least for awhile. I think I'll make a list and see how much I can get at the grocery store tomorrow for my $5.00.

And who could have imagined how much **joy** I could get out of one $5 bill? There was a time in my life when having only $5.00 in my purse would have been completely unacceptable, and I'd have considered myself broke. But now - I'm not only thrilled to have it, but I'm actually enjoying all the plotting and planning; figuring out how to get the most food for my money. It's a pleasant surprise – and yet one more learning experience, (as well as some much-needed training for whatever God has in store for me).

Let's see... according to the newspaper ads this week, (which I found at the laundromat), I should be able to get a loaf of bread, a sack of potatoes, a jar of peanut butter, a dozen eggs, some cheap margarine, and maybe even a few packages of Top Ramon. That's a lot of food, especially for someone who eats as little as I do, and I'm having more fun than I thought possible just sitting here making my little grocery list. I'm already excited about my trip to the grocery store tomorrow.

But don't worry, I'm far from starving, (because I know my Lord would never let that happen), but I AM to the point of having to use all the old cans of vegetables and soup I bought long ago, (probably when they were on sale - and so cheap that I couldn't resist). And now, even though I don't especially like canned mixed vegetables and pork and beans, they are serving me well, and I still have more cans in my cupboards. But pork and beans or not, I can already just imagine the taste of that peanut butter - and maybe a fried egg with toast. Yummy!

So all is well - and I am truly blessed. Now I just have to wait for the new Blue Water Resort and Casino to open so I can earn enough money for a computer, learn to use it, and design a website which I'll call "poetry on the road". And while I'm parked here in my dirt field behind the vendor booths, I'll use that time to get to know some of the people I met at my shows at the library, the garden club, the Senior Center, the Soroptimist Club and the church. The delayed casino opening has actually turned out for the best - because tomorrow I have several people stopping by to talk; mostly troubled brothers and sisters who are having problems and just need someone to listen - someone who cares, and someone to remind them that they are NEVER alone because the Lord is with them. .

And speaking of the Lord, He certainly does work in mysterious ways… and as always - there is a silver lining to the cloud. Every minute I spend here waiting for the casino to open is turning out to be "time well spent".

chapter 60

April 3, 1999

What a glorious, beautiful morning... just one more in a string of never-ending blue-sky days. I remember when the citizens of Gold Beach told me that I would eventually get tired of looking at the ocean and how I refused to believe them... and now I have to wonder if here in the desert, do the people ever get tired of waking up every day to the sunshine?

Just in case I needed to be reminded of how much better it is to give than to receive, yesterday I was blessed with the perfect reminder... and it's a story I'll cherish for the rest of my life.

I was so excited about going to the grocery store with my $5.00 and seeing how much food I could get with it, that as soon as I'd finished my morning bible reading, I was all smiles and humming cheerfully as I climbed onto my bright red Western Flyer bicycle I call Candy, and rode a few blocks across the dirt field, past the casino and McDonalds, and into the grocery store parking lot. My mouth was already watering at the thought of all the goodies I was planning to buy, and I asked an employee, a young man who was gathering shopping carts, if it would be alright for me to lock my bicycle to the rack where customers leave their carts in the parking lot.

"Sure," he answered. "Wow, that's a really cool bike," he added with obvious appreciation. "I'll try to keep my eye on it for you, because around here, they'll cut that lock right off to get a bike like yours."

"Why thank you, young man. You're very kind. But don't worry if it gets stolen, I won't hold you responsible," I assured him with a laugh. "I know you've got a job to do, and I'll bet they keep you pretty busy around here."

He nodded in agreement, but still insisted that he would watch my bike. So off I went - five dollars in my pocket, a smile on my face, and dreams of the lunch I was going to have already making my mouth water. **And that's when I saw him.**

His face was almost completely covered by a full beard and mustache, and his skin was dark brown in color, as though he had spent many long hours in the hot desert sun. The one thing that stood out the most on his almost completely hidden face was his unbelievably bright blue, soul piercing eyes. They obviously weren't clouded by drugs or alcohol, and even though he was dirty and disheveled, his eyes gave him an air of intelligence and intense clarity of thought. As I approached him, he was in the process of removing a huge backpack, which was completely coated in desert dust; so much so that there was no way to tell what color it was… just like his clothes, his hair, and his beard. He wasn't tall, I'd say pretty close to my 5'8", but his movements as he took off the backpack and set it on the cement were strong and smooth… and by the time I reached him, his pack was already on the ground, and he turned toward me and gazed directly into my eyes as he spoke.

"Excuse me, ma'am," he said - just as I was about to pass him by and enter into the grocery store. "I'm mighty hungry, and I wonder if you could spare enough for a meal?"

Oh-no… I thought to myself. How can I possibly feed both of us on five dollars? I can't – even though I really wanted to.

"I'm **so** sorry, sir," I answered with sincere regret, "but all I have is $5.00 - and I was hoping to buy enough groceries to last for a few days.

If I had more, I'd be honored to give it to you... but I don't. I'm so sorry I can't help," I said, thinking of how many other people I'd passed on the road; some holding signs that said "will work for food", or "I'm hungry", and others just asking for help... and yet I'd never **once** felt the way I did at that moment when I had to tell this complete stranger that I didn't have enough money to feed him. Why? I have no idea... but even as I told him "no", I could feel the tears beginning to well up behind my eyes – and my throat began to ache.

"That's ok, ma'am," he said respectfully. "You're right; you should keep your $5.00. I'm sure somebody else will come along soon," he smiled kindly, as if he was the one trying to make ME feel better, rather than worrying about his own hunger.

"I really **do** wish I could help you," I said again, compelled for some reason to repeat myself as I sadly turned away and walked through the door and into the grocery store.

But something had just touched my heart... and I can't even find the words to describe how sick I felt to my stomach as I walked away from that man; a man I'd never even met before... and yet I couldn't get his eyes out of my mind. Suddenly the thought of peanut butter, or eggs, or potatoes didn't sound so appealing anymore. Even as I walked up and down the aisles, locating the articles I'd been so eager to buy just a few minutes earlier, I couldn't bring myself to remove them from the shelf and put them in my still empty basket.

"What have I done?" I asked myself, feeling so sick to my stomach with shame that I actually began to cry. Finally I couldn't stand it anymore and I abandoned my cart right there in the middle of the aisle and hurried back outside to find the hungry man.

But it was too late and he was gone... and I was so disappointed that I wanted to sit down right there in front of the grocery store where I had first seen him and cry. How could I have been so selfish – when the Lord has been so generous to me? And yet... there I was, too self-centered and too enamored by the "things" I could buy with that $5 bill to realize that

I had just missed out on an opportunity to return some small portion of the unbelievable charity that has been shown to me.

My stomach was still churning as I literally raced to my bicycle; running like someone was chasing me... as the other shoppers stopped and stared in amazement - probably wondering what was going on or who I was running from. But the fact was, I wasn't running "from" anyone; I was running "to" someone. I was in such a hurry that as I frantically tried to enter the combination that would open my bicycle lock, it took me three tries to get it right. There was no logical explanation for my almost desperate need to find this hungry man - and through him... to right a wrong that I had so selfishly and shamefully committed. I just felt driven – and I didn't care why.

As I searched the parking lot of the grocery store, the casino and Mc-Donalds, I couldn't figure out how he could have possibly gotten so far away in such a short amount of time. Nor did I understand why he had left his shady place by the door of the grocery store; especially when he had gone to all the trouble of removing his back-pack, and had assured me that someone else would come along. I hadn't been inside the store for more than 5 minutes, but still, I couldn't find him anywhere. Determined not to give up, I raced up and down street after street... still crying and kicking myself as I pedaled my bicycle as fast as I could – praying the entire time for the Lord to help me find this stranger who had, for some unexplainable reason, touched my heart so deeply.

And then suddenly, just as I turned a corner, there he was... walking down the sidewalk, carrying his dirt covered backpack. I've never been so relieved to find anyone in my entire life, (except for the time my 4 year old son, Jeremy, was lost in the woods).

"Hello there," I yelled when I was still 25 feet away, so excited that I couldn't wait until I caught up with him to announce my arrival. "Do you remember me?" I asked as I finally pulled up along side him and got off my bike. "I'm the lady you talked to outside the grocery store; you know... the one who had $5.00 and was so selfish that I refused to share

it with you. I'm ashamed that I did that – which is why I've been looking all over town for you; because I needed to apologize... and because I
want to buy you dinner," I gushed, talking so fast that he broke into a big
grin, probably wondering if I was ever going to stop and breathe.

"No, you don't," he said calmly, and with one of the most beautiful
smiles I've ever seen. "You don't OWE me anything, sister."

"But I do," I explained. "We ALL owe each other, because we're family. You are my brother-in-Christ, and I've been so blessed... which is
why I HAVE this $5.00 in the first place, so it would be my very great
HONOR if you'd let me share it with you. I'm so ashamed of my first
reaction... and I can only hope that you'll forgive my selfishness. I let
myself get so caught up in thinking about everything I could buy with
that $5.00 that for a moment I forgot what's really important. So please,
brother, won't you let me buy you a meal at McDonald's?" I asked, as I
pointed to the golden arches which were now several blocks away.

"Why yes, ma'am" he answered. "I'd like that very much. I'm afraid I'm
too dirty to go inside," he said as he looked down at his dust-covered clothing, "because I wouldn't want to offend anyone while they're eating, but I'll
wait outside, and whatever you bring me will be greatly appreciated."

So together... with me walking my bicycle, (rather than riding), and
him carrying his dust-covered back pack over one shoulder, rather than
on his back, we headed for the Golden Arches. As we walked and talked,
I noticed that he was extremely well-spoken and seemed well-educated,
which made me wonder what circumstances had brought him to living
a life on the streets and having to ask for food. But of course I couldn't
ask, because I didn't want to embarrass him. I'm sure he had his reasons,
and they weren't any of my business. All I knew was that for some reason,
I was drawn to this man... in a very spiritual way.

When we arrived at our destination, I honored my new friend's request
and left him waiting outside, while I went in to see how much food I
could get for $.5.00. Suddenly the canned goods I still had in my cup-
boards sounded just fine... so I stared at the menu board, trying to see

how much I could get for my new friend, no longer wanting anything for myself. And the feeling I had while I was standing there studying the menu was so amazing – it was like I was *high* on the joy of helping him - and that $5 bill was now bringing me MORE joy than it did when I was walking into the grocery store planning to buy food for myself. But I still didn't know what he liked to eat?

As I stood waiting in line, and trying to decide what to buy, suddenly someone tapped me on the shoulder. I was so deep in thought that it startled me and I jumped a little before I turned around to see who it was… and when I did, I just about fell over in shock. There stood JOHN AND MARY. I hadn't seen them since I drove away from our spot in the desert outside Quartzsite, (which seemed like years ago), with me so determined to spend time alone - and yet so thankful to them for all they had done for me… and here they were!

It was reunion time and we hugged, and hugged… and almost simul-taneously asked each other "how we were doing - and what we were doing here in Parker". That's when John, (a very smart and observant man) asked me, "So what are YOU doing buying lunch at McDonalds? If I remember right, we practically had to drag you into a restaurant. So I'm really curious; why are you here?"

That's when I told them about the man I met in front of the grocery store. It was almost my turn to order, so I gave them the VERY abbrevi-ated version; just telling them that this exceptional man, who for some reason had touched me beyond explanation, was standing outside the grocery store and had asked me if I could spare the money for a meal. I was ashamed to admit it, (even to John and Mary), but because I only had $5.00, I'd been selfish and told him "no". But then, when I went inside - I just couldn't bring myself to do it… I couldn't buy food for myself when this hungry man was standing right outside the door. So I searched until I found him - and here we are!

My version may have been abbreviated, but the three of us had spent enough time together for them to know me pretty well - and the tears of pure emotion in my eyes were obvious. Nothing more needed to be said - and they both reached out and hugged me again... and not one of us said another word; we just enjoyed a three-way hug with no explanation needed.

But then John broke the silence and asked, in that strong yet kindly voice of his, "So where is this man now?"

I suddenly remembered how many hours both he and Mary had preached to me about being careful as a woman alone on the road, so I fully expected another lecture on the subject when I answered, "He said he was too dirty to come inside, so that's him standing out there next to the window."

John and Mary both turned to look, and thank goodness my new friend was busy leaning over his backpack, either looking for something or rearranging his possessions, but I found myself greatly relieved that he didn't see us talking and then looking at him.

And that's when John just took over! He literally stepped in front of me in line and ordered two Big Macs, two large orders of french fries, and the largest super-sized coke they had. He and Mary were smiling the whole time – and I could see that now they too, were getting in on the joy! I was so happy!!! My $5 would never have bought all that food. And I was even happier when I saw John stick a $20 bill into the bag of burgers and fries. Praise God! And praise all of our brothers and sisters who love and serve our Lord, like John and Mary.

"Thank you, guys. Thank you so much!" I said, as I took the bag and the drink and headed towards the door.

"No problem," John answered. "But wait a minute; I just have one favor to ask you. We just pulled in a few minutes ago, and to tell you the truth, we saw Lucky parked in that big dirt field so we parked over there by you. Why don't you come over for dinner tonight so we can catch up on everything?"

"That sounds great!" I answered. "I'll look forward to it... but now I'd better get this food out to our friend before it gets cold," I explained as I hurried toward the door, almost as if I was afraid he would disappear again.

"We love you," they both chimed in as I left - and I turned, blew them a kiss, and silently mouthed the words, "Thank you. I love you, too."

When I got outside and took the rather large bag of goodies to the man whose name I still didn't know, he looked at me with those beautiful blue eyes and said, (as though he'd read my mind), "They just call me Coyote around here, and I'd like to thank you for your kindness, ma'am."

I decided not to mention the $20 bill... but I did say, "You are more welcome than you could possibly know, Mr. Coyote. And please, do me a favor - and **don't** throw that bag away until you check out everything that's inside. And don't worry – whatever you find in there isn't from me – in fact, I didn't even have to pay for the food. You have MANY brothers and sisters in Christ who love you; and two of them just happen to be named John and Mary; and they're still inside eating lunch right now. The fact is - I don't deserve any of your gratitude because," I said as I happily pulled out my $5 bill and held it in the air for him to see, "You may have your lunch - but I still have my money for groceries! Isn't our Lord amazing? He took care of both of us!"

And then, even as he protested because he was so dirty, I hugged him... and I truly loved that man. I loved him in a way that I can't possibly explain, but will never forget.

So... back I went to the grocery store, and this time the potatoes and peanut butter looked mighty good, and I was once again feeling happy and thankful for the food I was about to buy, (not to mention the fact that Mary is a great cook - so I knew that I had a first class dinner in store for me that night).

And when I got back to my RV with my groceries, I saw that John and Mary's beautiful coach was parked across the field about 50 yards from mine, and I had to laugh out loud filled with the pure joy of life... and all the wonders it has to offer. Sometimes it takes having "nothing" to really appreciate having "something" and I felt like being poor was truly a blessing from my Lord... a chance to learn how to appreciate the things I always taken for granted. And now – because of this experience...I'm richer than I've ever been; and it's the kind of riches you CAN take with you!

Later that afternoon, Sister Sarah brought two of her Indian friends over to meet me and we talked about everything from Christianity to the art of basket-weaving. For some reason, I thought I'd ask and see if any of them had ever heard of Coyote, and when I did… they all looked at each other in wonder and disbelief.

"You actually met Coyote?" they asked, almost in unison.

"Why yes, I did, just a couple of hours ago, and for some reason, that man touched my heart in a way I can't even put into words. That's why I was wondering if you knew anything about him," I asked.

"I'm afraid no one knows anything about Coyote. He's the desert preacher. Everybody says he spends all his time just walking around the desert, day after day, winter and summer, handing out bibles and praying with the desert rats; you know… homeless people who live in tents and tarps and under the shade of a cactus. Coyote just seems to appear out of nowhere – and then when he's done talking about Jesus and praying, he leaves them a Bible and he's gone; poof… just like that. No one knows where he comes from – and no one knows where he goes. But we all know who he is; he's the Angel of the Desert."

And that's when my emotions finally got the best of me and I let the tears go… and no, even though my guests were surprised to see me crying and wanted to know why, I couldn't bring myself to share the story of what had happened that day - not only because I didn't want to sound like I was trying to make myself look generous or special, but because it seemed like what happened was something special; just between Coyote and me, (and John and Mary). I only got to spend a few minutes with him and yet he taught me so much in that short time that I will never forget him. And besides, WE knew what had happened, (Coyote and I); and that was more than enough. At least now I understood why I felt something was different about him from the moment I first looked into those bright, beautiful blue eyes, and I couldn't wait to tell John and Mary what I had learned.

That night when I arrived at their coach for dinner, I could already smell the wonderful meal in store, and as we ate, I told them what my Indian friends had said about Coyote. John was… well, how do I describe it… he was up like a shot, and calling for Mary and I to follow as we jumped into his car and together, the three of us, searched every single street, store, bar and tavern in Parker – looking for Coyote.

I have no idea what John had in mind when (or if) we found him, (although I have a feeling he wanted to give him money for more Bibles... which is just a guess), but John was like an arrow - shot from a bow and determined not to stop until he found his target, Coyote. But as the Indians had all three told me earlier... Coyote was gone... and not only was John unable to find him that night, - but I never saw him again either.

But my brief encounter with Mr. Coyote, the angel of the desert, touched my heart in a way that it's never been touched before... and I shall treasure our meeting forever!

May God bless and keep you, Mr. Coyote. You truly **are** the "*angel of the desert*".

chapter 61

April 10, 1999

John and Mary joined me in my dirt field for three days, explaining that they couldn't stay any longer because they were on their way back to California and had family waiting for them. I really enjoyed their company and once again, I am 100% sure that the Lord put them in my path for a reason. Yes, we have free agency, but I also think some things are "written"... and these events only require us to have "ears to hear" and "eyes to see"; such as my meeting with John and Mary, who obviously had "ears to hear", and I will be forever grateful to them for their love, their guidance and their encouragement.

I ate a delicious dinner cooked by Mary all three nights that they stayed in Parker, so my $5.00 worth of groceries lasted longer than I expected, but certainly not long enough to keep me fed until the opening of the Blue Water Resort, which I had thought was going to be in a couple of weeks, but now, according to the lady at the Human Resources Division, might not be for another month... or even more.

When John and Mary left, I hadn't learned that unpleasant fact, because I had arranged to check with the Human Resources Office once a week, and it wasn't time for my weekly visit yet. When they drove away,

I thought I'd be starting real soon, so I assured them that I was in good shape financially and that they didn't need to worry about me.

On our final night together, they insisted on coming over to **my** place to visit, (which was highly unusual because they have much more seating space in their coach compared to what I have in Lucky), and as we parted ways the next morning, we hugged, got a little weepy eyed and then held hands in prayer… which included the hope that we would see each other again someday; if not HERE - then in the HEREAFTER. I'll miss them, but so much is happening that I don't have enough time to think about getting lonely.

And speaking about things happening every day; the day before yesterday, I was making my daily drop-in at the vendor's tents just before noon, (in case someone wanted me to cover for them while they ate lunch so I could earn a few dollars), when suddenly everyone started yelling, "Look out! Put everything away! Hurry! Run! It's a big one!" Panic was sweeping through the vendor booths and as I looked up to see what all the excitement was about, I couldn't believe my eyes when I saw a big, black, rumbling cloud that looked like a dark curtain, so huge that it blocked the entire sky in the direction from which it was coming. It was still pretty far off in the distance, but to me, (being an "ocean lady"), it looked like a giant tsunami… but instead of water, it was dirt.

As I watched it moving closer, (and believe me - it was moving FAST), it also reminded me of the great mounds of dirt, boulders and ash that flowed from Mt. St. Helens as I watched it erupt in 1980; turning day into night and leaving behind several inches of dark, talcum powder-like ash in it's wake. (I still carry a jar of the ash I scooped off my car with me as I travel, just so I can look at it and remember what it was like.)

But this dust storm was a first for me, and I found myself caught up in the excitement as everyone around me began running to and fro, not quite in a state of panic - but obviously adrenalin driven and (excuse the trite old farm saying), running around like chickens with their heads cut off; and believe me, that's one thing I HAVE seen first hand… and they DO run around, even without their heads!

I asked what I could do to help and was told to begin stuffing boxes into cars and trucks, pulling down tents and whatever other assignments the harried vendors could think of. But then, in a matter of minutes, it was time to stop working and take shelter... because the storm was almost upon us and had gone from being a black, rolling background to a massive, swirling curtain of dirt that was now filling the entire sky, and I raced for Lucky, with just enough time to close the last window before it hit... full force.

At first, I thought my RV was going to roll over onto its side when the sheer force of the storm struck, but since there was nothing I could do about it but wait and see what happened, I grabbed my camera and tried to capture it on film. Later, when I looked at the pictures, I discovered that my effort was in vain because it was so dark outside, (even at noon), that the flash was triggered and the light from the flashbulb reflected back from the window glass and ruined the pictures. All I ended up with was one big, bright spot in the middle of each photo.

But that didn't matter. Even without pictures, I would never forget that huge, black cloud of wind and dirt that seemed to gobble up everything in its path. I can close my eyes and see it even now, as it got closer and closer. It was like a giant black monster that swallowed Lucky up, and as we rocked back and forth in the darkness, I couldn't even *see* my hand in front of my face. (Gee, I'm just FULL of trite old sayings today.)

It's funny, but each traumatic experience, (like the dust storm and the bee attack), are blessings in disguise, because every time something dangerous happens; especially something we share... like the dust storm, brings me closer to the very Indians who hated me when I first drove into Parker. I know it's only a few at a time, (maybe a dozen now), but gradually, they are getting to know ME as Abigayle the Christian and Poet, rather than as that *skinny white woman who always smiles*, (and that's a direct quote from one of the Indians who admitted that that's how they refer to me). It's interesting how difficulties and danger seem to bring us together, and I'm hoping that working alongside them in the casino will have the same effect. But whatever it takes, I'm looking forward to any opportunity I can get to break down the age-old barriers that lie between us, and hopefully, one day we'll all just be "God's children", regardless of color.

And speaking of blessings in disguise, I'm thankful for that dust storm for yet another big reason. Because I live alone, (and always put everything in its proper place and wipe up any mess I might make immediately), I don't have to spend much time cleaning my RV. The last time I did any deep cleaning was after the bee attack and now - once again after the dust storm. The talcum-powder like dirt had found its way into every nook and cranny possible, so of course, I began to clean - eventually removing the table cloth and placemats from my kitchen table, which is where I found the $50 bill.

Gee, I wonder where that came from. There was no doubt in my mind that John and Mary had left it for me, which would explain why they wanted to come to **my** RV on their last night in Parker, rather than me going to their coach. They must have tucked that $50 under the placemat and figured I'd find it after they were gone.

I can't think of a more perfect example of what Jesus meant when he said "charity" was one of the most important qualities we should strive for. True charity is given without the need (or hope) for recognition or even so much as a 'thank you'. I wrote a poem on that subject a long time ago, and it's become such an audience favorite that I turned it into a song. If I ever again have enough money to make donations to good causes, (not counting tithing, of course), I would **always** do it anonymously - because it would defeat the whole purpose of charity if I was expecting to be rewarded, even in the form of respect or gratitude. The only reward a truly charitable person needs is the happiness of the person (or group) they are helping - and their riches in Heaven, (which to me means being as close to God as possible).

So thank you, John and Mary. You had no idea that I would run out of food while waiting for the casino to open, and yet once again, you have been there when I needed you most. And their timing couldn't have been better - as I was even out of the old canned goods. And then – just when I need it most, I find the $50 bill... which I can make last a long time if I'm careful.

I am so blessed, again and again! I just dream of the day when it will be **my** turn to help those who are in need - and I know that somehow, that day will come. (But I sure do wish the resort would hurry up and open!)

chapter 62

April 17, 1999

Another week has gone by... and the personnel office is still saying they don't know when they'll be ready to open. I asked if they had any brochures printed so I could see what the resort will look like, and the nice lady at the front desk, (who is getting to know me pretty well since I pester her every week), handed me one - and it was far more beautiful than I had even imagined. The brochure included directions to the building site so I decided to ride out there on my bicycle and see for myself how things were going.

I knew from talking to the various vendors, as well as my new Indian friends in town, that the Colorado River serves as the western border of Parker, but the dirt field where I'm parked is nowhere near the river, so I haven't actually seen it yet. But when I read the brochure and discovered that the new Blue Water Resort and Casino was located right on the banks of the river - and would have 200 boat slips and even a restaurant on the water to serve people in a "boat drive-up" window... I thought it would be fun to see it for myself ... and boy, am I ever glad I did!

The map said that it was a little over two miles north of town just off the main highway, and although you can't actually see the resort itself from the road - there would be a big sign announcing the Blue Water Resort and Casino, and a paved road that leads directly to the resort.

I sure wish I'd thought of riding out there earlier this month because already there's a non-stop wagon train of RV's leaving the area, which, according to the locals, is a yearly mass-exodus as the snow birds and tourists escape before the temperature becomes unbearably hot. But guess what... not only am I NOT among those who are leaving town, but it's already so HOT that my two-mile bicycle ride to the casino would have to be an early morning adventure, starting at first light; hopefully before the temperature hits the 90's.

So, off I went – early this morning, riding my bicycle on the side of the highway on a very narrow and rocky shoulder, smiling and waving nicely to everyone who honked at me, as though I thought they were saying hello... rather than angrily urging me to get farther off the road, (which is what I knew they really meant). But there was no way I could - because a water run-off ditch runs right next to the highway, which didn't leave enough room for me to move over.

And even though it was already **hot**, (even at 6:30 in the morning), I stuck to the advice John gave me and wore long, loose-fitting pants and a long-sleeved shirt, which left me dripping wet by the time I spotted the huge sign that said, "future home of the Blue Water Resort and Casino". Hip-Hip-Hooray! I found it... and right next to the sign was a brand new paved road, (just like the map on the brochure described), so I turned onto it, circling around the barriers that were meant to keep the public out, and rode for maybe a quarter of a mile before I saw yet another sign, and a fork in the nice new blacktop road. The sign had two arrows, and one pointed to the right and said, "Blue Water RV Park" and the other one pointed straight ahead and said "Casino, hotel and parking".

I couldn't believe my eyes. There's actually an RV Park right next to the casino! That means that when I start working, I can rent a space and either walk or ride my bike to work every day. I as so happy and relieved when I saw that sign... because I'd been pretty worried about how I was going to get to and from work everyday, especially in the summer heat, (which I understand gets up into the 120's) and here it was; the answer I hadn't dared to hope for - an RV Park right next door. I was so excited about the RV Park that I decided to check it out first, so I took the fork that said "RV Park" rather than the one going to the Resort. But after riding another quarter of mile or so, the road suddenly dropped off - and became such a steep hill that I was afraid to ride DOWN it, let alone have the strength to pedal back up ; at least not in this heat!

So after spending a few minutes debating with myself at the top of the dauntingly steep hill, hating to give up and yet really wanting to see the RV Park, I decided it was best to turn back, retrace my steps and go directly to the Resort instead. At least now I knew there **WAS** an RV Park and with that wonderful bit of information, the long, hot ride on my bicycle was already well worth the effort. Now I was anxious to see the Resort itself; the place where I would eventually be working.

It was at least another half a mile or so before I first spotted the huge building off in the distance and it was absolutely gorgeous! It looked like one of the grand hotels in Las Vegas, with tons of glass, rows of palm trees everywhere and a building constructed of huge blocks of stone.

It was such a large and spread out complex that I couldn't even see the river from the road, so I decided to circle around the side and see if I could find a way to get a look. But as I rode to one end of the building, I discovered that I couldn't get any further on my bicycle because the building went all the way down to the water. That's when I decided to leave my bike and see if I could walk around the building, at least far enough to peek around the side of the hotel… and that's where I got my first glimpse of the boat docks and the huge outdoor amphitheater. I also saw that the entire riverfront side of the almost finished building, and it was nothing but 6 stories of glass – and it was absolutely gorgeous!

And speaking of gorgeous… the Colorado River itself was just as stunning. No wonder they named the new casino "Blue Water Resort and Casino… as the river water was bright blue and almost completely still because of the dam that bordered the south end of the casino. It may have been the Colorado River, with Arizona on one side and California on the other, but here… next to the dam, it looked more like a crystal clear blue lake… and as hot as I was, I had the sudden urge to jump into the water.

Of course I decided against it, (since they had barriers up all over the place), but I still had a long, hot ride ahead of me to get back to Parker - and I was wishing I had the nerve to jump in the water. But at least my day has already been a success… even without seeing the RV Park or taking a swim, so I'd just try it again another day… but this time, I'd leave even earlier; as soon as it got light enough to see.

So I began the long hot ride back to Lucky, smiling all the way… but by the time I got there, I was one tired puppy. Because I don't have electricity, I don't have air-conditioning, so I bought a soda which I felt gave me the right to sit down at a nice cool table in McDonalds and read my bible while I cooled down.

That's when one of the people I've come to know in the area joined me at my table and I told them about my ride to the casino and my discovery of the RV Park.

"That RV Park has been there for years," my friend Tory explained. "They even had to close part of it because the Indians took the land for the casino. And there's another way to get there, without having to climb that big hill," she continued. "You just keep going down the highway **past** the casino sign, for another mile or so, and you'll see a road off to your left. It's called "Blue Water Drive. Then you follow that road back towards the casino, for a little less than a mile, and you're at the entrance to the RV Park. In fact, I think that's where it the road ends, now that they've built the new resort."

"You've got to be kidding." I shook my head in amazement. "You mean that RV Park is open right now, and it's not part of the Blue Water Resort?"

"Nope," she answered. "It's been there for about 20 years, and the people who run it aren't even Indians. If I remember right, there was quite a battle when the Indians took part of the RV Park for the casino, because according to the newspaper the owners had a hundred-year lease, and the Tribal Council only gave them 24 hours to get off the property before they bulldozed whatever was left," she informed me, leaning forward and speaking quietly as though it was a subject you didn't want to be heard talking about in front of the wrong people. "But in this town, there's no way you can fight the Tribal Council, even if they did sell every other lot to the whites, at least in the town of Parker, anyway."

"You mean they actually deeded lots and sold them to the whites?" I asked, surprised that the Indian tribes would do such a thing.

"They sure did," Tory answered, again leaning forward and almost whispering; "Clear back in the early 1900's, and those Chiefs weren't stupid. They knew that if they sold every other lot in town to the white folks, they'd put in water, sewer, electricity, sidewalks, and even plant trees. Then the Indians would get it all for free - because they owned the lots in between. It was pretty smart, if you ask me," she said as she nodded, almost conspiratorially. .

"I guess you're right," I raised my eyebrows in agreement. "That's one way to get things done. But how could they go back on a hundred year lease?"

"Simple," she said, this time leaning in even closer and looking around to make sure no one was listening before she spoke. "This is tribal land - a separate nation; so American laws don't have any jurisdiction here. The Indians can do anything they want and there's no legal recourse. I've seen houses burned to the ground because the Indians sold an unsuspecting white family a hundred-year lease for land on the riverbank, and then the rich folks from California who bought the lease, planning to build a vacation home on the river, built a million dollar home, and then, as soon as they were finished, the Indians cancelled the lease and took the land back, house and all."

"You've got to be kidding," I said. "I can't believe they'd do that. So who burned the house down?" I asked.

"The people who built it," she answered. "They tried to fight back, but short of guns and an Indian war, there was nothing they could do legally… except to make sure that the Indians didn't get the house, which is why they burned it down."

"Wow," I exclaimed. "I had no idea all this was going on. I wondered why there were so many white people here in Parker, and why the mayor was white… and why they even had two police departments, one Parker Police and one Tribal Police. That fact that the Indians sold every other lot explains everything. But going back on those leases – that's downright dirty."

"Yup," she agreed. "But the Indians are laughing all the way to the bank."

"And those poor people who built the house," I sympathized. "Was that a one-time thing or is it pretty common?" I asked, hoping I wasn't stepping into the middle of a 20th Century Indian war.

"They do it all the time. You'd think people would eventually learn, but sometimes the Indians actually let them stay on the land for quite a while – like the RV Park… just long enough for other people to feel secure and that way the Indians can sell more leases. And that's exactly what they did to the RV Park, and it's been there for at least 20 years."

"Unbelievable. Boy, this is really going to be interesting working at the casino. I took a look at the waitresses at the old one next to the grocery store, and it looks like the employees are mostly Indians, so I have a feeling it'll be a real challenge getting them to accept me."

"Oh, I don't think I'd go shoot for 'acceptance' if I was you. I'd settle for being tolerated. See, every Indian on the reservation owns a piece of the casino, so they can't be fired. In fact, they don't even have to show up for work unless they feel like it. I ought to know because I took a job at the old casino for a while and it was awful. While I was there, one of the Indian girls punched one of the white girls right in the face, and the white girl didn't even hit her back… and guess who got fired?"

"Don't tell me - it was the white girl," I guessed… already getting a pretty clear picture of the situation. "Boy - I'm sure glad we had this conversation. I had no idea what was going on, and now that I do, I'll have to be a little more careful about what I say and who I say it to."

"Yaa," she laughed, "good luck with that," she said as she got up to leave. "Let me know how it goes," she added with a smile as she waved and walked out the door.

Now I really needed to think. First, there's the lecherous Food and Beverage Manager, and now there's the closest thing to an Indian war I'm ever likely to see. Normally I'd consider the hatred between the Indians and the whites as nothing more than an opportunity to make a difference... but that lecherous manager is what bothers me most; and the fact that I'll be stuck selling hamburgers for minimum wage - thanks to him.

Yup — I need some time to think, study my Bible and pray. Luckily, all the vendors that line the road in front of the dirt field where I'm parked go home at night - so even though I'm right on the edge of town, it's completely deserted and quiet once they close and I can be alone... to think. I really need some guidance, Lord. I need to know if stopping here in Parker to earn a computer and get a website up and running is **really** what you want me to do. Because after talking to Tory, I feel like I might just be stepping right into the middle of a hornets nest, (and you know how I feel about bees!)

chapter 63

April 19, 1999

Something funny happened today - and I'm still laughing about it, as are my sons back in Oregon… I'm sure. The timing was perfect because today is my oldest son Scott's birthday, so I had planned to use the long distance card I bought to call him this evening… but I never got the chance.

I was sitting in my RV, enjoying an early morning cup of tea, when a Parker Police car pulled up. Uh-oh, I thought. They're going to tell me I can't park in this field anymore, and now where am I going to go? I hurried to the door and greeted the officer before he even had time to knock, and this is what he said:

"Excuse me, ma'am. Are you Abigayle?" Of course he used my "real" name, which I never use, except when I must, (like to apply for a job), because whatever the Lord has called me to do, even the writing of this book, is not about me. It's about faith, joy, trust, obedience, serving our Lord and glorifying God… so my name is unimportant – and besides that, fame would be a curse.

"Yes, sir, I am. What seems to be the problem?" I asked

"Oh, I don't think there's any problem, except with your sons. I guess they've been calling all over Arizona trying to find you. They didn't know your license plate number but they described the vehicle and you - and then we remembered the killer bee incident.

"My sons are looking for me?" I asked. "That's funny because I was just planning on calling them today."

"Well, I'm afraid the officer who answered the call probably put quite a scare into them when he said, "Oh… you must mean the bee lady", because, (I think he said his name was Jeremy), well… he seemed pretty shocked when he heard that."

I couldn't help but laugh as I imagined what he must have thought when he heard me referred to as the 'bee lady', since both my sons have watched me run from every bee in the country the entire time they grew up – and even watched me eat most of our family picnics in the car because of the bees hovering around the food at the table. Now they hear me referred to as the "bee lady"? I'm sure it must have been quite a surprise.

"Your son asked me if I would drop by and tell you to give them a call. He said there wasn't any emergency at home… but that they're worried about you. So I promised I'd pass the word along."

"Thank you very much, officer. I really appreciate your taking the time to do that. I've got a job at the new casino so I'm just parked here waiting for it to open," I explained, hoping to assure him that I didn't plan on being a permanent resident of this dirt field.

"Well, you better be careful," he responded with genuine concern. "There's some unsavory types coming through here, and a woman alone, such as yourself, needs to be mighty careful," he warned me as he smiled, waved and walked back to his patrol car.

"Thank you so much. I'll be sure and do that," I assured him as I also waved goodbye. Well, at least that ought to help - because now the local police know that I'm just parking here while I wait for the casino to open, so hopefully I won't have to worry about them knocking on my door and telling me to leave.

And now I need to call my sons – which I was planning to do anyway. Let's see, it's an hour earlier in Oregon… so I guess I'll call them a little later, after their both home from work. I can't wait to hear their reaction when I tell them about the "killer bees".

Later – Same Day

It was so good to hear their voices again. The reason I don't call home more often is that it makes me sad… and brings me back to the life I lived BEFORE the Lord called me. I try not to let any negative thoughts or sad feelings affect my attitude, but now, after our conversation, I am once again flooded with memories… cherished pieces of my past that someday I'll be able to bring back to the forefront; but for now – must be left in the farthest recesses of my mind. They are blessings I am **so** very grateful for… but I have other work to do now; like figuring out how to best use the gifts the Lord gave me to do His work… and my previous life was all simply training for whatever it is I must do.

I knew that the Lord would take care of my family while I was gone, so I wasn't surprised to hear that my boys are doing fine… still roommates, best friends, and healthy and well. They tell me that my granddaughter, my father, Roma, and my brother are all doing fine too… so I'm glad I called, even if I do miss them even **more** now than I did before I heard their voices. But when I hung up the phone, I cried, and I shouldn't have done that. When Jesus told the apostles to leave everything behind and follow Him, they didn't even get a chance to say goodbye, so I, too, must be strong and willing to give up everything to serve Him; without question and without tears.

When I told Jeremy about my job, and about how I'm waiting for the casino to open, and about the RV Park I discovered right next door, he offered to call the Park manager and use his credit card to pay for a month's rent in advance so I can get out of this dirt field and into a safer place. I assured him that I wasn't in any danger here, but that I might just take him up on his offer when the casino actually opens - because working or not, I won't have a payday for the first couple of weeks, (or maybe even a month – depending on how often they pay), so I'll need rent for that first month while I wait. Jeremy is struggling financially himself right now, so it really was a generous offer, but I'd rather not have to take him up on it. And if I do, you can bet I'll pay him back as soon as I'm working.

He said to let him know and he'd make the call, so I feel better knowing that I don't have to pull up to that RV Park with no money - and talk the owners into letting me stay there for free until I get my first paycheck. Whew! What a weight off my shoulders!

I love my sons, my grandchildren, and all of my earth family so much! I know I don't mention them very often because I'm trying to focus on other things. Because I was a single mother for most of their lives, I was the center of the family... and they all revolved around me. Sunday dinners were always at my house, every Holiday spent together, (again at my house), and I was always there when they needed advice or encouragement. I even cut the umbilical cord on all three of my grandchildren.

But both of my sons were there on the day of the flood, and were witnesses to the miracle of the Bible, and of course.... knowing me as they do, they believed every word I said when I told them that the Lord had spoken to me. The fact is, I think they're actually kind of proud that their mother is now working for the Lord, even though I'm not sure exactly what I'm supposed to be doing yet - or even if I'm on the right course, but my family knows that no matter how much I love them... I would give up anything or anyone God asked me to. God is first in my life... because my family is HIS family too, and I serve them all. But at least they all know how much I love them!

Now that Jeremy has offered to pay for my first month, I wish I could drive over there right now; just so I'd have air conditioning, and television. And with the RV Park right on the Colorado River, I could even escape the intense heat by going swimming in the crystal clear blue water. That sounds like Heaven on Earth to me... but it would be a waste of money that I might need later, and it would serve no purpose other than my own pleasure – which means it can wait.

In the meantime, I'll just keep checking in at the casino Human Resources Department and hoping that my job will begin soon. Each time they tell me that they don't know when, I pray and ask my Lord if Parker is really where He wants me to be... at least for now. But then I get my answer when every time something goes wrong, like the bees… or running out of money… or whatever the problem; somehow He takes care of it - so I feel like He's still paving the way – and I'm still on the right path.

I guess as each new problem arises, I also have to assume that it could be Satan trying to scare me away. I don't need signs from God, nor do I look for them. I just need the strength and the courage and strength to face whatever obstacles I meet, and as long as the Lord keeps providing that, I'll follow the Spirit. And so far, staying here on this Indian Reservation and creating a website where I can share my story of faith, adventure and complete trust in God with the world, feels like the next step in my journey.

So now I'll just have to see what tomorrow holds – and thank you, Jeremy, for easing yet another burden.

chapter 64

April 21, 1999

Two days later

Oh my gosh! I think I just came face to face with Satan last night, (or at least on of his minions), and I'm about to start Lucky's engine and head for the relative safety of the RV Park my son Jeremy offered to pay for - because what happened last night was just what I needed to convince me that it was time to move!

I didn't look at the clock, but I'd guess it was about midnight when it was finally cool enough for me to step outside and enjoy the night air and the brilliant star filled Arizona sky. I shut the door and walked around to the front of the RV, planning to use the bumper as a place to sit as I enjoyed the complete quiet and the awesome beauty of God's handiwork, when I got the surprise of my LIFE!

There, already sitting on the bumper I had been planning to use - was the tallest, skinniest, blackest man I've ever seen. I've had many African-American friends, and would **never** judge a person by their color, but when I say "black", I mean blacker than I thought was humanly possible. The whites of his eyes and his teeth stood out like they were florescent, and he was so tall, (maybe 6'6", at least) and unbelievably skinny, (making me look plump and shapely), that he reminded me of a snake, and he looked more like he was curled around my bumper than actually sitting on it.

"Who are you and what are you doing here?" I asked, still stunned and caught by such surprise that I didn't have time to think of anything else to say.

That was when he stood up, towering over me and leaning forward as he answered in a deep, gruff voice that I'll never forget, "I'm Revelation... and I've come for YOU!"

"What do you mean 'you've come for me'? I asked, still more surprised than afraid. For the first time since I drove away from Gold Beach, I actually wondered if I was dreaming... but I knew better; especially when he grabbed the front of his shirt and literally ripped it open – buttons flying and bare chest exposed.

And on that blackest of black chest were dozens of huge, wide scars, crossing over each other until they almost made a pattern. Then he put his arms out toward me, palms up and yelled, "See these! See these scars!"

And that's when I looked at his pink palms and saw that they, too, were covered with fat, angry scars, and that's when the first pangs of fear began to creep into my mind.

"**This** is what I do every time I want a woman! I cut myself! I make myself hurt! This is 16 years worth of pain and torment" he literally screamed as he looked down at his chest. "This is what I did while I was waiting for the woman Satan promised me. And now you're here... and I've come so we can be together - forever," he said as he continued to stare directly into my eyes; either trying to intimidate me or convince me - which one I'm not sure. But suddenly I knew that if I let him get the upper hand, even psychologically, I'd be in even worse trouble than I already was... which is why I refused to look away from his almost black eyes – and instead returned his evil glare with what I hoped was equal intensity, as I stared right back at him, unblinking... and trying with every drop of power inside me to be just as intimidating as he was.

"Well then," I said without raising my voice, (like he was), and yet with all the dominance and strength I could possibly muster, "I'm afraid we've got a problem," I said, realizing that if he believed in Satan then he must also believe in God and Jesus, "because I've already given myself to **Jesus**. You must have the wrong woman - because I belong to my Lord... so Satan has absolutely no authority over me, and neither do you!"

If there was ever a moment in my life when I needed to use everything I had ever learned about people; about manipulation through tone of voice, choice of words, gestures and body language, it was NOW. I had already looked around to see if any of the roadside vendors had decided to spend the night - hoping there was someone close enough to hear my screams if the situation got worse... but they were all gone. There wasn't a single car in sight and the nearest telephone booth was too far to run without him catching me. That meant my only hope was to out-maneuver him... that and the help of my Lord and Savior.

"That faggot, Jesus!" he screamed in fury, looking wild-eyed and ready to explode at any moment. "He always takes the credit! He's nothing but a weakling runt... and yet everyone thinks He's something special! I know where the real power is, and YOU belong to ME!"

This time I showed fierce and genuine anger and literally shouted at him as I said, "Don't you **DARE** call my Savior a faggot!" I rebuked him. "Satan is the liar of all liars - and he's the one who set you up! He's the one you should be made at because he knows good and well that I already belong to Jesus. I'd suggest that you get out of here right now because there's no possible way I'll EVER be your woman; I'd die first!"

"I'm not going anywhere," he said as he took a step closer and put his face just a few inches from mine, close enough that I could smell his putrid breath... but I still refused to back up, afraid of showing any weakness. His eyes were so black... and so evil... that I felt like I was looking directly into the eyes of Satan himself, as he shouted, spraying spittle on my face in his wrath, "I've waited for 16 years and I'm not waiting another day! You're mine!"

"Well, then, "I responded as calmly and seemingly unaffected by his evil venom as I possibly could, hoping to show him that he was powerless and that I wasn't the least bit afraid of him, "I guess you've got a problem then - because I'm under the protection of my Lord Jesus Christ, and I love him with all my heart, and that means neither YOU nor Satan have any power over me whatsoever."

As I said those words, I spoke with such quiet calm and assurance, I sounded like a person who is using the tenor of their voice to hypnotize someone, smooth and soothing, yet strong and unyielding... while still refusing to break eye contact. But inside, I felt like I was in the middle of a battle, like David and Goliath, and since this man was not only twice my size but twice as fast, my faith in God would be my shield - and my devotion to Jesus would be my weapon. I knew that I had the power of the Lord on my side... so I refused to let one single doubt enter my mind, nor would I let this raving maniac see even a brief flash of weakness or fear in my eyes (or in my demeanor).

It must have worked - because for one brief moment, he seemed a bit confused; just a fleeting look that crossed his face before he once again regained his composure. But it was enough. Now I could tell that even if he wouldn't admit it, I had convinced him that I had God on my side... and he wasn't quite sure what to do about it.

And once I had seen that momentary break in his confidence, I knew that it was time to take advantage of his confusion, so I continued... quickly but calmly, as though nothing he had said was of any importance to me. "So, Mr. Revelation, I am going back inside my RV and get some sleep - and then in the morning, I'm leaving town... so you'll never see me again. I will pray for you though, because through Christ, even **you** can be forgiven, and I'm sorry that you've been fooled by the evil pretender, Satan. But as for me - I'm under the protection of my Lord and Master and I bid you goodnight."

As I turned calmly toward the door of my RV, he suddenly sprang into action and practically leapt around me, blocking the path between me and the door I had been so hoping to reach and get inside before he had time to even realize what was happening. If I could have just gotten in that door, I could have pulled the plug on the alarm John had insisted I take with me - and then hoped that someone was close enough to hear it... but apparently, that wasn't going to happen; at least not yet. Mr. Revelation wasn't quite finished, just somewhat taken aback for a moment... and quick to recover.

"Wait a minute" he yelled. "You're not going anywhere... and if you do, I'm going with you. You can't get rid of me if I have to hang on to your bumper. Now that I've found you, you're mine! Satan promised you to me and you may not know it now, but you will someday... which is why you're not going anywhere without me!" he insisted, but this time it wasn't spittle and screaming... it was more like he was trying to convince me - trying to change my mind. I considered the change in his attitude a sign of progress, and the fear I had felt just moments before began to fade - because apparently this demon of a man wasn't quite as smart as he thought he was; just insane or possessed... which I didn't know.

Now if I could just stall him long enough for a car to drive by - or if only the police would happen to patrol the area and see this huge tower of a man yelling at me... or if only - I don't know what else I hoped might happen, but I knew without a doubt that the power of God could never be thwarted by Satan. It's funny the things that flash through your mind during times of extreme duress, and as I stood there staring into his evil, (and now almost panicked), eyes... I remembered how God had told Satan that he could do anything he wanted to do to Job... anything but take his life. I knew God held all the power, so nothing this possessed man might say or do could change that. I had no reason to fear him, because I don't fear death, but I could see that it was time to use a different tactic. I needed to lull him into a sense of false security. I needed to stall him and get him to let his guard down long enough for me to either make it inside the door of the RV, (which he was still blocking) or keep him talking long enough for help to arrive in the form of another person (or persons).

"Ok," I said calmly, almost as if I was trying to be kind. "If you want to sleep out here on the ground, that's your choice. I certainly can't tell you where you sleep, nor does it matter to me... but I'm tired, so I'm going to bed," I said as I once again attempted to step around his huge, snakelike body that was still standing directly between me and the relative safety of my RV. "Goodnight, Mr. Revelation. I hope you find the woman you're looking for, but when I leave in the morning, I'd suggest that you don't hang onto my bumper; not unless you want to spend eternity with Satan starting tomorrow morning."

But as I tried to slip my head under his armpit and gain access to the door, he once again moved quicker than I thought such a big body could move and blocked my way, this time grabbing my arm, which I immediately shook out of his grasp with strength I didn't know I had. That move alone showed me something. He was so much stronger than I am that there was no way I should have been able to pull my arm out of his grasp... unless he was wavering - perhaps even becoming a bit unsure of himself. At last, I felt my hopes begin to rise.

And this time when he spoke, his voice was quieter, with almost a touch of pleading in it, as he said, "I told you you're not going anywhere until we settle this. I'm going to sleep on the ground right behind your tires so you'll have to run over me if you want to leave. And I know what that weakling faggot Jesus teaches his followers. You can't kill anyone on purpose - and that's your weakness! There's no way you'll run over me - so this is where I'll be sleeping; right here in front of your door... behind your front tires. That way tomorrow morning, we can leave together; just you and me."

As I realized that there was no way he was going to let me get inside the RV, I once again surveyed my surroundings, still stalling for time and wondering if I could possibly outrun him and race for the casino just a few blocks away. But even though I ran track in junior high school, and can still run like a gazelle, there was no way this 6'6" man wouldn't be able to catch me. And now that he seemed to have his temper under control, and was no longer screaming and ripping his clothes off, any sudden attempt I made at flight might just inflame him all over again. After seeing the uncontrolled rage and evil in his eyes earlier, I knew that if he got mad enough, he could easily kill me with a quick snap of my neck, or strangle me in a matter of minutes.

Every single one of my *human* senses were telling me to run... to get away from this crazy man, but instead I was praying for the guidance of the Holy Spirit and calling upon my Lord for help - so I controlled the urge to make a senseless attempt to escape and decided that my best bet was still to "out think" him.

And so I stood there for a moment, wondering what to say next... when it suddenly came to me. "Ok," I said, in an almost acquiescent voice, "If we're going to sleep outside tonight then at least let me get us a blanket. Just move away from the door so I can go inside and get one," I told him, hoping that he'd think he had won - and that I had decided to go along with him; hoping that I could get inside and pull the alarm. As I spoke, I was still staring directly into his eyes, knowing that I could match the intensity of his with my own, and perhaps even become the dominant party; he would give in. And I almost thought was working, especially when this time HE was the first to break eye-contact and looked at the ground, shuffling his feet while he was thinking it over.

But it didn't work. "What do you think I am - stupid?" he asked. "You'll get inside and lock the door and I'll be out here all alone. Nope —we'll sleep right out here on the dirt together before I'll let you lock me out and start honking your horn."

Ok, so he wasn't quite as stupid as I had hoped he was... but I was far from giving up.

"That's not a very nice way to treat someone you call your 'woman'", I said. "What kind of man would make his woman sleep in the dirt with scorpions and bugs," I complained, intentionally looking like my feelings were hurt and that I was disappointed in him - if that was how he planned to take care of me.

And that's when I saw it... a small pickup truck was pulling up next to one of the empty vendor tents less than 50 yards away from where we were standing. That was almost half a football field, so it wouldn't work if

I took off running and he chased me, but perhaps there was another way. If the driver saw him chasing me, he could go for help, but I'd probably be dead or at least severely injured by the time the police arrived... so I needed to keep this insanely evil man calm. I needed to use wisdom and understanding as my weapons, and hopefully things wouldn't escalate to that point. But somehow, I needed to get to that car without this crazy man chasing me... and then tell the driver to call the police. That was what I needed to do, and I suddenly knew just how to do it.

"Ok," I said with a sigh...and in an acquiescing tone. "You win. But if you insist on sleeping outside on the ground tonight, and you won't let me go inside my RV, we still need a blanket," I insisted. Then I suddenly pretended to notice the small truck that had pulled up next to the vendor's booth.

"Oh, what perfect timing," I exclaimed, smiling as though something wonderful had just happened. "There's a friend of mine over there - and he always carries an extra blanket in his truck. Just a minute and I'll go get it. Don't worry, I'll be right back," I assured him, already walking toward the car backwards even as I spoke, still smiling... and using every drop of acting ability I could muster as I made the words sound like he was actually going to get to hold me in his arms all night. Before he'd fully comprehended what was happening, and was still reveling in what he thought was his victory, I was already getting closer to the truck.

I've often been nicknamed "flash" because I love to run, but I'm also a "pro" at speed walking, which means I can cover more ground than a jogger and NOT look like I'm running. I knew that if I started running, he'd smell a trick and tackle me... but if I didn't show any fear and, in fact, looked like I was on his side – perhaps I had a chance.

"Wait a minute," he yelled as I got farther away, sounding even more confused this time, which was much better than angry. "I'm going with you."

"No," I argued, in a kind and caring voice – as I turned to face him without so much as a break in stride. "I don't think that's a good idea because you are a big and powerful man... and if he sees you coming, he just might be afraid and run for the police. Please, I know this man; he's a friend... so just let me handle him, and I'll get the blanket. I'll tell him everything is fine... and we can decide what to do in the morning. And you're right," I said, now far enough away that I, too, was practically shouting, " I wouldn't run over you - but I am going to make sure we have a blanket because I hate bugs," I insisted, watching his face contort in confusion as I was getting closer and closer to the truck. I think the fact that I was walking, (and still communicating calmly with him), rather than running in fear, seemed to be convincing him that I really was just getting us a blanket - and that he had nothing to worry about.

And so far, it was working, but those last few yards seemed to take forever and I had to fight the urge to keep from breaking into a run as I power-walked the remaining distance to the little pick-up truck. And once again, as I neared what I hoped would be help... I called upon the power of the Lord to give me both strength and wisdom as I battled this obviously evil threat to my life.

And then I was there... standing at the driver's window of the little red truck. The driver had apparently pulled over to sleep, because I had to knock on his window before he sat up and opened his eyes... looking not only surprised but a little uncomfortable, as though he thought it might be the police telling him to move.

My first thought was that I could just jump in his vehicle and tell him to get us out of here – fast! But then I saw that the entire bed of his pick-up was filled to the brim with what looked like all of his worldly possessions, and even the passenger seat was piled high with junk, so I decided the next best thing to do was to ask him to go call the police, ASAP. Then I'd ask him if he had a blanket I could use, which I could already see that he did, (since it was covering his lap), and that way, I could return to Revelation with the promised blanket so he wouldn't think I had betrayed him - and kill me before the police could arrive.

OK, plan "B" it is, I thought to myself. "Excuse me, sir," I said as he hurriedly rolled down his window. "Would you please do me a big favor and go call the police? I also need to borrow your blanket, just until the police get here, but I'd really appreciate it if you would go **right now** – and tell them that there's a lady parked in that dirt field outside of town who needs their help."

"You need help?" he asked, obviously wide awake now and trying to figure out what was going on. "Well then," he said with pride, "I'm not going anywhere or calling anyone… I'll just help you myself," he insisted.

"Sir, I do need help… but I've got the situation under control. I'll be fine if you'll just give me that blanket and then go call the police. See, that's why I told that man over there," I said as I pointed toward my RV – holding my hand low enough that Revelation couldn't see me pointing, "that I was coming over here to borrow a blanket. So everything will be fine if you just loan it to me and then casually drive away, like you're NOT going for help, but just moving along… and we'll let the police handle him. He's very strong and definitely insane, and yes… he's dangerous, but if YOU try to help, then both of us could get killed. It would be better if you'd just get the police while I keep him calm."

"Sorry, lady, but there's no way I'm leaving you here with a crazy man," he said as he looked over toward my RV and saw Revelation standing there glaring at us. "Just get my wheelchair out of the back of the truck, because I'm not going anywhere," he stubbornly insisted. Great, a hero who just happened to be a paraplegic, and I was running out of time. Revelation was probably beginning to wonder if I'd been tricking him. How long could it take him to kill a paraplegic and a woman? I wasn't sure what to do – but I knew I didn't have any more time to argue with my paralyzed hero friend. And right now, that was what I needed most… time; time for the police to get here, whether this man called them or whether they just happened by on patrol.

One more time, I thought… just one more time. "Sir, please… I'm begging you. Just go for help. He's going to come over here any minute and then we'll BOTH be in trouble."

But of all the people who could have come to my rescue, I just happened to get the most stubborn paraplegic in the world. I couldn't figure out why… it was possible that he'd been drinking and had pulled over to sleep it off, but whatever the reason, this man adamantly refused to listen - and there was no way he was going to call the police. There was no use arguing with him any longer as he insisted on being the one to save me.

"I said get me my wheelchair and I'll take care of that creep!"

Oh boy, things weren't exactly going as I'd hoped, but now I had no choice as I saw Revelation began taking steps in the direction of the truck. "OK," I relented. "I'll get it,"

The wheelchair was easy to spot, lying right on top of the pile of junk filling the bed of his truck, so I pulled it down and set it next to the front door and he used his hands to prop himself up and swing over onto the seat of the wheelchair. He appeared to be just a few years younger than me, so I was thinking "Vietnam War Vet" and as I studied his quick and precise movements as he slipped easily from the truck into the chair, I decided he probably wasn't drunk and just wanted to be a hero, or perhaps *needed* to be a hero.

When I was living in Gold Beach, the Siskiyou National Wilderness where we rode our horses on hundreds of miles of trails was filled with Vietnam Vets; soldiers who could no longer deal with society after they returned and chose to live a life of solitude and freedom from society. Many of them were sometimes violent and most of them were emotionally damaged, and I'd taken much joy in befriending as many of them as possible. It helped - living next door to the only Tavern in town… because they came down once a month to cash their disability checks and then spend it on a several day bender right next door to me. Eventually, they adopted me as their little sister, their pastor or their voice of reason in a world filled with confusion and anger, and now I had a little better idea why this injured soldier refused to leave.

As I struggled to push his wheelchair through the 3-inch deep dirt, after reminding him to put the blanket on his lap, he was so full of adrenalin that his arms were turning the wheels faster than I could push the chair, so I ended up just walking behind - with him doing all the work. Obviously, even though he had just been sleeping, he was ready for a fight... and I knew I had to do something fast or the situation was going to explode into violence.

"What's your name?" I asked my stubborn but brave friend.

"Mike," he answered, but kept his focus on getting his wheelchair through the deep dirt as quickly as possible.

"Well listen, Mike. I just spent almost an hour with this man, and believe me; he's insane so please DON'T make him mad! He could easily kill both of us, so let's use our brains instead of brawn - and together we can trick him... rather than fight him. I told him you were a friend of mine, so PLEASE promise me that you won't do or say anything to set him off. I mean it," I whispered now that we were getting close to the RV, "he's criminally insane... so it won't take much to set him off, and if he flies into a rage we'll both regret it. Let's be smarter than he is," I continued to whisper, as we were only a few yards away and Revelation was walking toward us. "Together, we can outsmart him."

I was just about to hold up the blanket and say, "See, here's our blanket. I'd like you to meet my friend Mike. He's the one who was nice enough to loan us his blanket;" - but I never got the chance to say a single word before everything broke loose when Mike started shouting at the top of his lungs, saying, "Hey, You get out of here right now and leave this lady alone!"

Oh great, I thought. That's the worst thing he could have possibly done, and now we were BOTH in trouble. Revelation didn't even bother to answer, but his face contorted in uncontrolled fury as he covered the 10 feet between us in what seemed like one big step and grabbed the wheelchair in both hands, one gripping each armrest, and lifted it up into the air, shaking it violently, as though Mike's weight was nothing - and he was merely swatting a fly.

Mike was hanging on for dear life and I could see that if his upper body strength hadn't been so well developed, he would have flown out of the chair. That's when I jumped into action! With no time to think, and the Holy Spirit putting every word in my mouth, I yelled at the top of my lungs, "Wait a minute," I said as I grabbed Revelation's arm and put my face as close to his as I could, (considering the height difference between us). "Stop that right now!" I ordered, like a mother reprimanding an errant child. "What are you doing?" I asked him… still shouting, but in a voice filled with authority rather than panic.

"You should be thanking this man!" I demanded, as I gripped his arm with every drop of strength I could muster. "He's defending your woman! You say I belong to you, so wouldn't you WANT him to protect me? Isn't that what any man would want for his woman?" I asked, trying to confuse him. "Mike is my friend, and he doesn't know you… so he's just trying to protect me. If I belong to you, like you say I do; then you should be glad he's trying to protect me! You should be thanking him! Now put that chair down," I ordered as I pulled even harder on his arm until I was practically hanging from it.

Finally Revelation took his eyes off Mike and turned to me as he said, "Then he better shut his mouth right now!" he demanded as he reluctantly lowered the wheel chair to the ground. I could see that Mike was in a state of shock, and since I didn't know what kind of health he was in, as far as I knew - he could be on the brink of a stroke or a heart attack.

"Just shut up for a minute and listen to me!" I insisted, putting my face so close to Revelations that once again I could smell the stink of his breath. "Mike brought us a blanket, so doesn't that tell you something? And yes, he yelled at you – but that's because he doesn't know you. He thinks he's protecting me, so why would you hurt him for doing that. You said I was your woman, so why aren't you thanking him for taking care of me?" I asked, with my hand still on his arm, pressing but no longer fighting… trying to calm him down and get both Mike and I out of this deadly situation.

"Because nobody talks to me like that; nobody who lives to tell about it anyway!" Revelation growled as he still held on to the chair that was sitting on the ground, refusing to release his grip on it as he talked to me but stared threateningly at Mike.

Seeing the panic-stricken look on Mike's face after his brutal shaking, I knew that he now understood what I'd been trying to tell to him. We needed to keep Revelation calm… whatever it took, until we figured out a way to get help.

I could see it was a struggle for Mike to say the words, but he finally seemed to break out of his shocked stupor and said, "Yaa, man… I'm sorry I yelled at you. I just didn't want you to hurt this nice lady."

"Well you better be sorry, because I'd a' killed you if it weren't for her. Now I got my blanket, so you can just get out a' here. We don't want you here - so get lost, NOW!"

"Let me just push him back to his car," I insisted, "He's a sick man, and you can see that he's crippled. I give you my word," I said as I stared directly into those black, angry eyes. "I'll just push him back to his truck and he'll go away and leave us alone. Then we can talk some more; just you and me… about our future."

That seemed to do the trick, and even though I could see that Mike still didn't want to leave me with a crazy man, he finally understood why he had no choice - and I didn't give him time to say another word before I began pushing him towards his truck.

"Now do you see why I wanted you to call the police?" I whispered to Mike as we crossed the field. "You are a very brave man… and I thank you - but this is going to take men with weapons and handcuffs. So please, just get in your truck and **slowly** drive away. Don't let him think you're going for help - or then I WILL be in trouble. This is a small town so I'm sure the police can be here in minutes. Thank you, Mike. You were so brave, but now… please, just do as I ask."

"I don't like it, but I suppose you're right," he reluctantly agreed, trying to hide the fact that he was trembling… and two minutes later he slowly drove towards town. I took my time walking back to the RV, wanting to use up some of the time it would take for the police to get here, and leaving me less time to spend with a still irate crazy man.

"Thank you for letting Mike go. He really did mean well, but at least now we have a blanket," I said as I stalled for time. "Where do you think is the best place to put it?" I asked, slowing circling the RV?

But he didn't answer my question, as he was still too furious. "You know… if you weren't my woman I'd a' killed that freak."

"I know you would have – but you did the right thing… which means there's some good in you." I knew the police should be arriving any minute, so reckless or not, I couldn't help trying to plant a seed. "You know you shouldn't have talked about Jesus like that… and you know that Satan is the liar, Mr. Revelation. You've been following him most of your life – and how happy have you been?" I asked him, so calm that I might have been chatting with a neighbor. "Do you think that if Satan really has all the power you'd have had to hurt yourself so many times?"

"I don't know," he said, looking puzzled but not even close to convinced. "All I know is Jesus never did nothing for me."

"But have you ever asked him?" I argued quietly. "Why do you think I love him so much? Do you think I'm stupid? No, you know I'm not – or you wouldn't want me for your woman. But Satan thinks that **you** are – and he's counting on that to keep you miserable and alone. Jesus is the one who loves you, and Satan doesn't want you to know that. If you follow Satan you'll be even MORE miserable than you are right now. And you'll be that way for eternity. Do you have any idea how long that is? I've seen HELL… in a vision, and it was torment and pain beyond your comprehension. Can you imagine spending eternity screaming in pain? Well that's what Satan wants for you! But not Jesus… He wants you to be happy – and he wants you to be loved… forever."

And then there was no more time, with Revelation looking confused instead of angry, four police cars, sirens wailing and lights flashing, turned the dirt field into a cloud of dust as they surrounded Lucky. Two of them were marked "City of Parker Police" and two were marked "CRIT Reservation Police", and the minute they stopped, 8 men jumped out, guns in hand and ran toward us.

They didn't even bother to identify themselves, (like you always see on television), they just jumped on him, bringing him to the ground and pulling his arms behind him as they handcuffed him. Everything happened so fast, I'm not sure whether it was a Parker Police car or a Reservation Police car, but four of the officers drug the struggling man into the backseat and that car sped away, with one more following behind, lights still flashing and sirens screaming.

As they drove away, I could see Revelation in the back seat looking at me… and Heaven help me, I couldn't help but feel sorry for him. I don't feel hatred very often, in fact I can't remember the last time I did, but I **hated** Satan right then!

But along with the sadness, I felt such immense relief that I can't even describe it. It took almost an hour to make my statement to the police and afterwards the polite and concerned officer said, "Ma'am, you don't know just how lucky you are. That's one dangerous man we just took in. He escaped from the Institute for the Criminally Insane, where he was remanded after he killed his first victim. I don't know how he does it, but every so often, he manages to escape again, and all we can do is return him to the same place he keeps escaping from. Once the Court declared him "insane", they don't even bother with a trial anymore, and believe me - he's hurt more than a few people on his little freedom runs. It looks like you were his target this time, and since they can't seem to keep him from getting away, I'd suggest **you** get as far away from here as you possibly can, just in case."

"Well, sir, "I answered, still upset, but more angry at Revelation for calling Jesus a faggot and almost hurting Mike than anything else, "I'm afraid I can't leave town because I've got a job at the new casino as soon as it opens. I'll move into the RV Park next to the casino first thing tomorrow morning, so I should be safe there. If you don't mind, maybe you could come to the Park and check on me every now and then… you know - just in case?" I asked the Parker Police officer.

"Sure, we'll do that. In the meantime, you'll be safe tonight because we'll keep him in lockup for a day or two before we take him back to the Institute. He's hurt so many people, crazy or not, someone needs to just plain shoot him. You can bet we wouldn't make a federal case out of it if they did."

"Well, sorry, but I don't carry a gun," I laughed – trying to ease the tension as well as assure the officer that I was fine. "I wanted to thank the man that called you, but he didn't come back. Since I'll be moving to the RV Park in the morning, if you see him would you tell him I said thank you?"

"Oh, you mean Mike. We all know Mike, and it's a pretty sad story, losing his legs in Vietnam and getting a check so small he can't afford a place to live; at least not with his gambling habit. If you'll be working at the new casino, I'm sure you'll be seeing Mike again so you can thank him yourself."

"Ok officer. Thank you, again… and may God bless you for risking your life every day just to keep us safe," I added sincerely.

"It's my pleasure, ma'am," he said as he tipped his hat. "You be safe, too… and welcome to Parker."

So first thing this morning, (after a rather short night's sleep), I got everything off the counters, table cleared and I'm ready to head out to the RV Park. With the two-hour time difference, I decided to call Jeremy after I was all ready to go, and he promised to call the RV Park as soon as we hung up.

Just think… I'm going to have electricity and air conditioning! And yes, they even have cable television, so I can catch up on the news and politics, and I can even go swimming in the Colorado River! How blessed can I be!

One thing I've learned since leaving Gold Beach; the more you follow the path our Lord wants you to, and the more good you can do by glorifying God and influencing others to do the same, the harder Satan will try to stop you. So now…I'm more convinced than ever that I **need** to stay here in Parker and earn the means with which to share my story with the world. First came the lecherous Food and Beverage Manager – then came the killer bees, and now Revelation, (the epitome of evil). The bees killed four people that weekend, but I wasn't harmed. Revelation has hurt (or killed) many people, and yet I wasn't harmed. Surely it's the protection of my Lord, and now… other than surviving financially while I wait for the casino to open and dealing with the "man" (and I use that term lightly), who will be my boss, all obstacles have been conquered, and I'm not only fine but sure that this is where the Lord wants me... at least for now.

So, now it's off to "living in the lap of luxury" at the RV Park next to the Casino - and right at the rivers edge, (thank you, Jeremy). I suppose it would be too much to expect, but I'm still hoping I can find a spot to park where I can see the blue water of the beautiful Colorado River from my windows. Wouldn't that be a great place to write!

chapter 65

April 24, 1999

Three days, and so much has happened I don't even know where to begin. I guess I'll start with the ONLY negative thing so the rest of the story will be pure JOY. I don't know if it's from the stress of my encounter with killer bees, my battle with Revelation or concerns about dealing with a lecherous boss, but I'm having a bout with boils. It's been a lifelong problem of mine; but usually it only happens when I'm under extreme stress, so I can't imagine why I'm getting a two big ones on my face right now. But I guess if that's the worst of my problems, then I'm doing GREAT!

Now for the WONDERFUL NEWS – AND LOTS OF IT!

I'm all settled into my new home at the Blue Water RV Park. The managers, Bill and Janey, welcomed me as if I were a long lost family member. As I drove up, (having had no problem finding the back route Tory told me about), I pulled up to the managers trailer, (located right on the water's edge, of course) and both Janey and Bill came running out to greet me; asking if I was Abigayle. They said my son Jeremy had called them and they had a spot ready and waiting for me. It was the nicest reception I've ever had at an RV Park, and they really made me feel like I had come home.

As he had told me he would, my son Jeremy had paid a full month's rent, ($240), and although the parking spots near the water were already occupied by permanent residents, Janey directed me to one that if I stepped outside, I could see the river. It was the only space with a big tree right behind it, which was not only covered with beautiful flowers but it offered something quite rare out here in the desert... shade from the hot, afternoon sun.

It took me a while to get level, because the pads are gravel rather than cement, but with Janey's help, it wasn't long before I shut off my engine, signed in relief ... and jumped out to give her a big thank you hug. (If Jeremy was here, I'd have hugged him too!)

It was still fairly early in the morning, so I decided to walk around my new "home" and get the layout of the land. I saw that they not only had a public shower, but a Laundromat as well. That really made me happy because I'm sure I'll have plenty of uniforms to wash and Parker is several miles away, which is a long, hot ride on my bicycle, (especially carrying laundry) in the hot summer sun.

Then I decided to wander along the waterfront, feeding the ducks and thanking God for bringing me to such a beautiful place where I could work, write and rest. To me, working a regular job **is** rest, because it's something definite. You go to work at a certain time, do the very best job you can at whatever it is you're doing, and then you punch out and go home. You make money, pay your bills, and you have food to eat. It's the "easiest" of lifestyles - because you don't have to worry about "where to go next" or "whether the engine will start", or "where your next dollar is coming from".

Staying here at such a lovely RV Park on the Colorado River and working a low-stress job; meaning the kind where you don't have to answer to shareholders or a Board of Directors, aren't responsible for other employees and get to leave your job at work when you go home at night, (unlike the ones I'm used to doing), will be a real treat. Owning my own business was 24/7 – 365 days a year, and although the money won't be nearly as good, I couldn't be happier. I figured it would take me quite a while to save enough to buy a computer, (with all the necessary accessories), then learn how to use it, and finally, design a web-site; especially if I was stuck making minimum wage at the hamburger stand… as I'd been told to expect by Mr. Lecherous, (my nickname for the Director of Food and Beverage).

After my tour of the RV Park and a pleasant walk along the river, I spent a couple of hours at Bill and Janey's trailer getting better acquainted, and they are absolutely wonderful people. When I left their house, I decided to sit down at my kitchen table and study my Bible, after kneeling and giving thanks to God for so many things that I couldn't possibly list them all. And then, as I sat there reading, that was when I began to hear that all too familiar hum. Oh no, not bees again, I thought.

I looked out the window but I didn't see anything, so I checked every window in the RV, and still - just a few bees, (a number I would call unpleasant, but not unbearable). But then I looked out the back window, (the one that faces the huge flowered tree), and wouldn't you know it; it was literally "alive" with bees. The flowered branches were actually moving from the weight of them as they flew from flower to flower, and the hummmm was a steady drone.

OK… I know that these are only honey bees, or they wouldn't be so busy pollinating the only flowering tree in the RV Park, but after my recent experience in the desert, it still gave me the chills… and I realized that I either had to give up the blessing of having shade, or learn to live with the bees. I finally decided that I wasn't going to let a tiny insect that the Lord created for a necessary purpose, frighten me away from the coolest spot in the Park… which is why I decided it was time to learn to live with my greatest fear; bees.

I also needed to open my awning, (and I mean NEEDED), because without one - the hot sun heats up the metal sides of the RV until it actually radiates heat, and the door handle becomes too hot to touch without holding a cloth in your hand. I decided to wait until the cool of the morning to do it; hopefully before the bees were out — because I'll have to climb the ladder at the back of Lucky, (right next to the flowering tree), and then spend quite a bit of time using duct tape to piece together all the rips and tears that age and weather have caused in the canvas. It'll be quite a job, but with enough duct tape, (and as few bees bothering me as possible), I'll get it done.

So now I have a home, but I still needed a job. When I told Janey and Bill about Mr. Lecherous and how long I'd been waiting for the casino to open, they were surprisingly upset on my behalf. Of course, the Indians and the casino are a sensitive subject for them, (since they'd had to close almost half of the RV Park when the Indians decided to cancel their lease and took the land back, with only 24 hours notice), so I can understand why they'd be leery... but they were adamant when they insisted that I shouldn't believe a single thing that the Food and Beverage Director told me, and that I should go to the Human Resources Department every single day... so my job didn't get given to someone else who was more receptive to Mr. Lecherous.

After listening to them, I was convinced; now was not the time to get comfortable and let the one big trial I have left to overcome before I settle down here in Parker, (for who knows how long)..Yesterday morning, I thought I'd ride my bike to town and check with the lady at the office again, but Bill and Janey wouldn't hear of me riding up that big hill and since they had planned to go to the grocery store anyway, they insisted that I ride along with them. In this heat... that was more than a relief; it was a blessing, and I gratefully accepted.

So off we went; Janey and Bill to the grocery store and me to the Casino Department of Human Resources. When I walked inside and up to the counter, I said hello to the lady I've become so familiar with and she said, "I hate to tell you this, dear, but I'm afraid we're not in charge of the new resort anymore and all the applications have been thrown away. Now you have to go directly to the new casino - and start all over again with the new managers."

"What?" I asked in shock and disbelief. "You mean I don't have a job anymore, after waiting all this time?"

"I'm afraid so," she said as she shook her head back and forth and looked at me with true empathy in her eyes. "The people we had running this little casino just weren't up to the task of running the new one – and the way they were going, it never would have opened. That's why the Tribal Council voted to bring in some big outfit from Las Vegas who's in charge of everything now, from top to bottom. But to tell you the truth," she said softly, "I think it might be a better deal all the way around," she concluded, almost whispering as though there were some people in the office who wouldn't exactly appreciate hearing her admit to such a thing.

"OK", I said with a smile and hope still in my heart. "I guess it's over to the new casino for me then. Thank you so much for all your help. It's been a pleasure getting to know you."

"You, too," she answered as we shook hands one last time. "Good luck!" she almost whispered as I turned to walk out the door.

As I waited next to Bill and Janey's big, white diesel truck for them to finish their grocery shopping, I had time to think... and since Mr. Lecherous was my last big obstacle, (and I trust God with all my heart and soul), I wasn't discouraged in the least; in fact, I had a feeling that this, too, was a blessing. As soon as they returned, I told them the whole story and they nodded their heads in agreement, as if saying, "See, we told you to check in every day," but were much too courteous and kind to actually say the words.

"Well I guess as soon as we get back to the Park," I thought out loud, "I'll just ride my bike over to the casino and put in a new application. So far, the Lord has taken care of every single obstacle in my path, so I have a feeling that this time is no different and that everything is working out for the best."

"Yes, I agree" Bill said, "you should head over there immediately - but you're not riding your bicycle up that big hill. Let Janey and I put our groceries away while you get your clothes changed and then I'll drive you over." See what I mean about nice people?

Then Janey added, "And be sure to put our telephone number on your application because we'll be happy to come over and get you when they call."

"Thank you so much... both of you! It'll be great not to be dripping wet and out of breath when I walk in - and you're right, I do need a telephone number. I can't tell you how much appreciate your kindness."

It was about two o'clock in the afternoon yesterday when I finally walked in the front door of the beautiful new Blue Water Resort and Casino for the first time, and sitting at a desk right in the middle of the entryway, obviously screening anyone who came inside, was a receptionist.

"Hi there," I announced myself. "My name is Abigayle, and I put in an application with the Human Resources Department at the old casino. I've been waiting for over a month for the grand opening... and now I understand that they've called in the 'pros' to take over and I need to start again. Could you please tell me who I should speak to about that, ma'am?" I asked politely.

"Well, young lady, I just happen to have an application packet right here," she said as she handed me yet another huge stack of papers. "You'll need to fill these out, and bring along any resume' you might have, and then we'll make you an appointment to meet with the new Food and Beverage Director.

"Great," I said as I took the papers from her outstretched hand. "Could I possibly go ahead and make that appointment for tomorrow morning because I'll have these filled out today and I'm living at the RV Park right next door, so I'd like to get in as soon as possible."

"Sure", she said as she looked down at her appointment book. How does 10:00 A.M. sound?" she asked.

"That sounds perfect! I'll be here with bells on... and papers in hand," I laughed. The receptionist was a middle-aged white woman, well-dressed and very professional, and I felt free to show her just how happy I was.

"I'll see you then – or should I say 'hear' you then," she laughed, (referring to my 'bells'), and we shook hands before I turned around and headed back out the front door.

Bill had insisted on waiting for me, even though I had no idea how long it would take, but as it turned out, it was only a10 minute errand and I was so relieved not to have to walk all the way back to the RV Park. I can't believe how HOT it is already! Living here is going to be some adventure for a girl from the temperate Oregon Coast!

Bill took me back to Lucky - where I began filling out the papers… again. Suddenly Jim, the WWII Vet and Lions Club President, knocked on my door. "Surprise, surprise," he said as I welcomed him inside. "I'll bet you're wondering how I found you?"

"Not really," I answered. "You must know every single person in Parker so it probably didn't take you five minutes to figure out where to find me."

"Well, you're right about that," he laughed, "and I'm glad to see you somewhere besides that dirt lot. In fact, this is pretty nice; even close to the river. Now all you need is a little raft so you can get your exercise rowing."

"Yaaa," I agreed. "That's a great idea… so maybe after I start working I'll just buy myself one."

"There's no need for that," he offered. "Actually I came out here to ask you to put on a small show for a group of handicapped people - and the volunteer mentors who work with them. I know there won't be any money in it for you — but I just happen to have a little two-person rubber raft and a couple of oars I haven't used for quite some time so I'm thinking that you could probably put it to very good use."

"Oh my gosh," I exclaimed as I hugged him gratefully. "That would be wonderful! And Jim, you know that I don't expect money and would be happy to speak to your group, raft or no raft. It's all God's work anyway; I'm just the conduit."

"I know," he smiled and gave me another hug. "It just makes me feel better to be able to do something for you for a change. That all…"

I thanked him again - and then, as we arranged for him to pick me up on Saturday, Jim noticed that my table was covered with papers. "Well," he said, "I can see that you're busy so I'd better get out of your hair and let you get back to work," which is exactly what he did… and with all that paperwork still waiting for me, I was glad he was polite enough to see that I didn't have time for our usual two hour conversation.

I spent the entire evening filling out all those forms and wondering who I would be meeting with in the morning. I was a bundle of nerves, with a stomach full of butterflies… and barely got a wink of sleep, even though the steady hum of my rooftop air conditioner kept the RV at a comfortable 75 degrees and should have lulled me to sleep.

Since there was no way I would ask Bill for another ride to the casino in the morning, as kind as they'd already been, I planned to leave 30 minutes early and walk up the big hill and the half-mile on the blacktop road to the Casino entrance. But about an hour before time to leave, just as I was ironing a nice blouse and light slacks, Janey knocked on my door and told me they would to pick me up at a quarter to 10:00. I never even asked them, and yet... there they were, ready and willing to do anything they could to help me. How blessed could I possibly be? Not only do I have a nice place to park, a month's rent paid in advance, but now I have two guardian angels in the form of Janey and Bill.

Of course, I thanked her profusely, and true to her word, at a quarter to ten, I heard the truck horn honking outside, with Bill at the wheel. This was it... I thought to myself as I climbed into the truck. In just a little while, I'll know whether I have a job or not. I just hope it's not that same Food and Beverage Manager, (Mr. Lecherous), and that the new team from Las Vegas decided to get rid of him. But I guess there was only one way to find out – and that was to get this interview over with.

As I walked into the huge entryway, (one of several, but the only one that was open), there was the same lady sitting at the desk. "Hi," she welcomed me with a smile as I walked toward her desk. "I see you have your application all ready to go," she added as I held out my stack of papers. "That good; now I'll just let Mr. George know you're here. It shouldn't be more than a few minutes," she said as she took my papers and disappeared down a side hall.

Whew... at least it wasn't the Mr. Lecherous who was in charge any-more; it was Mr. George - and although I had no idea who he was, or what he was like, I was absolutely thrilled. I couldn't help but laugh out loud as I waited for her to return. If Mr. George was part of the profes-sional team they brought in from Las Vegas to straighten out the mess the locals had made, you can bet he's all business - so my spirits were soaring! Now this is more like it!

And true to her word, it wasn't even 5 minutes before she and Mr. George appeared and he held out his hand for me to shake. As I introduced myself, I could see that he was appraising me… but NOT in a man/woman way. He was appraising me as an applicant, and as a human being – which is just what an employer should do. (I'd hired a few people myself at our resort in Gold Beach, so I understood what he was looking for.)

"Please," he said politely as he motioned with his hand toward the hallway, "let's step into my office so we can discuss what position you're interested in, and I'll see what I can do for you."

I can only describe Mr. George as a well-dressed, almost bald, 50-something year old man; very businesslike and yet very friendly - a far cry from Mr. Lecherous, so I was pretty sure that I might not be stuck selling hamburgers for minimum wage after all.

Mr. George guided me to an office not far down the hall, where he politely pulled up a chair for me across from his desk as he quickly browsed through my paperwork… all neatly and legibly done, and no blank left unfilled, just as a prospective employer would expect.

The entire interview couldn't have taken more than 15 minutes, with him asking me about my background, (rather than reading it on the generic application forms), and a few other well-put questions; like why I thought I would be a good addition to the team - and why I wanted to serve in the Fine Dining Restaurant.

I was completely honest with every response, no matter how corny it might sound. I told him that I love people, and to me *serving* them is my opportunity to make them happy. I want every single customer I serve to walk out of that restaurant saying "Wow – now that's what I call service", and I know how to make them feel that way because it's something you can't fake; it's because you really DO care – and they can sense it. I also told him that because I'd owned my own business, I knew how important obedience and dependability were; whether it was being on time every day for your shift, or sticking to the rules - even when no one was looking. I believe in doing whatever I'm told by my superior, even if I don't agree, (as long as it's legal and moral, I added with a smile), but I'm not afraid to make polite suggestions that I think might improve things. That's when he set my papers down on the desk in front of him and leaned back in his chair, smiling.

"OK...I think I've heard enough," he said as he stood up behind his desk and held out his hand, as if to shake mine. "It sounds like I've got my first Fine Dining server," he said as we shook hands. I'm afraid we're not quite ready to open yet - because the locals left us with quite a mess to clean up... but I'd say it shouldn't be more than a month at the most. But in a couple of weeks I could sure use some help stocking the kitchen, organizing the wine cellar and getting the restaurant ready to open. Would you be interesting in helping out... at a fair wage with full benefits, of course?" he asked.

"I most certainly would," I said enthusiastically as I shook his hand. "Just call me at the number on my application, which is at the RV Park right next door, so I'm available any time," I added. "Thank you, so much, Mr. George. I won't let you down."

"I have no doubt about that," he said. "Now I'm hoping I can find six more just like you. The Fine Dining Restaurant is small and expensive, so we'll only need a staff of 7, and now I only need 6 more just like you," he said as I let his hand go. "We'll have a fine dining training seminar before we open, so of course you'll get paid for that too, so don't worry about not having any experience. You've got what it takes; now we'll just teach you the finer points," he added as I turned to leave his office... literally walking on air and restraining the urge to jump up and click my heels together... twice!

"Thank you so much, Mr. George. I'll be waiting to hear from you, and by the way, I don't care what kind of work it is you need done before you open. I'm willing to do anything from cleaning to unloading trucks... so just give me a call."

And there you have it... problem number four; **eliminated**. First the killer bees, then Revelation, then a place to live near work and now Mr. Lecherous... all problems solved!. And the best thing of all... while I'm earning my computer and designing my website, I'll have a wonderful job where I actually get paid to make people happy! I'd do that for free… so how much better can it get? Halleluiah! Thank you, Jesus!

When I walked outside the building, I didn't expect to see the big white truck still waiting in the parking lot because I had told Bill that I had absolutely no idea how long this interview was going to take and I insisted that he go home. But of course, he didn't pay any attention and the truck was idling, nice and cool from the air conditioning, as I walked out the door and jumped into the cab, so happy I was laughing and woo-hooing!.

"Boy, talk about service!" I exclaimed as I got in. "I thought I told you to go home and I would walk back to the Park."

"Yaaa, I suppose you did. But you just ask Janey how well I take orders - and we've been married for almost 40 years now," he said as we drove out of the casino parking lot and into the RV Park I now called home. "Sounds like things went pretty well," he said as he heard my "woo-hoo" and saw the smile on my face.

"Let's wait until we get to your place and I'll tell both you and Janey all about it. But it's absolutely wonderful, Bill… everything is wonderful!

So, two more weeks… and at least I'll be doing something to earn money. That means I should have enough money to buy groceries **and** pay another month's rent when it's due, but Bill and Janey insisted that I not worry about money for rent. They know I'll pay it when I have it… and according to them - food is much more important. Now even that burden has been removed.

Sometimes I'm so happy and so blessed that I could just cry. Here I am, on an Indian Reservation that's pretty close to war with the white folks, working at a casino owned by Indians, living in an RV Park that is close enough to walk to work, (especially if I can find a way around the fence that goes out a few feet out into the water so I can avoid the big hill altogether and walk to work along the riverbank. I'm so close to the water that I can carry my little raft to the river for all the fun in the sun I can stand and even my boils are getting better, I've got food in my cupboards, new friends, (both Indian and white) and my air conditioning is working perfectly. What more could I ask?

And guess what? Even the bees aren't going to be a problem anymore. Just a little while ago, Janey came over and told me that the people who park on the second space in from the water, (one where you're only 30 feet from the river and can see it from almost every window) are leaving this year. I guess the elderly gentleman who spends winters in Parker is too ill to travel anymore, and although I hate to see my blessing come as a result of someone else's hardship, I just happen to be the lucky person that Bill and Janey chose to move into the now open spot. Wow! Now I can feed the ducks from my own patio and things just keep getting better and better!

And Bill and Janey didn't have to give me that spot by the water either. There's a long waiting list for the spaces up front because they're so coveted that even people who only spend the winter here, pay for their empty spot all year long... just so it's available when they need it. That's why the park looks deserted right now, but half the spaces are being paid for. Strange... but I can't blame them for wanting to be close to the water, and now that's where I'll be!

Although I have no idea how long I'll be staying here in Parker, Arizona, I do know that even though this "Poetry on the Road" might not be on the *road* for a while, I'll still take every opportunity to make a difference in the lives of both those whom I'll be serving and the all the other employees I'll be working with. I'd like to see if I can form some sort of bridge between the Indians and the whites, and Don is a good place to start - as he is active in all kinds of local politics and knows the Indian Council Members personally. I'll put on my shows anywhere and everywhere they'll listen, (including my customers at work) and I'll study my Bible, stay in constant touch with my Lord, and try to take one more step toward righteousness each and every day.

I feel like the time I spend here in Parker is just one more rung on the ladder that will eventually lead me to whatever my Lord wants me to do... and while I'm here - I'll get to learn more about my American Indian brothers and sisters and hopefully help them understand more about us white folks. And by working in a casino, I'll have many opportunities to encourage and hopefully inspire people who are being held captive by addictions to gambling.

And just as a side note; living in one of the hottest places in the United States will be yet another new experience in my book of life. There are vast deserts to explore, new people to meet and so much to learn. And best of all... this isn't the end; it's only one more in a long string of new beginnings.

And yes... my future is still a blank slate - and I have no idea what the Lord has in store for me or how I can best use the gifts He has given me to make a difference in this very big and confusing world. But one thing I DO know for sure: No matter what happens; no matter how difficult or how pleasant things may be - I will always have the blessing of being able to close my eyes... and hear that powerful, loving and oh-so familiar voice when He spoke to me after the flood, saying **"Do not worry – everything will be fine!"** (And it is!)

P.S. One of my favorite Psalms 139:23, 24 (King James Version)

Search me, O God, and know my heart; try me and know my thoughts:

And see if there be any wicked way in me; and lead me in the way everlasting.

Excerpt from

Book Two

Midnight was the hour in which I chose to make my escape from Parker, Arizona; an escape from the comfort and contentment that made it feel like a trap of ease – a place so stress free and pleasant that it could tempt me away from whatever it is the Lord wants me to do with the rest of my life. It took me longer than I expected to save the money for a computer – and almost as long for me to figure out how to use it… but now my reasons for staying in Parker are finished… and it's time to get on with my journey.

So far, it's been a long, hot 4 hours driving west on Interstate 40 through the hot, barren desert on my way to Central California. My family is holding a reunion at Yosemite National park in a couple of days and I thought it would be a wonderful opportunity to let everyone know I'm still alive and kicking. And the timing couldn't be better since the Lord has allowed me to prosper beyond my wildest expectations because I not only managed to save enough money for a computer but I also bought a small color television, a VCR, and even a digital camera with which to record the wonders I have no doubt are yet to come. And even MORE amazing is the fact that I'm leaving the Reservation with $3,000 cash in my pocket, which will more than cover my travel expenses as well as any repairs I might need along the way. I still can't believe how blessed I am... because for the first time since leaving Oregon, I don't have to worry about breaking down and I can even spend the night in an RV park and revel in the luxuries of electricity and water without feeling guilty for wasting the money. Thank you, Lord.... thank you so very much - which is what I repeated over and over again as I started up the engine and pulled out of the parking spot in the RV Park I had come to think of as "home".

The Food and Beverage Manager at the casino begged me not to leave, and even offered me the position of Restaurant Manager if I would stay. And yes, it was tempting... parked right next to the Colorado River, enjoying the never-ending sunshine with my many new friends and touching the lives of the customers I served at the "River Willow Restaurant". Every night I shared my poetry and bore witness to everyone I could, and it was great - but something was telling me that this **wasn't** the end of my journey - and that Parker, Arizona was simply a stop on my way to somewhere else.

And wouldn't you know it, today was a day of record setting heat, (even for July in the Mohave Desert), which is why I decided to leave at midnight. But even at that late hour, it was still 110 degrees outside and since Lucky has been parked for months, I can only hope that I don't break down on some deserted stretch of road without power to operate the air conditioner. In this heat, motor homes quickly turn into metal ovens... so engine trouble doesn't mean just being delayed or stuck somewhere you don't want to be; out here it's a matter of life and death.

But so far, so good. I've got a spray bottle filled with water I'm using to keep my right leg wet so it doesn't *cook* from the heat of the motor rising up through the cracks in the rotting wood surrounding the interior engine cover, and so far Lucky's running like a top... that is if you don't count the fact that I have no dash lights and have to use a flashlight to check my gauges - or if you don't count the fact that it took an extra hour just to get **out** of Parker in the first place, (even AFTER I left the

RV Park), because when I was filling my gas tanks at the local service station, (and left Lucky idling in case the engine wouldn't start again), suddenly there was a big "pop" and a giant cloud of hissing steam came from the engine as water flooded the pavement around me. Great, I thought. I'm not even out of town yet and I'm already having trouble!

Fortunately, the gentleman who ran the station hurried over to see what the problem was and discovered that my radiator cap hadn't been tightened properly so when the pressure built up, it "shot" off like a rocket, and hot water sprayed out like an erupting geyser. Great! Just what I needed! And I had tried so hard to make sure that Lucky was *road ready* before I left. I even hired a young worker from the casino to change my oil, check my fluid levels and flush my radiator - and still I couldn't seem to get out of town. Oh well, I thought to myself; there was nothing I could do about it but refill the radiator, put the cap back on, (which I found almost 50 feet away), and pray. If something **was** truly trying to keep me from leaving - I would NOT let it win!

It took almost an hour, but with the help of the gas station attendant and a kindly trucker who happened to be filling up his rig when it happened, we got the radiator refilled, both gas tanks topped off, air in my tires, (thank goodness the trucker noticed), and a jump start to get me running again. At last, I was actually leaving town - and that's when I discovered I had no dash lights; a minor problem and one easily solved with a flashlight.

It didn't take long before I fell into the routine of spraying my leg until it was dripping wet, then pointing the flashlight at the gauges, then taking a drink of water, (much needed in the 110 degree heat with no air conditioning - especially after my ordeal at the gas station), and then checking my map to make sure I didn't miss a turn while singing songs of joy and praise the whole time. I did it, I thought to myself; I actually got away.

It's strange, but I haven't seen a single car since I got gas for the second time tonight at a service station in Barstow a couple of hours ago. My plan is to drive through the night, and then by the time the sun rises in the morning, (and the heat becomes unbearable), I should be in Tehacha-pi; the last town before I hit the mountain pass that leads to Bakersfield, California. When I get there, I'll find an RV Park, hook up to electricity, turn on the air conditioner and sleep through the hot daytime hours be-fore once again driving during the comparative cool of the night tomor-row. Sounds like a plan – that is if I don't get lost on one of the many construction detours that keep taking me off the highway.

According to the map, I'm about 35 miles from the town of Tehachapi and it feels strange with no other cars on the road; like I'm the only per-son on earth with nothing but the steady hum of the engine to keep me company. I've spent the last few hours climbing the Bristol and Cady Mountains in the Mohave Desert with my overheated engine glowing redder and redder with each steep hill. But at last, Highway 40 quit climbing and it looks like it might be all downhill from here, which hopefully will give my engine a chance to cool down. "Just 35 more miles, Lord", I said as I took a long deep breath. "Please just get me 35 more miles so I can rest!"

And then it happened! KA-BOOM - and suddenly Lucky was filled with smoke so thick I couldn't even see my own legs - let alone the road as I tried to pull onto the shoulder before I rolling to a stop – and won-dering if this might be my last few moments on Earth. Smoke meant fire – and I knew that the propane tanks could explode any minute.

That's when my survival instinct took over… with pulse pounding and heart racing, I thought, "OK… Lucky's on fire! I've got to get out of here fast, but what should I take with me? Is my **life** worth anything in-side this RV?" All those questions and more; a myriad of thoughts racing through my mind… and yet it couldn't have been more than two seconds before I was up and moving. It's amazing how fast you can think during times of extreme duress, because during those two seconds I actually had time to wonder if the offer of a cushy job at the resort, the unsecured radiator cap, the dash lights refusing to work, an overheated engine burn-ing my wet leg, the all-time record setting high temperatures that forced me to leave in the middle of the night… and now Lucky catching on fire were all the result of Satan trying to keep me from leaving – to keep me from doing whatever it is I can do to serve God.

And then I remembered the fire extinguisher that had been hanging next to the door since I first bought Lucky and my spirits soared. Now I had a weapon to use against the fire. I hurriedly searched the passenger seat in the dark, feeling for my purse and my tape recorder, thinking at least I'll have identification and a way to capture this crazy night on tape… and then I'll grab the fire extinguisher on my way out the door!

I knew that my bicycle was lying down in the aisle so I carefully stepped over it in the dark to the cupboard where I had hidden the $3,000. I felt guilty for taking the extra 3 seconds it took to get the money when I knew that the propane could explode at any time, but I also knew that it might be my only means of getting another vehicle if Lucky was destroyed. So many questions running through my mind - and so many decisions to make; it was like I was watching myself in a movie. But what surprised me most was that instead of feeling panic, I felt strangely calm and in control as I retrieved the money and then grabbed the fire extinguisher before leaping out the door.

Once I was safely outside, I hurried to the front of Lucky and used the light from the flames that were leaping out of the grill to read the instructions on the red cylinder. I instantly regretted not bringing my flashlight, but it was too late now so firelight would have to do. "Pull yellow pin, hold upright and squeeze handle, aiming low," it said.

Still calm, but wondering how long I had before the propane tanks exploded, I wasted no time pulling the pin, pointing it toward the blue and yellow flames… and squeezing. But that's when my heart sank.

Rather than the steady flow of flame-smothering foam I had expected to see, there was nothing but a weak little "puffff" as a small stream of grey powder came out of the shiny red cylinder… traveling maybe 10 or 12 inches before falling uselessly to the ground. **The fire extinguisher was empty!**

Blue Water Casino and Resort at Parker, AZ

My first drawing for my flyers.

The miracle Bible that survived the flood.

Lucky and our first palm tree.

Abigayle was born in the town of Tillamook on the Oregon Coast in 1951 and graduated from Oregon City High School in 1969. She has always been an inspirational poet and songwriter… always a "cheerleader" for the underdog… and always undaunted by challenges, no matter how intimidating or unusual.

She is a wilderness woman, nature lover, animal trainer, athlete, and yes - even a bit of a recluse… yet her gift for inspiring and encouraging people has kept her in the center of the action for most of her life, using her gift of communication to share the love of Jesus!

Abigayle was an Army child, then an Army wife, then a tour-traveling athlete… which took her to almost every state in this Great Nation, as well as to several foreign countries, even before she began this most recent 7 year journey. But as Dorothy in the Wizard of Oz said, "There's no place like home," and for Abigayle, even though she lives in Branson, Missouri now, (a lovely place)… home will always be the Oregon Coast.